History and Interpretation in
New Testament Perspective

Biblical Interpretation Series

EDITORS
R. ALAN CULPEPPER
ROLF RENDTORFF

ASSISTANT EDITOR
DAVID E. ORTON

EDITORIAL ADVISORY BOARD
JANICE CAPEL ANDERSON
MIEKE BAL
PHYLLIS A. BIRD
ERHARD BLUM
ROBERT P. CARROLL
WERNER H. KELBER
EKKEHARD STEGEMANN
ANTHONY C. THISELTON
VINCENT L. WOMBUSH
JEAN ZUMSTEIN

VOLUME 54
HISTORY AND INTERPRETATION IN
NEW TESTAMENT PERSPECTIVE

History and Interpretation in New Testament Perspective

BY

E. Earle Ellis

Society of Biblical Literature
Atlanta

HISTORY AND INTERPRETATION IN NEW TESTAMENT PERSPECTIVE

Copyright © 2001 by Koninklijke Brill NV, Leiden,
The Netherlands

This edition published under license from Koninklijke Brill NV,
Leiden, The Netherlands by the Society of Biblical Literature.

All rights reserved. No part of this work may be reproduced or transmitted in any form or by any means, electronic or mechanical, including photocopying and recording, or by any means of any information storage or retrieval system, except as may be expressly permitted by the 1976 Copyright Act or in writing from the Publisher. Requests for permission should be addressed in writing to the Rights and Permissions Department, Koninklijke Brill NV, Leiden, The Netherlands.

Authorization to photocopy items for internal or personal use is granted by Brill provided that the appropriate fees are paid directly to The Copyright Clearance Center, 222 Rosewood Drive, Suite 910, Danvers, MA 01923, USA. Fees are subject to change.

Library of Congress Cataloging-in-Publication Data

Ellis, E. Earle (Edward Earle)
　History and interpretation in New Testament perspective / E. Earle Ellis.
　　p. cm. – (Biblical interpretation series ; v. 54)
　Sequel to: The making of New Testament documents.
　Includes bibliographical references and index.
　ISBN-13: 978-1-58983-250-3 (pbk. : alk. paper)
　ISBN-10: 1-58983-250-7 (pbk. : alk. paper)
　1. Bible. N.T. – Criticism, interpretation, etc. I. Title.

BS2395.E45   2001b
225.6–dc22

2006026262

Printed in the United States of America
on acid-free paper

To the memory of my mother
Lois Belle McBride Ellis
24 October 1894–14 December 1939

CONTENTS

Preface ix
Abbreviations xi

I. HISTORICAL-LITERARY CRITICISM—AFTER
   TWO HUNDRED YEARS 1
   Origins 1
   Aberrations 3
   The Necessity and Contribution of Historical
      Criticism 10
   Limitations 14

II. PSEUDONYMITY AND CANONICITY OF NEW
    TESTAMENT DOCUMENTS 17
    The Views of the Baur Tradition 18
    Attitudes Toward Pseudepigrapha in Antiquity 22
    Apostolic Authority in the First-Century Church 24
    The Deceptive Character of Apostolic
       Pseudepigrapha 25
    Conclusion 28

III. DATING THE NEW TESTAMENT 31
     Historical Evidence for Dating New Testament
        Books 32
     Early Literary Criticism 38
     Twentieth-Century Developments and Critique 44
     Conclusion 49

IV. 'THE END OF THE EARTH' (ACTS 1:8) 53
    The Use of the Phrase in Acts 53
    The Use of the Phrase in Classical Writings 56
    The Connotation of the Phrase in Acts 58
    Implications for the Dating of Acts 60

V. THE ORIGIN AND COMPOSITION OF THE
   PASTORAL EPISTLES 65

	Canonicity and Authorship	65
	Occasion and Date	71
	The Historical Setting	75
	Composition: Literary Criticism	77
	Themes	82
VI.	PAUL AND HIS CO-WORKERS REVISITED	85
	Long Term Co-Workers	85
	Four Frequent Designations	87
	Other Categories of Co-Workers	92
	The Classification of Co-Workers' Activities	95
VII.	THE INTERPRETATION OF THE BIBLE WITHIN THE BIBLE ITSELF	99
	The Character of New Testament Usage	99
	The Presuppositions of New Testament Interpretation	112
VIII.	HOW JESUS INTERPRETED HIS BIBLE	121
	The Bible Received by Jesus	121
	Jesus' Attitude Toward His Bible	122
	Jesus' Principles of Biblical Interpretation	126
	Conclusion	131
IX.	PREFORMED TRADITIONS AND THEIR IMPLICATIONS FOR THE ORIGINS OF PAULINE CHRISTOLOGY	133
	The Making of the New Testament Documents	134
	Implications of Preformed Traditions for the Authorships and Dates of the Letters	142
	Implications of Preformed Traditions for Pauline Christology	144

Indexes of Passages 151
Index of Modern Authors 171
Index of Subjects 176

PREFACE

The present volume stands on its own, but in many respects it represents a sequel to my previous work in the *Biblical Interpretation Series*, *The Making of the New Testament Documents*.[1] In the first instance it places that book within the context of the historical-literary criticism of the past two centuries.[2] It then examines in detail a number of issues that are treated briefly in the earlier volume. Specifically, it critiques the hypothesis of 'innocent' apostolic pseudepigrapha in early Christianity[3] and investigates historical and literary evidence for dating New Testament documents,[4] for Paul's mission to Spain[5] and for his subsequent composition of the Pastoral Epistles.[6] It also gives extended attention to the identity and various roles of Paul's co-workers.[7]

With respect to preformed traditions, a major topic of *The Making of the New Testament Documents*, the present book devotes more attention to the rationale and techniques in the use of a special kind of preformed tradition, that is, Old Testament texts and expositions in the New Testament[8] and specifically in the teaching of Jesus.[9] In conclusion it draws out the implications of preformed traditions for the origins of Paul's christology.[10]

The book is a revision and/or updating of essays that have appeared in an earlier form at various times and places. To the editors and publishers of those volumes a word of acknowledgment and appreciation is here gladly given.[11]

---

[1] E. E. Ellis, *The Making of the New Testament Documents*, Leiden 1999.
[2] See below, chapter I, 1–16.
[3] See below, chapter II, 17–29; cf. Ellis (note 1), 322ff.
[4] See below, chapters III and IV, 32–38, 44ff., 60–63; cf. Ellis (note 1), 307–310.
[5] See below, chapter IV, 65–83; cf. Ellis (note 1), 278–283, 391n, 422–425.
[6] See below, chapter V, 65–77; cf. Ellis (note 1), 422–425.
[7] See below, chapter VI, 85–98; cf. Ellis (note 1), 39, 89ff., 326f., 420f.
[8] See below, chapter VII, 99–120; cf. Ellis (note 1), 31f., 60f., 78–81, 95f., 99–103, 105f., 114f., 117–138, 156f., 159ff., 166ff., 173–179, 345–348, 350f., 407n, 417.
[9] See below, chapter VIII, 121–132; cf. Ellis (note 1), 31f., 175f., 178f., 247n, 249, 314f., 350, 354.
[10] See below, chapter IX, 133–150; cf. Ellis (note 1), 74–77, 79ff., 87–90, 103f., 108f.
[11] Chapter I: *The Proceedings of the Conference [Debate] on Biblical Inerrancy*, edd. M. Ashcraft *et al.*, Nashville TN: Broadman Press, 1987, 411–421. Chapter II: *Worship, Theology and Ministry in the Early Church. FS R. P. Martin*, edd. M. J. Wilkins

My mother was born in Paradise Township, Indian Territory (after 1906 the State of Oklahoma), and travelled with her family by covered wagon to Oakland Park, Florida. There and in nearby Dania she spent her adult life. She was a vivacious personality, active in home, church, business and social affairs. She loved, nurtured and disciplined me in my formative years and taught by example the Godly virtues of a cheerful spirit, of joy in serving and of patience in suffering. I dedicate this book to her memory.

For assistance in the research I am most grateful to Roberts Library at Southwestern Seminary, the Tyndale House and the University libraries at Cambridge and The British Library in London. I also thank my assistants, J. M. Givens and David Yang, for proof-reading, for creating the indices and for other labors; and my secretary, Mrs. Carla Works, for efficient service in preparing the manuscript.

I am deeply appreciative to Professor Alan Culpepper for again accepting this second contribution to the *Biblical Interpretation Series* and to Ms. Mattie Kuiper and Ms. Anita Disseldorp of Brill Academic Publishers for guiding the manuscript through the press.

As we again celebrate Christ's resurrection and 'look for the blessed hope, even the glorious appearing of our great God and Savior Jesus Christ,'[12] I pray that this book may in some measure bless his church and illumine his Word.

Easter 2000

E. Earle Ellis
Southwestern Baptist Theological Seminary
Fort Worth, Texas

---

and T. Paige, Sheffield UK: SAP, 1992, 212–224. Chapter III: 'Dating the New Testament,' *NTS* 26 (1980), 487–502. Chapter IV: '"Das Ende der Erde" (Apg 1,8),' *Der Treue Gottes trauen. Beiträge zum Werk des Lukas für Gerhard Schneider*, edd. C. Bussmann und W. Radl, Freiburg: Herder, 1991, 277–287. Chapter V: 'Pastoral Letters,' *DPL* (1993), 658–666. Chapter VI: 'Paul and his Co-Workers,' *DPL* (1993), 183–189. Chapter VII: 'Interpretation of the Bible Within the Bible Itself,' *The International Bible Commentary*, ed. William R. Farmer, Collegeville MN: The Liturgical Press, 1998, 53–63. Chapter VIII: 'How Jesus Interpreted his Bible,' *CTR* 3 (1989), 341–351. Chapter IX: 'Preformed Traditions and their Implications for Pauline Christology,' *Christology, Controversy and Community. New Testament Essays in Honour of David Catchpole*, edd. David Horrell and Christopher Tuckett, Leiden: E. J. Brill Academic Publishers, 2000, 303–320.

[12] Tit 2:13.

ABBREVIATIONS

†	Date of death
ABBL	*Allgemeine Bibliothek der biblischen Literatur*
AH	Irenaeus, *Adversus omnes Haereses*
AJBI	*Annual of the Japanese Biblical Institute*
ANF	*Ante-Nicene Fathers*, 10 vols., edd. A. Roberts and J. Donaldson, Grand Rapids 1951 (1885–92)
ANRW	*Aufstieg und Niedergang der römischen Welt*, edd. H. Temporini and W. Haase, Berlin 1972–
ANT	*The Apocryphal New Testament*, ed. J. K. Elliott, Oxford 1993
AÖAW	*Anzeige der österreichischen Akademie der Wissenschaften*
Ant.	Josephus, *Antiquities of the Jews*
ARN	*Aboth according to Rabbi Nathan*
ASTI	*Annual of the Swedish Theological Institute*
ATR	*Anglican Theological Review*
BAFCS	*The Book of Acts in its First Century Setting*, 6 vols., ed. B. W. Winter, Grand Rapids 1993–97
BAR	*Biblical Archeology Review*
BBR	*Bulletin for Biblical Research*
BC	*The Beginnings of Christianity*, 5 vols., edd. F. J. F. Jackson and K. Lake, London 1920–32
BHH	*Biblisch-Historisches Handwörterbuch*, 4 vols., ed. B. Reicke und L. Rost, Göttingen 1962–79
Bib	*Biblica*
BJRL	*Bulletin of the John Rylands Library*
BK	*Bibel und Kirche*
BR	*Biblical Research*
BS	*Bibliotheca Sacra*
BT	Babylonian Talmud
BZ	*Biblische Zeitschrift*
CAH	*Cambridge Ancient History*, 12 vols., ed. S. A. Cook, Cambridge ²1925–39
CAP	*The Apocrypha and Pseudepigrapha of the Old Testament*, 2 vols., ed. R. H. Charles, Oxford ²1963 (1913)
CBQ	*Catholic Biblical Quarterly*
CGT	*Cambridge Greek Testament*

CIL	*Corpus Inscriptionum Latinarum*, Berlin 1863–
CR	*The Classical Review*
CTJ	*Calvin Theological Journal*
CTR	*Criswell Theological Review*
ct.	contra; contrast
Compendia	*Compendia Rerum Judaicarum ad Novum Testamentum*, edd. S. Safrai *et al.*, Assen 1974–
CurTM	*Currents in Theology and Ministry*
DBI	*Dictionary of Biblical Interpretation*, 2 vols., ed. J. H. Hays, Nashville TN 1999
DBS	*Dictionaire de la Bible. Supplément*, ed. Louis Pirot, Paris 1928–
DCA	*A Dictionary of Christian Antiquities*, 2 vols., edd. W. Smith and S. Cheetham, London 1908
DCB	*A Dictionary of Christian Biography*, 4 vols., edd. W. Smith and H. Wace, London 1877–87
DGRA	*Dictionary of Greek and Roman Antiquities*, 2 vols., edd. W. Smith *et al.*, London ^{3}1890
DGRBM	*Dictionary of Greek and Roman Biography and Mythology*, 3 vols., ed. W. Smith, Boston 1859
DJD	*Discoveries in the Judaean Desert*, edd. J. T. Milik *et al.*, Oxford 1956–
DJG	*Dictionary of Jesus and the Gospels*, edd. J. B. Green *et al.*, Downers Grove IL 1992
DLNT	*Dictionary of the Later New Testament*, edd. R. P. Martin *et al.*, Downers Grove IL 1997
DPL	*Dictionary of Paul and His Letters*, edd. G. F. Hawthorne *et al.*, Downers Grove IL 1993
DRev	*Downside Review*
DT	Dutch Text (Translation)
EB	*Encyclopedia Biblica*, 4 vols., edd. T. K. Cheyne and J. S. Black, London 1899–1907
EdF	*Erträge der Forschung*
EE	*Estudios Eclessiásticos*
EGT	*The Expositor's Greek Testament*, 5 vols., ed. W. R. Nicoll, London 1910
EJ	*Encyclopedia Judaica*, 10 vols., edd. J. Klatzkin and I. Elbogen, Berlin 1928–34
EQ	*Evangelical Quarterly*
ET	English Text (Translation)

ET	*Expository Times*
ETL	*Ephemerides Theologicae Lovanienses*
EvT	*Evangelische Theologie*
f. (ff.)	following page, verse (two pages, verses)
fl	flourished
Flor	Florilegium
FS	Festschrift (or memorial volume)
FT	French Text (Translation)
GCS	*Die Griechischen Christlichen Schriftsteller*
GP	*Gospel Perspectives*, 6 vols., edd. D. Wenham *et al.*, Sheffield UK 1980–86
GT	German Text (Translation)
HDB	*Dictionary of the Bible*, 5 vols. (4 + extra volume), ed. J. Hastings, Edinburgh 1898–1904
HE	Eusebius, *Ecclesiastical History*
HJ	*Heythrop Journal*
HTR	*Harvard Theological Review*
HUCA	*Hebrew Union College Annual*
IDB	*Interpreter's Dictionary of the Bible*, 4 vols., ed. G. A. Buttrick, New York 1962
IDBSuppl	*Interpreter's Dictionary of the Bible. Supplementary Volume*, ed. K. Krim, Nashville 1976
IEJ	*Israel Exploration Journal*
IF	Introductory Formula
ILS	*Inscriptiones Latinae Selectae*, 3 vols. in 5, ed. H. Dessau, Chicago 1979 (1892–1914)
INT	*Interpreting the New Testament*, edd. D. A. Black *et al.*, Nashville TN 2001
Int	*Interpretation*
IQR	*Irish Quarterly Review*
*ISBE*²	*International Standard Bible Encyclopedia*, revised ed., 4 vols., ed. G. W. Bromiley, Grand Rapids 1979–88
IT	Italian Text (Translation)
J	Jerusalem (Palestinian) Talmud
JB	The Jerusalem Bible
JBL	*Journal of Biblical Literature*
JBR	*Journal of Bible and Religion*
JCBRF	*Journal of the Christian Brethren Research Fellowship*
JE	*The Jewish Encyclopedia*, 12 vols., ed. I. Singer, New York 1901–06

JPT	*Jahrbücher für protestantische Theologie*
JR	*Journal of Religion*
JRS	*Journal of Roman Studies*
JSJ	*Journal for the Study of Judaism*
JSNT	*Journal for the Study of the New Testament*
JSS	*Journal of Semitic Studies*
JTS	*Journal of Theological Studies*
Loeb	The Loeb Classical Library, edd. T. E. Page *et al.*, London 1912–
LQHR	*London Quarterly and Holborn Review*
LXX	The Septuagint
M	Mishnah
Mek	Mekilta de-Rabbi Ishmael
MPG	*Patrologia Graeca*, 162 vols., ed. J. P. Migne, Paris 1857–66
MPL	*Patrologiae. Series Latina*, 221 vols., ed. J. P. Migne, Paris 1879–90
Ms(s)	Manuscript(s)
MT	Masoretic Text, Hebrew Old Testament
n	note, footnote
NBD	*New Bible Dictionary*, ed. J. D. Douglas, Wheaton ^{2}1982
ND	*New Documents Illustrating Early Christianity*, edd. G. H. R. Horsley *et al.*, Sydney 1981–
Neot	*Neotestamentica*
NPNF	*Nicene and Post-Nicene Fathers, First and Second Series* 13 + 14 vols., edd. P. Schaff and H. Wace, Grand Rapids 1961 (1890–1900)
NSHERK	*The New Schaff-Herzog Encyclopedia of Religious Knowledge*, 12 vols., ed. S. M. Jackson, New York 1908–12
NT	*Novum Testamentum*
NTA	*New Testament Apocrypha*, 2 vols., ed. W. Schneemelcher, Cambridge ^{2}1992
NTAb	*New Testament Abstracts*
NTR	*New Theology Review*
NTS	*New Testament Studies*
OCD	*The Oxford Classical Dictionary*, edd. N. G. L. Hammond and H. H. Scullard, Oxford ^{2}1970
OED	*The Compact Edition of the Oxford English Dictionary*, 2 vols., Oxford ^{2}1972
ODCC	*The Oxford Dictionary of the Christian Church*, edd. F. L. Cross and E. A. Livingstone, Oxford ^{3}1997

OTP	*Old Testament Pseudepigrapha*, 2 vols., ed. J. H. Charlesworth, Garden City NY 1985
par(r)	parallel(s)
PT	Portuguese Text (translation)
PTR	*Princeton Theological Review*
PW	*Real-Encyclopädie der klassischen Wissenschaft*, edd. A. Pauly, G. Wissowa, W. Kroll, Stuttgart 1893–
Q	Traditions common to Matthew and Luke
R	*Midrash Rabbah*, edd. H. Freedman *et al.*, 10 vols., London 1951
RB	*Revue Biblique*
RBen	*Revue Bénédictine*
RE	*Review and Expositor*
RÉG	*Revue des Études grecques*
RGG³	*Religion in Geschichte und Gegenwart*, 7 vols., ed. K. Galling, Tübingen ³1957–65
RQ	*Revue de Qumrân*
RSR	*Recherches de Science Religieuse*
RTL	*Revue Théologique de Louvain*
RTP	*Revue de Théologie et de Philosophie*
SB	*Sitzungsberichte der Preussischen Akademie der Wissenschaften*
SBL	Society of Biblical Literature
SC	*Sources Chrétiennes*
SEÅ	*Svensk Exegetisk Årsbok*
SH	*Scripta Hierosolymitana*
SIG	*Sylloge Inscriptionum Graecarum*, 4 vols., ed. W. Dittenberger, Hildesheim 1982 (³1915–24)
SJT	*Scottish Journal of Theology*
SNTS	Studiorum Novi Testamenti Societas
SNTU	*Studien zum Neuen Testament und seiner Umwelt*
Socino	*Babylonian Talmud. Socino Edition*, 18 vols., ed. I. Epstein, London 1948–52
SP	*Studia Papyrologica*
SPat	*Studia Patristica*
ST	*Studia Theologica*
SWBTS	Southwestern Baptist Theological Seminary
SWJT	*Southwestern Journal of Theology*
T	Synoptic Gospels, Triple Tradition; Tosefta
TB	*Tyndale Bulletin*
TBeit	*Theologische Beiträge*

TCERK	*Twentieth Century Encyclopedia of Religious Knowledge*, 2 vols., ed. L. A. Loetscher, Grand Rapids 1955
TDNT	*Theological Dictionary of the New Testament*, 10 vols., ed. G. Kittel, tr. G. Bromiley, Grand Rapids 1964–76 (1933–73)
Tg	Targum
ThTijd	*Theologisch Tijdschrift*
TLG	*Thesaurus Linguae Graecae: CD Rom #D*, Irvine CA 1992; cf. *Thesaurus Linguae Graecae. Canon of Greek Authors and Works*, edd. L. Berkowitz *et al.*, Oxford 1990
TLZ	*Theologische Literaturzeitung*
TR	*Theologische Rundschau*
TRE	*Theologische Realenzyclopädie*
TS	*Theological Studies*
TSK	*Theologische Studien und Kritiken*
TU	*Texte und Untersuchungen*
TWNT	*Theologisches Wörterbuch des Neuen Testaments*
TZ	*Theologische Zeitschrift*
TZT	*Tübinger Zeitschrift für Theologie*
USQR	*Union Seminary Quarterly Review*
VF	*Verkündigung und Forschung*
War	Josephus, *The Jewish War*
WdF	*Wege der Forschung*
WTJ	*Westminster Theological Journal*
WUNT	*Wissenschaftliche Untersuchungen zum Neuen Testament*
WW	*Word and World*
ZDPV	*Zeitschrift des Deutschen Palästinavereins*
ZNTW	*Zeitschrift für die neutestamentliche Wissenschaft*
ZTK	*Zeitschrift für Theologie und Kirche*

CHAPTER ONE

HISTORICAL-LITERARY CRITICISM—AFTER
TWO HUNDRED YEARS

Origins

In 1787 two events occurred that may serve to mark the beginning of the discipline of 'higher' criticism in biblical studies. One was the publication of the second edition of J. G. Eichhorn's *Introduction to the Old Testament* in which, apparently, the term 'higher criticism' was first applied to the study of Scripture.[1] The term was identified by Eichhorn with an analysis of the 'inner constitution' (*Beschaffenheit*) of the biblical books, that is, their sources, literary composition and historical origins as determined by their internal characteristics. In time this approach came to be known as historical-literary criticism or the historical-critical method.

A second event of relevance for our topic was the inaugural lecture of Eichhorn's pupil, J. P. Gabler, on the 'distinction between biblical and dogmatic theology.'[2] Gabler argued that the original meaning of Scripture, with its mix of cultural and trans-cultural teachings, could be discerned by a careful linguistic, historical and literary analysis (181, 187f.) and that this 'biblical theology' could be classified into two categories, 'those things which ... refer most immediately to their own times and ... those pure notions which divine providence wished to be characteristic of all times ...' (185). While the former were 'merely premises,' the latter were intended to be

---

[1] J. G. Eichhorn, *Einleitung ins Alte Testament*, 3 vols., Leipzig ²1787, I, vi: 'I had to apply the greatest effort to a previously unworked field, the investigation of the inner constitution of the individual writings of the Old Testament with the help of the higher criticism (*der höheren Kritik*)—a new name to no humanist.'

[2] J. P. Gabler, 'On the Proper Distinction between Biblical and Dogmatic Theology and the Specific Objectives of Each' (30 March 1787), tr. J. Sandys-Wunsch and L. Eldredge, *SJT* 33 (1980), 134–144, from J. P. Gabler, *Kleinere Theologische Schriften*, Ulm 1831, 179–198. Further on Gabler cf. B. Ollenburger, 'Biblical Theology: Situating a Discipline,' *Understanding the Word*, ed. J. T. Butler, Sheffield UK 1985, 37–62; R. Morgan, 'Gabler's Bicentenary,' *ET* 98 (1986–87), 164–168. See below, note 27.

'a part of Christian doctrine' (189). We 'must so build upon these firmly established foundations of biblical theology . . . a dogmatic theology adapted to our own times, [teaching] the harmony of divine dogmatics and the principles of human reason' (193). 'Only from these [exegetical] methods can those certain and undoubted universal ideas be singled out, those ideas which alone are useful in dogmatic theology' (192).

Gabler anticipated a number of developments in later criticism: (1) a canon within a canon, (2) the identification of abiding revelation with universal ideas rather than with historically conditioned events and teachings and (3) a conviction that careful historical-literary criticism was an objective science that would produce a consensus about the original meaning of a particular biblical passage if not about its meaning today. His optimism regarding the outcome of this approach was doubtless shared by his mentor, J. G. Eichhorn.

Of course, Eichhorn and Gabler had predecessors in the use of a historical method both in Germany[3] and even earlier in Deistic circles in England.[4] But they provided the programmatic framework for subsequent biblical criticism, and their work may be regarded as the bench-mark for the beginning of the discipline.

Although a historical approach to the Bible has been useful in numerous respects, the high hopes of these two pioneers and a myriad others like them can now be seen, in the light of two centuries of effort, to have failed. Not only is there no consensus about the reconstruction of the various events in biblical history, there is also no agreement among critical scholars about the meaning of even one substantive passage in the whole Bible. When a majority of scholarly opinion is claimed for this or that viewpoint, about the most one can say in light of the history of research is that the majority is probably wrong. For there is more than a little truth in the fictional obituary notice of one scholar which stated that he was the leading authority on the Gospel of John from March to December

---

[3] For example, J. A. Ernesti, C. G. Heyne and G. T. Zachariae.

[4] For example, Edward Herbert (Lord Cherbury), John Locke and Matthew Tindal. Cf. W. Baird, *History of New Testament Research I*, Minneapolis 1992, 33–43; W. G. Kümmel, *The New Testament: The History of the Investigation of its Problems*, Nashville 1972, 52–107 = GT: 55–128; Sandys-Wunsch and Eldredge (note 2), 144–158; H. G. Reventlow, *The Authority of the Bible and the Rise of the Modern World*, Philadelphia 1985, passim; A. Richardson, *History Sacred and Profane*, London 1964, 17–53.

1938. Scholarly majorities are a transient and often a localized phenomenon in the world of biblical criticism.

In this state of affairs, while most have continued to pursue the traditional critical method,[5] at least one scholar has declared the method to be bankrupt and another regards it as moribund and near to its end.[6] Still others have moved to various kinds of language analysis[7] or to symbolic and psychological exegesis reminiscent of allegorical and of other non-historical methods in the patristic and in the medieval church.[8] Moreover, many in the pews and among the pastors of the churches regard historical criticism as either irrelevant or detrimental to the true understanding of Scripture. These attitudes seem to have arisen not only from the lack of any assured or abiding results in the use of the method but also from the seeming abstraction or hostility of many critical studies for the meaning of the Bible in the church. How is it that a method which began with so much promise could have reached such a confused and disordered state?

ABERRATIONS

The interpretation of Scripture is subject, of course, to the same errors as the analysis of other historical documents. However, it has been plagued with problems and disagreements that may, I believe,

---

[5] Cf. E. Krentz, *The Historical Critical Method*, Philadelphia 1975; E. E. Ellis, 'Historical Method,' *Christ and the Future in New Testament History*, Leiden 2000, 243–246.

[6] W. Wink, *The Bible in Human Transformation*, Philadelphia 1973, 1: 'Historical biblical criticism is bankrupt;' G. Maier, *The End of the Historical-Critical Method*, St. Louis 1977; idem, *Biblical Hermeneutics*, Wheaton IL 1994, 247–306. For Roman Catholic objections, reactions and suggested new directions in biblical criticism cf. R. E. Brown, 'All Gaul is Divided,' *USQR* 40 (1985), 99–103 (a critique of three French Catholic scholars: J. Carmignac, C. Trestemont and R. Laurentin); D. Farkasfalvy, 'In Search of a "Post-Critical" Method . . .,' and I. de la Potterie, 'Reading Holy Scripture "in the Spirit" . . .,' *Communio* [USA] 4 (1986), 288–325.

[7] For example, 'Literary Theory,' 'Reader Response Criticism,' 'Structuralism and Deconstruction' in *DBI* II, 77–85, 370–373, 509–515; B. C. Lategan and W. S. Vorster, *Text and Reality*, Atlanta 1985. But see V. S. Poythress, 'Philosophical Roots of Phenomenological and Structuralist Literary Criticism,' *WTJ* 41 (1978–79), 165–171; A. C. Thiselton, 'Structuralism and Biblical Studies: Method or Ideology?' *ET* 89 (1977–78), 329–335; J. A. D. Weima, 'Literary Criticism,' *INT*.

[8] For example, Wink (note 6), 19–83. Cf. G. Aichele, *Limits of Story*, Philadelphia 1985, 36–46, 121–128; D. S. Greenwood, 'Post-Structuralism and Biblical Studies:

be largely attributed to two mistaken assumptions, one concerning the nature of historical knowledge and the other concerning the competence and the role of human reason. Let us consider these factors in turn.

The Subjectivity of Historical Knowledge

In the nineteenth century it was widely believed that history-writing was a science that could recreate the past 'as it actually occurred' (*wie es eigentlich gewesen*), to use the oft repeated phrase of Leopold von Ranke.[9] Certainly Ranke towered above contemporary historians in his effort 'to divorce the study of the past from the passions of the present' and in his insistence on the use of primary and contemporary sources in the writing of history.[10] But it is doubtful that he gave his phrase the objective ring that was given it by others or that he regarded his work as disinterested science since, as he put it, it was philosophic and religious interest and the hope to come nearer to God that drove him to history.[11]

In fact, modern history-writing has often been highly subjective and, intentionally or not, has served the national, economic or ideological interest of the particular historian. In general terms this can be seen in the Prussian School[12] and in various British historians including both those who sought to write 'scientific history' and those who viewed 'history as literature.'[13] More specifically, it was evident

---

Frank Carmode's, "The Genesis of Secrecy,"' *Studies in Midrash and Historiography* (*Gospel Perspectives* 3), edd. R. T. France and D. Wenham, Sheffield UK 1983, 263–288. Certain affinities between the 'dehistoricizing' existentialist hermeneutic of R. Bultmann and second-century Gnosticism have been noted by W. Rordorf, 'The Theology of Rudolf Bultmann and Second-Century Gnosis,' *NTS* 13 (1966–67), 357–362. Cf. also O. Cullmann, *Salvation in History*, London 1967, 24–28 = GT: 6–10.

[9] The phrase occurred in the preface to the first edition of Leopold von Ranke, *Geschichte der romantischen und germanischen Völker von 1494–1514*, 3 vols., Leipzig ³1885 (¹1824), I, vii: '[Der gegenwärtige Versuch] will blos zeigen wie es eigentlich gewesen.'

[10] G. P. Gooch, *History and History Writing in the Nineteenth Century*, London 1928, 101f.

[11] Gooch (note 10), 77.

[12] Gooch (note 10), 130–155 (discussing, among others, G. Droysen and H. v. Treitschke).

[13] Cf. John Kenyon, *The History Men: The Historical Profession in England since the Renaissance*, London ²1993 (from Sir Walter Raleigh to G. R. Trevor-Roper). Further on the problem see K. Mueller-Vollmer, *The Hermeneutics Reader*, New York 1985, 1–53; H. S. Commager, *The Study of History*, Columbus OH 1966, 53–60.

quite early for those of us from the American South who were weaned on oral family traditions of the War between the States and on such books as Jefferson Davis' *The Rise and Fall of the Confederate Government* and who later experienced in school the interpretations of, say, the historian Charles A. Beard.[14]

The myth of the objective critical historian was shattered above all by the devastating critique of Carl Becker.[15] For the modern historian, he wrote,

> it is the concept that determines the facts, not the facts the concept.... Instead of 'sticking to the facts,' the facts stick to him, if he has any ideas to attract them (534)...
>
> [He] is detached from any fixed idea in religion, placing himself 'too far off—for espousing the cause of either good or evil.' But he knows well that he must espouse, with fine enthusiasm, the cause of not espousing any cause (534f.)...
>
> But it is difficult not to take sides if sharp contrasts and impassable gulfs are permitted to appear. If one could serve neither God nor Mammon, it is necessary to dispense with both. The modern historian has therefore a concept, a preconcept, of continuity and evolution, with 'natural law' at the back of things.... Facts which do not contribute to establish these concepts will not be selected; they may be unique, but they are judged not important (535).

Becker's observations bring to mind a story about Georg Hegel's lectures on the philosophy of history at the University of Berlin. At some point a student protested, 'But, Herr Professor, the facts are otherwise.' Hegel replied, 'So much the worse for the facts.' His point, I suppose, was that historical 'facts' take on meaning only in the context of interpretation and that interpretation, therefore, is the more important component of historical knowledge.

In nineteenth and twentieth-century biblical studies the historical-critical method was assumed to have an objectivity, a 'scientific' character, that endowed it with an almost irresistible authority. It

---

[14] J. Davis, *The Rise and Fall of the Confederate Government*, 2 vols., London and Cranbury NJ 1958 (1881). Cf. the discussion in D. H. Fischer, *Historians' Fallacies*, New York 1970, 24–31; C. A. Beard, *The Rise of American Civilization*, New York 1933.

[15] C. L. Becker, 'Detachment and the Writing of History,' *The Atlantic Monthly* 106 (1910), 524–536 = *Detachment and the Writing of History: Essays and Letters...*, ed. P. L. Snyder, Ithaca NY 1958, 3–28. For an opposing view cf. Fischer (note 14), 41ff.

was thought to give the 'historical facts' in contrast to the dogmatic pictures of the biblical story traditional in the church. Unfortunately, it only substituted one dogma for another, philosophical for theological. One may illustrate this briefly by three examples, (1) the reconstruction of Old Testament history popularized by J. Wellhausen, (2) the Quest for the 'historical' Jesus and (3) F. C. Baur's reconstruction of early Christian history.

Wellhausen's theory of the origin and composition of the Pentateuch, which determined his own understanding of Old Testament history and which continues in a modified way to influence contemporary reconstructions,[16] could have been produced and found acceptable only in the late nineteenth century when the then dominant evolutionary ideas of progress and Hegelian theories of history provided the conceptual magnet to which Wellhausen's selected facts could stick.[17] Likewise, writers on the 'Quest of the historical Jesus' from H. S. Reimarus to W. Wrede, brilliantly reviewed by Albert Schweitzer,[18] sought to recover a Jesus freed from theological dogma but only succeeded in finding a 'liberal' Jesus congenial to their own interests. They were like men peering into a well, who sought an object in its distant depths but saw only the reflection of their own faces.

---

[16] J. Wellhausen, *Komposition des Hexateuchs*, Berlin ⁴1963 (¹1885). Cf. J. Van Seters, *Prologue to History*, Louisville KY 1992, 8–23; B. S. Childs, *An Introduction to the Old Testament as Scripture*, Philadelphia 1979, 112ff., 119–124; O. Kaiser, *Introduction to the Old Testament*, Oxford 1975, 39f.; O. Eissfeldt, *The Old Testament: An Introduction*, Oxford 1965, 164–170. Otherwise: G. C. Aalders, *A Short Introduction to the Pentateuch*, London 1949; U. Cassuto, *The Documentary Hypothesis and the Composition of the Pentateuch*, Jerusalem 1961; I. M. Kikawada and A. Quinn, *Before Abraham Was: The Unity of Genesis 1–11*, Nashville 1985. Cf. the discussion and critique of G. J. Wenham, *Genesis 1–15*, Waco TX 1987, xxv–xlv; idem, 'Pondering the Pentateuch: The Search for a New Paradigm,' *The Face of Old Testament Studies*, edd. D. W. Baker *et al.*, Grand Rapids 1999, 116–144. Cf. C. Houtman, 'Pentateuchal Criticism,' *DBI* II, 260f.

[17] Cf. H. J. Kraus, *Geschichte der historisch-kritischen Erforschung des Alten Testaments*, Neukirchen 1956, 286f.; W. F. Albright, *History, Archeology and Christian Humanism*, London 1965, 136–140. Re W. Vatke, cf. J. W. Rogerson, *Old Testament Criticism in the Nineteenth Century*, Philadelphia 1985, 69–78.

[18] A. Schweitzer, *Geschichte der Leben-Jesu Forschung*, Tübingen 1984 (1906); now a full English translation in idem, *The Quest of the Historical Jesus*, London 2000. J. D. Crossan, *The Historical Jesus: The Life of a Mediterranean Jewish Peasant*, San Francisco 1991, is reminiscent of those 'Lives' with the grave-clothes changed to contemporary dress. Written in the Baur tradition, it rejects much of the first-century New Testament evidence, uncritically accepts much later apocryphal material and rep-

The original Quest ended in failure,[19] and subsequent 'quests' that produced an 'apocalyptic' or 'existentialist' or 'revolutionary Jesus,' also carried the brand-marks of their times and of their authors.[20] The 'historical' Jesus was inevitably the historian's Jesus. All such reconstructions are necessarily interpretations since history, in this sense, is itself interpretation.[21] For the church they will succeed only to the degree to which they accord with and explain the 'historical' Jesus presented by the Evangelists, those prophetically inspired interpreters who provide the church's standard by which all other works are to be measured. They have often failed because they set their interpretations over against the Gospels and wrongly supposed that their own constructions carried an 'objectivity' that was lacking in others.

In the mid-nineteenth century F. C. Baur carried out a thoroughgoing reconstruction of early Christian history that imposed a diachronic pattern upon the relationship of the New Testament documents based, like Wellhausen's views, upon Hegelian philosophy.[22] He interpreted the whole of that history on a supposedly enduring conflict between the party of Paul ('thesis') and that of Peter ('antithesis') which was slowly reconciled in later generations ('synthesis'), and on this basis he dated most of the New Testament books to a post-apostolic period. His largely theoretical reconstruction, which in fact not only was philosophically determined but also misunderstood the nature of the conflicts reflected in early Christianity, became a dominant factor in the criticism of both the Gospels and the New Testament letters and continues to be influential in New Testament

---

resents a rather tendentious historian's Jesus. See Ellis, 'The Historical Jesus and the Gospels,' 'Background and Christology of John's Gospel' (note 5), 3–19, 70–88.

[19] Cf. G. Bornkamm, *Jesus of Nazareth*, New York 1960, 13: 'Albert Schweitzer... has erected its memorial, but at the same time has delivered its funeral oration. Why have these attempts failed? Perhaps only because it became alarmingly and terrifyingly evident how inevitably each author brought the spirit of his own age into his presentation of the figure of Jesus.' See Ellis (note 5), 3–7.

[20] E.g. Crossan (note 18). Cf. J. W. Bowman, *Which Jesus?* Philadelphia 1970.

[21] Cf. B. Lonergan, *Method in Theology*, New York 1972, 175–234: 'The word, history, is employed in two senses. There is history (1) that is written about, and there is history (2) that is written. History (2) aims at expressing knowledge of history (1)' (175).

[22] Cf. especially F. C. Baur, *Paul*, 2 vols., London ²1876 (1845); idem, *The Church History of the First Three Centuries*, 2 vols., London 1878 (1853); idem, *Ausgewählte Werke*, 5 vols., Stuttgart 1963–1975. See below, 41ff.

scholarship today.²³ Nevertheless, while he freed exegesis from some mistaken traditional models and demonstrated the importance of conflicts in early Christianity for understanding its history, he did so only to lead New Testament study into a Hegelian captivity from which it has not even yet escaped. And primarily for this reason he was, as a historian, much less reliable than, say, his compatriots, Augustus Neander and Theodor Zahn, or his counterpart in the British Isles, J. B. Lightfoot.²⁴

The Syndrome of Rationalism

A second factor detrimental to the contribution of historical criticism was the assumption that human reason in itself was competent to determine the meaning, at least the historical meaning, of Scripture. In part it was the product of the eighteenth century's 'autonomous man,' or what Karl Barth has called 'absolute man,'²⁵ filled with the self-confidence not to say the hubris associated with the scientific and political enlightenment of 'man come of age.' In part it was derived from a Cartesian and earlier rationalism that affected in diverse ways the approach to the Bible of both traditional Protestant 'high orthodoxy' and Deistic-influenced scholarship.²⁶ In biblical criticism from J. P. Gabler to the present the assumption of the omnicompetence of human reason has reflected a confidence that method was master of Scripture and that, if the right tools were rightly

---

²³ Cf. E. E. Ellis, 'Ferdinand Christian Baur and his School,' *The Making of the New Testament Documents*, Leiden 1999, 440–445; idem, 'Paul and his Opponents,' *Prophecy and Hermeneutic in Early Christianity*, Tübingen 1978, 86–95, 100–105; idem, *Paul and His Recent Interpreters*, Grand Rapids ⁵1979, 18ff. For a contemporary defense of Baur's viewpoint cf. G. Lüdemann, *Opposition to Paul in Jewish Christianity*, Minneapolis MN 1989, 35–115; M. D. Goulder, *St. Paul versus St. Peter: A Tale of Two Missions*, Louisville KY 1995.

²⁴ E.g. A. Neander, *History of the Planting and Training of the Christian Church*, London ³1851; T. Zahn, *Einleitung in das Neue Testament*, 2 vols. in 1, Wuppertal 1994 (³1907) = ET: 3 vols., Grand Rapids: Kregel 1987; J. B. Lightfoot, 'St. Paul and the Three,' *Saint Paul's Epistle to the Galatians*, London ¹⁰1892, 292–374. Cf. H. Harris, *The Tübingen School*, Grand Rapids ²1990, vii–xvi, 181–237; S. Neill and T. Wright, *The Interpretation of the New Testament 1861–1986*, Oxford ²1988, 20–64; Ellis, *Prophecy* (note 23), 84–95.

²⁵ Cf. K. Barth, *Protestant Theology in the Nineteenth Century*, London 1972, 33–79, 37 (*absolutistische Mensch*): 'The man of the eighteenth century approaches even Christianity with the belief in the omnipotence of human capability' (83); H. Thielicke, *The Evangelical Faith*, 3 vols., Grand Rapids 1974–1982, I, 49–53.

²⁶ Cf. J. B. Rogers and D. K. McKim, *The Authority and Interpretation of the Bible*, San Francisco 1979, 187f., 247f.; Reventlow (note 4), 411f.

applied, the historical meaning of the text would become apparent.[27] This assumption, which flew in the face of Paul's indictment of autonomous human reason in I Cor 1:18–3:20, led to a dismissal of the Holy Spirit from the task of historical criticism even if, in orthodox circles, a *pro forma* nod to the illumination of the Spirit was still given. Among scholars who worked within a 'closed' naturalistic world view, criticism became even more narrowly anthropocentric.

A mythological interpretation of biblical accounts of miracles, which pushed out an earlier rationalism,[28] is usually associated with the name of Rudolf Bultmann although 'the myth school' has roots going back to D. F. Strauss and J. P. Gabler.[29] For Bultmann it rested upon a philosophical assumption and determined his understanding of historical-literary criticism. In one article[30] he wrote,

> The historical method includes the presupposition that history is a unity in the sense of a closed continuum of effects in which individual events are connected by the succession of cause and effect....
>
> This closedness means that the continuum of historical happenings cannot be rent by the interference of supernatural powers and that therefore there is no 'miracle' in this sense of the word. Such a miracle would be an event whose cause did not lie within history.... [Historical science] cannot perceive such an act... [but] understands in terms of that event's immanent historical causes.
>
> It is in accordance with such a method as this that the science of history goes to work on all historical documents. And there cannot be any exceptions in the case of biblical texts....

---

[27] Cf. K. Stendahl, 'Method in the Study of Biblical Theology,' *The Bible in Modern Scholarship*, ed. J. P. Hyatt, Nashville TN 1965, 196–205, and the (quite convincing) response of A. Dulles in the same volume (210–216). Stendahl's essay stands in the tradition of J. P. Gabler. Cf. L. T. Stuckenbruck, 'Johann Philipp Gabler and the Delineation of Biblical Theology,' *SJT* 52 (1999), 139–157, 154–157.

[28] For example, as espoused by H. E. G. Paulus (*Das Leben Jesu als Grundlage einer reinen Geschichte des Urchristentums*, 4 vols. in 3, Heidelberg 1828), who explained miracles as the onlookers 'misunderstanding of natural events.' This psychological approach had its background in David Hume's, 'Of Miracles,' *An Inquiry Concerning Human Understanding*, London 1748, Section 10. Cf. Schweitzer, *Quest* (note 18), 50–55 = GT: 91–95; 'Rationalism,' *OED* II, 2421.

[29] On its background in German theology cf. C. Hartlich and W. Sachs, *Der Ursprung des Mythosbegriffes in der Moderne Wissenschaft*, Tübingen 1952. For its most notorious representative piece cf. D. F. Strauss, *The Life of Jesus Critically Examined*, Philadelphia 1972 (^{4}1840).

[30] R. Bultmann, 'Is Exegesis Without Presuppositions Possible?' *Existence and Faith*, New York 1960, 291f. = GT: *TZ* 13 (1957), 11. For a critique of Bultmann's point of view cf. Richardson (note 4), 139–147; T. F. Torrance, *Theological Science*, London 1969, 312–337.

One observes here how Bultmann's confessional commitment to a particular philosophical, essentially Epicurean, dogma determined his understanding of history and thus of historical criticism. It had particularly perverse effects for understanding the biblical documents because it imposed a confessional norm and world view that succeeded in silencing the very affirmation that the biblical writers wished to make, that is, their conviction and experience of the redemptive action—including miraculous action—of God in time and matter and history.

Nevertheless, historical criticism as such should not be identified with the rationalistic assumptions on which it has sometimes been pursued. There are signs today that it is moving beyond the 'closed' world view of rationalism toward a renewal of theistic assumptions and an openness to transcendence in its analysis and interpretation of the Scriptures.[31]

Errors in historical criticism are also due, of course, to a faulty use of the method. They may include mistakes in understanding the words, grammar and syntax, in identifying the literary genre and in perceiving the historical origins, context and relationships of a given passage or document. It is important to remember, however, that such errors are common to all historical and literary analysis and that they can be corrected only by a better use of the method.

THE NECESSITY AND CONTRIBUTION OF HISTORICAL CRITICISM

Given the uncertainties in the art of historical reconstruction and the variety and subjectivity in interpretation, one may be tempted to the cynical remark of Voltaire that history, after all, is only a pack of tricks that the living play on the dead. Certainly, the discipline of history, like other social sciences, is more an art than a science. It is a *Vermutungswissenschaft*,[32] in which subjective elements are unavoidable. This does not mean, of course, that every historical reconstruction is equally defensible. Some can be shown to be unten-

---

[31] For example, in the work of P. Stuhlmacher, *Historical Criticism and Theological Interpretation of Scripture*, Philadelphia 1977, 61–91. Cf. E. E. Ellis, *The Old Testament in Early Christianity* (*WUNT* 54), Tübingen and Grand Rapids 1991, 148–151; idem, *Making* (note 23), 3–19; idem (note 5), 254–278.

[32] 'Supposition-science.' See M. Hengel, 'Der Jakobusbrief als antipaulinische Polemik,' *Tradition and Interpretation in the New Testament. FS E. E. Ellis*, ed. G. F. Hawthorne with Otto Betz, Grand Rapids and Tübingen 1987, 252.

able by a proper use of historical method, but none achieve the degree of objectivity of, say, the natural sciences. History, after all is said and done, remains interpretation.

However, Christians can never forget that ours is a historical faith, our salvation a salvation in history, and our confessed 'Word of God written' a collection of documents composed by prophets, i.e. pneumatics in specific times and places. The historical analysis of Scripture is for us, therefore, not an option but a necessity, a necessity that has become more urgent because of the heightened historical consciousness and enterprise of the world in which we live. Pursued properly, it is also a part of the Christian's responsibility to 'love the Lord your God... with all your mind' (Mt 22:37) and, if one is called to do so, to fail to pursue this avenue of mental endeavor is to sin.

To paraphrase Winston Churchill's comment about democracy,[33] historical-literary criticism is the worst method of interpretation ever devised by man, except for all the others that have been tried. This is perhaps an exaggeration since the Apostle Paul, using rabbinic methods, brought forth the Word of God from the Scriptures more abundantly than anything modern historical studies have been able to produce. Nevertheless, for our time and place in the church historical criticism, as a method, has offered more in terms of explanation, clarification and heuristic probing of the biblical texts than other approaches, traditional or speculative. From the exegetical-historical work of, say, a J. B. Lightfoot, a Theodor Zahn or an Adolf Schlatter I am fully persuaded of that.[34]

Historical analysis has two virtues that set it apart: it is falsifiable and it is self-corrective. (1) Although as a method it cannot identify the certain and true meaning of a passage, it can set out various options and in some cases show that a given interpretation is erroneous. (2) When it is misused, others are able to point out what went wrong and to offer a more defensible interpretation of the matter. This may be illustrated in New Testament studies by two issues,

---

[33] Cf. *The Oxford Dictionary of Quotations*, edd. B. Darwin *et al.*, Oxford ³1980, 150.

[34] For example, the oft-reprinted J. B. Lightfoot, *St. Paul's Epistle to the Galatians*, Peabody MA 1994 (¹⁰1892), T. Zahn, *Das Evangelium des Matthäus*, Wuppertal 1984 (⁴1922); idem, *Einleitung in das Neue Testament*, 2 vols. in 1, Wuppertal 1994 (³1907); and A. Schlatter, *Der Evangelist Matthäus*, Stuttgart 1959 (²1933).

the form criticism of the Gospels and the authorship of certain New Testament letters.

Classical and Contemporary Form Criticism

The classical form criticism of the Gospels rested on historical and literary assumptions that can now be shown to have been mistaken and that, consequently, must be revised. It assumed, among other things, that Jesus' acts and teachings were first transmitted exclusively in an oral manner and that, like folk traditions, they were freely transformed by any jackleg preacher who cared to do so.

As has been argued elsewhere,[35] this 'oral transmission' theory was thought to be supported by the early Christians' expectation of a near-term end of the age and arrival of God's kingdom, which caused them to eschew the writing down of Jesus' teachings. This idea foundered with the discovery of the library of the Qumran sect, which had the same expectation and produced many writings. It also was at odds with the facts (1) that education had a long tradition in Palestinian Judaism, (2) that teaching children to read and write was commanded by the Law (Josephus)[36] and (3) that some written transmission of Jesus' teaching would probably have been needed for his sedentary adherents in Judea and in Galilee during his three to five-year earthly ministry.[37] There was, in fact, no pre-literary stage in early Christianity. The theory of an 'oral period' propounded by the classical form criticism had its background not in the practices of first-century religious Judaism but in J. G. Herder's eighteenth-century conception of the Gospel traditions as 'oral saga.'[38]

The theory of a 'folk-tradition' transmission of Jesus traditions has even less historical basis.[39] It also had its background in Herder's

---

[35] Ellis, *Making* (note 23), 21–27; *Prophecy* (note 23), 242–247.

[36] Josephus, *Against Apion* 2, 204: γράμματα παιδεύειν ἐκέλευσεν; cf. idem, *Ant.* 4, 211. Cf. Dt 6:6f.; 11:19f.; *Testament of Levi* 13, 2; Philo, *Embassy to Gaius* 115; 210; R. Riesner, *Jesus als Lehrer*, Tübingen ³1988, 97–206.

[37] Ellis, *Prophecy* (note 23), 242–247; cf. R. Riesner, 'Jesus as Preacher and Teacher,' *Jesus and the Oral Gospel Tradition*, ed. H. Wansbrough, Sheffield UK 1991, 193–196. Jesus' ministry probably extended from autumn AD 28 to spring AD 33. See Ellis, *Making* (note 23), 248–251; B. Reicke, *The New Testament Era*, Philadelphia 1968, 183f.; on the problem cf. J. Finegan, *Handbook of Biblical Chronology*, Princeton 1964, 259–273, 291–300.

[38] Cf. Kümmel (note 4), 80–83 = GT: 94–99.

[39] Cf. E. E. Ellis, 'Gospels Criticism,' *The Gospel and the Gospels*, ed. P. Stuhlmacher, Grand Rapids 1991, 37–41 = GT: 38–43; idem, *Making* (note 23), 19–27, 26f.

romanticism, evidenced little knowledge of first century Jewish practice and was at odds with the cultivated and controlled 'receiving' (παραλαμβάνειν) and 'delivering' (παραδιδόναι) of religious tradition characteristic of rabbinic Judaism and of early Christianity, as O. Cullmann, H. Riesenfeld, B. Gerhardsson and R. Riesner have shown.[40]

Historical criticism enables us today to correct these previous errors and to set forth a better form criticism showing that the traditions of Jesus were carefully cultivated, transmitted by an authorized leadership and fixed in writing much earlier than was formerly supposed.

Criteria for the Authorship of New Testament Letters

The self-correcting character of historical-literary criticism may also be illustrated by the discussion of the authorship of certain New Testament letters. Nineteenth-century scholars observed that some Pauline letters, for example, differed from others in vocabulary, style and theological expression. Some of these scholars, in particular F. C. Baur, rejecting both the Pauline attributions in the letters and the testimony of the patristic church, concluded that Paul could not have authored them. Under the influence of Hegelian dialectic they dated them to a time long after Paul's death.[41] A major assumption underlying this viewpoint, an assumption shared by traditional and speculative scholars alike, was that Paul either sat down on a Sunday afternoon and penned his letters or that he dictated them verbatim to a secretary. It provided the basis for arguing that a different style, vocabulary and theological expression meant a different author. However, more recent historical and literary criticism has shown that the assumption was mistaken.

In antiquity, expert amanuenses, i.e. secretaries, were regularly employed to write letters and other documents of any length, and

---

[40] Cf. M Aboth 1:1; Lk 1:2; Acts 16:4; Rom 6:17; I Cor 11:2, 23; 15:1–3; Col 2:6ff.; II Pet 2:21; Jude 3. See Ellis, 'The Making of the New Testament Letters,' *Making* (note 23), 53–59. Cf. O. Cullmann, 'The Tradition,' *The Early Church*, London 1956, 57–99; H. Riesenfeld, *The Gospel Tradition*, Philadelphia 1970, 1–29; B. Gerhardsson, *Memory and Manuscript*, Grand Rapids ²1998; Riesner (note 35), 353–502; Ellis, *Making* (note 23), 54. Otherwise: W. H. Kelber, 'Die Anfangsprozesse der Verschriftlichung im Frühchristentum,' *ANRW* II, 26, 1 (1992), 3–62; idem, *The Oral and the Written Gospel*, Philadelphia 1983, whose work is critiqued by B. Gerhardsson, *The Gospel Tradition*, Lund 1986, 30–42, 56f.

[41] They placed these letters at the 'synthesis' stage of the dialectic. See below, Chapter Five, 66ff.; Ellis, *Making* (note 23), 440ff.; idem, 'The Pastorals and Paul,' *ET* 104 (1992–93), 45–47.

they exercised a variable degree of freedom in their composition. They also would include, as the author might direct, previously written materials that were pertinent to the topic.[42]

Paul also employed secretaries in the writing of his letters, persons who in accordance with the practice of the day exercised some influence on the letters' style and vocabulary.[43] Even more important, he incorporated preformed traditions in virtually all of his letters and a considerable number in some. They make up over 40% of four letters (Ephesians, Colossians, I Timothy, Titus) and about 37% in I Thessalonians.[44] Some of the preformed pieces were authored by Paul, but others were composed by prophets and inspired teachers in his and allied apostolic missions.[45] Given the role of the amanuenses and the presence of preformed traditions, one can no longer use in any precise way internal criteria of style, vocabulary and theological expression to make judgments about the authorship of the letters attributed to Paul but must now give priority to external historical evidence. One can now see that nineteenth-century objections to Paul's authorship, which were made on the basis of internal criteria, were without literary or historical basis. And it was a better literary criticism that uncovered the fallacy of a viewpoint that made its case above all on literary criticism.

LIMITATIONS

In the nature of the case 'method' is a limited instrumentality for understanding the biblical texts.[46] It may be refined and utilized to the highest degree possible for human reason and still miss the meaning, even the historical meaning, of the text. There are at least two

---

[42] This has been demonstrated in the case of Josephus by H. St. John Thackeray (*Josephus*, 9 vols., London 1926–1965, II, xvf., xx–xxiv), for *The Letters of Pliny* (Oxford 1966, 538–546) by A. N. Sherwin-White and, with regard to secretarial usage, for Cicero by E. R. Richards, *The Secretary in the Letters of Paul* (*WUNT*[2] 42), Tübingen 1991, 23f., 127, 165–168; J. Murphy-O'Connor, *Paul the Letter-Writer*, Collegeville MN 1995, 6–16. Cf. Ellis, *Making* (note 23), 324–329.

[43] Rom 16:22; the postscripts at Gal 6:11; II Thess 3:17; Plm 19; cf. O. Roller, *Das Formular der paulinischen Briefe*, Stuttgart 1933; Richards (note 42), 194–198.

[44] Cf. Ellis, *Making* (note 23), 116, 139.

[45] It is assumed that only teachings of those recognized as pneumatics, that is, inspired teachers, would have been considered for inclusion.

[46] Further cf. R. E. Murphy, 'The Song of Songs: Critical Biblical Scholarship vis-à-vis Exegetical Traditions,' in Butler (note 2), 63f.

reasons for this, the limitations and frailties of historical knowledge, which we have observed above, and the nature of Scripture.

From the perspective of the biblical writers, and of Jesus as he is represented by them, the essential meaning of the Scriptures is revelation, also in their historical and literary dimension. As such, the meaning is understood to be either hidden or revealed to the reader at God's discretion and is never viewed as truth available, like pebbles on a beach. Thus, the meaning of a biblical text is said to be hidden because of wrong interpretation (Mt 15:6), because of a failure to read it christologically (II Cor 3:12–18) or because of God's purpose (Dan 12:8f.; Lk 9:44f.).

When the meaning is 'unveiled,' it is regarded as something attained not by human method or wisdom but by God's revelatory act. Consequently, when the messianic prophecies were connected to Jesus, he replied, 'Flesh and blood has not revealed this to you but my Father in heaven' (Mt 16:15ff.). Or he explained his disciples' understanding of, among other things, his biblical expositions with the words,

> To you it is given [by God] to know
> The mysteries of the kingdom of God.
> *Lk 8:10*

And he sometimes concluded a sermon with the phrase: 'He who has ears to hear, let him hear' (Mt 11:15). For the New Testament writers only the Holy Spirit can provide the ears by which the truth of the Bible will be received.[47]

As is the case in other aspects of Christianity, there is a paradoxical element in the biblical teaching on understanding the sacred texts. When the Word of God hidden in Scripture is unveiled, it is viewed as a divine disclosure, not a truth that one achieves but a truth that one receives from God. Nevertheless, one is not to remain passive in receiving it. One is commanded to pray, to study, and to meditate on the words of the prophets and apostles. And, following the example of the biblical writers, one may use 'method.'[48] It is in this frame of reference that God is pleased to unveil his prophetic word.

---

[47] On this 'patristic way of reading the Bible' and (from a Roman Catholic perspective) the need to rediscover it cf. de la Potterie (note 6), 310–313, 320–325. See Ellis, 'The Role of the Prophet in the Quest for Truth,' (note 5), 255–278.

[48] Cf. Ellis (note 31), 79–101.

Like all ministers, historical-literary critics are servants and not masters of the Word of God. They come or should come to the Bible to listen. Only in the context of listening in the Spirit,[49] even in the midst of historical-literary analysis, will they be enabled to discover the meaning of the texts both in their historical and in their present meaning. Using the Bible apart from the Spirit, whether in the pulpit or in the study, will inevitably lead to aberrations, if not the ones discussed above, then to others. The Reformation symbol of the Spirit-Dove above the open Scriptures should always be emblematic of our study.[50]

---

[49] This is essentially the view of the Reformers, John Calvin and Martin Luther. Cf. P. Stuhlmacher, 'The Hermeneutical Significance of I Cor 2:6–16,' in Hawthorne (note 32), 328f.

[50] Cf. Ellis (note 5), 273–278.

CHAPTER TWO

PSEUDONYMITY AND CANONICITY OF NEW
TESTAMENT DOCUMENTS

Ancient pseudepigrapha, that is, documents written under a name other than the true author, are to be distinguished from writings later misattributed to a wrong name, such as the book of Hebrews in the New Testament, Ecclesiastes in the Old and probably the Wisdom of Solomon in the Apocrypha.[1] They should also be classified to distinguish fictional romances and student exercises written in the name of a famous man, which did not and did not intend to deceive, from pseudepigrapha that were fraudulent and deceptive, whether for religious,[2] financial,[3] political, personal[4] or other motives. Only the latter may rightly be termed forgeries for, in the words of J. D. Denniston, 'with a true forgery, the attribution must be made by the real author himself, and there must be intention to deceive.'[5] Such forgeries were produced in abundance by both pagan and

---

[1] M. Smith, 'Pseudepigraphy in the Israelite Literary Tradition,' *Pseudepigrapha I*, ed. K. von Fritz, Genève 1972, 191–215, argues that Israelite literature, including Ecclesiastes and the Wisdom of Solomon (210), was customarily anonymous and then misattributed. Only under Greek influence did Jewish pseudepigrapha appear, apparently as the product of related sectarian groups (215). Otherwise: D. G. Meade, *Pseudonymity and Canon*, Tübingen 1986, 55–66.

[2] According to R. H. Charles (*Eschatology*, New York 1963 [²1913], 204f.) the general view that inspiration had ceased (cf. BT Sanhedrin 11a; Josephus, *Against Apion* I, 38–42) required apocalyptic writers after 200 BC to write under the name of an ancient prophet or patriarch in order to get a hearing.

[3] The physician, Galen (c. AD 200), wrote the tract, *On His Own Books*, to counter the sale of forgeries of his writings (*Galeni scripta minora 2*, Leipzig 1891, 91–124, cited in B. M. Metzger, 'Literary Forgeries and Canonical Pseudepigrapha,' *JBL* 91 [1972], 6). The libraries at Alexandria and Pergamum paid well for famous authors, and forgery flourished. Cf. J. S. Candlish, 'On the Moral Character of Pseudonymous Books,' *The Expositor: Fourth Series*, 10 vols., ed. W. R. Nicoll, London 1890–94, IV (1891), 95 = GT: in N. Brox, ed., *Pseudepigraphie in der heidnischen und judisch-christlichen Antike*, Darmstadt 1977, 11; J. A. Sint, *Pseudonymität im Altertum*, Innsbruck 1960, 116f.

[4] E.g. Pausanius, *Description of Greece* 6, 18, 4f.: To foster hatred against his enemy, Theopompus, Anaximenes forged a treatise in his name.

[5] J. D. Denniston, 'Forgeries, Literary I. Greek,' *Oxford Classical Dictionary*, ed. N. G. L. Hammond, Oxford ²1970, 444.

Christian writers.[6] But are they to be found in our canonical New Testament?

THE VIEWS OF THE BAUR TRADITION

The claim that pseudepigrapha are present in the New Testament began with the 'tendency' criticism of Edward Evanson over two hundred years ago.[7] Forty years later, with a Hegelian twist, it was more successfully advocated by F. C. Baur, who considered the General Epistles and all but four of Paul's letters to be pseudepigrapha.[8] With Adolf Hilgenfeld's increase of the genuine Pauline Epistles to seven,[9] the Baur School and its followers maintained a fairly fixed identification of New Testament pseudepigrapha. With few exceptions,[10] they are the root of all subsequent scholarship that assigned pseudepigraphal authorships to New Testament documents.

Although his chronology was telescoped and his Hegelian dialectic sometimes dropped, by the turn of the twentieth century Baur's 'tendency' criticism and diachronic reconstruction achieved a broader acceptance and in the work, say, of Adolf Jülicher was the assumed starting point. That is, the Baur hypothesis became the Baur tradi-

---

[6] Cf. W. Speyer, *Die literarische Fälschung im heidnischen und christlichen Altertum*, München 1971.

[7] E. Evanson, *The Dissonance of the Four Generally Received Evangelists*, Ipswich UK 1792, 255–289.

[8] He accepted only Romans, I–II Corinthians and Galatians as genuine. Cf. F. C. Baur, 'Die Christuspartei...' (1831), 136–205f., reprinted in *Ausgewählte Werke*, 5 vols., Stuttgart 1963–75, I, 1–146; idem, *Paul*, 2 vols., London 1876 (1845), I, 248f. = GT: 278f.; II, 106–111 = GT: 116–122; idem, *The Church History of the First Three Centuries*, 2 vols., London 1878–79, I, 122–131, 149f. = GT: 116–124, 143. Cf. E. E. Ellis, 'Foreword,' in H. Harris, *The Tübingen School*, Grand Rapids and Leicester ²1990, xi–xv; idem, *The Making of the New Testament Documents*, Leiden 1999, 440–445.

[9] He was a member of the Baur School. Cf. A. Hilgenfeld, *Historisch-kritische Einleitung in das Neue Testament*, Leipzig 1875, 246f., 330–334, who added Philippians, I Thessalonians and Philemon to the 'genuine' Pauline corpus.

[10] Bruno Bauer and the Dutch School (e.g. A. D. Loman, W. C. Van Manen), those A. Schweitzer calls the 'ultra-Tübingen' critics, were apparently also influenced by Evanson (note 7). Cf. A. Schweitzer, *Paul and his Interpreters*, London 1948 (1912), 117–150. Baur was the decisive figure although a few before him had rejected the genuineness of the Petrine and certain Pauline letters. Cf. W. G. Kümmel, *The New Testament: The History of the Investigation of its Problems*, Nashville 1972, 84ff. = GT: 100–102. See E. E. Ellis, 'Toward a History of Early Christianity,' *Christ and the Future in New Testament History*, Leiden 2000, 216–225.

tion.¹¹ This tradition was predominant in German New Testament studies throughout much of the twentieth century¹² and had a strong influence in America¹³ and, after mid-century, in England.¹⁴ Appropriately enough, it received its most notable converts in recent decades from those who honor tradition, Conservative Evangelicals¹⁵ and Roman Catholics,¹⁶ perhaps with the thought that any wine of a 150-year vintage can't be all bad.

---

¹¹ A. Jülicher, *An Introduction to the New Testament*, London ⁴1904, 16–30 = GT: 12–20, who is congenial with Baur's approach, regards the Pastorals and most of the General Epistles as pseudepigraphic (174–255) but ascribes the rest of the Pauline corpus to the Apostle with the possible exception of Ephesians (142–147). My teacher W. G. Kümmel's (*Introduction to the New Testament*, Nashville ¹⁷1975) revision of P. Feine–J. Behm's *Einleitung in das Neue Testament* (Leipzig 1965 [⁹1951]) reflects a similar shift and accommodation to the Baur tradition, as does J. Weiss (*The History of Primitive Christianity*, 2 vols., New York 1937 [1917]) vis-à-vis his father, B. Weiss (*A Manual of Introduction to the New Testament*, 2 vols., London 1887), who found no pseudepigrapha in the New Testament.

¹² In 1989 it was still defended by G. Lüdemann, *Opposition to Paul in Jewish Christianity*, Philadelphia 1989, whom J. L. Martyn (*USQR* 42, 1–2 [1988], 12) calls 'a sort of F. C. Baur redivivus.' See above, 8n.

¹³ With reference to Ephesians, the Pastorals and the General Epistles, J. Moffatt, *An Introduction to the Literature of the New Testament*, Edinburgh ³1918, 315–428; E. J. Goodspeed, *Introduction to the New Testament*, Chicago 1937, 222–239, 265–295, 327–355; with reference to Ephesians and the Pastorals, J. Knox, *Chapters in the Life of Paul*, Macon GA ²1987 (1950), 8f., 54; idem, *Marcion and the New Testament*, Chicago 1942, 58ff., 73–76.

¹⁴ With the waning of the influence of 'the Cambridge Three:' J. B. Lightfoot, B. F. Westcott, F. J. A. Hort. Cf. M. D. Goulder, *St. Paul versus St. Peter: A Tale of Two Missions*, Louisville KY 1995. For a survey of recent studies cf. T. D. Lea, 'Pseudonymity and the New Testament,' *New Testament Criticism and Interpretation*, edd. D. A. Black and D. S. Dockery, Grand Rapids 1991, 549–553; Meade (note 1), 1–16. See also D. Guthrie, 'Epistolary Pseudepigrapha,' *New Testament Introduction*, Leicester ⁴1990, 1011–1028; Metzger (note 3), 3–24.

¹⁵ I.e. who identify as pseudepigrapha a number of Pauline and/or Petrine letters. Cf. I. H. Marshall, *The Pastoral Epistles*, Edinburgh 1999, 57–92; idem, 'Prospects for the Pastoral Epistles,' *Theology for the People of God. FS J. I. Packer*, edd. D. Lewis et al., Leicester UK 1996, 136–155; R. J. Bauckham, *Jude, 2 Peter*, Waco 1983, 148, passim; J. D. G. Dunn, *Unity and Diversity in the New Testament*, London 1977, 147, 346, passim; idem, 'Pseudepigraphy,' DLNT 977–984. R. P. Martin, *New Testament Foundations II*, Grand Rapids ²1983, 232f., 305, passim; Meade (note 1), 118, 186, 190, passim; Metzger (note 3), 22; idem, *The New Testament*, Nashville ¹⁴1978, 214, 258f.

¹⁶ The Roman Catholic work, *The Jerome Biblical Commentary* (edd. R. E. Brown et al., London 1970, ²1990), identified only II Peter as a pseudepigraphon in the first edition. The revision (1990) followed Hilgenfeld's (note 9) list of Pauline/Petrine pseudepigrapha to the letter except for I Peter, where the patristic witnesses and Catholic tradition prevailed. A. Wikenhauser's *Introduction to the New Testament*, London 1958, identified only II Peter as ungenuine (515). Its revision by J. Schmid (1973), agreed with Hilgenfeld completely, with the possible exception of Colossians.

Critics of Baur's views, in earlier[17] and recent times,[18] raised two important queries: (1) Was his reconstruction historically based? (2) If it was, should the pseudepigraphal documents be retained within the New Testament canon? The present chapter addresses the latter question.

Baur thought that for the 'pseudo-Pauline' letters one should not think of 'deception and intentional forgery' (*Fälschung*). However, he continued, 'if it be asserted that the matter is not intelligible except on this hypothesis [of forgery], that cannot be maintained as an argument (*wäre diess keine Einwendung*) against its possibility and likelihood.'[19] Elsewhere, he states that one could, if one must, give up the canonicity of II Peter, the Pastorals and 'other smaller letters of our canon,' without giving rise to any danger for the historical foundation of Christianity.[20]

Most of Baur's adherents were not so easygoing on this matter. His colleague, F. H. Kern, took the Epistle of James to be forged in order to refute Pauline views but asserted that such an imposture would have been an acceptable and irreproachable practice of the time.[21] A. Jülicher contended that 'the ethical notion of literary property' is a modern conception and that for the early church forgery applied only to the heretical distortion of *religious* truth and not to

---

[17] E.g. J. B. Lightfoot, 'St. Paul and the Three,' *Galatians*, London [10]1892, 292–374; idem, *Essays on the Work Entitled Supernatural Religion*, London 1889, passim; (implicitly) T. Zahn, *Introduction to the New Testament*, 3 vols., Grand Rapids 1953 (1909) = GT: Wuppertal 1994 ([3]1907); A. Harnack, *Geschichte der altchristlichen Literatur II. Chronologie*, 2 vols., Leipzig 1958 (1896), I, viii: 'In the whole New Testament there is, strictly speaking, only one single writing that can be called pseudonymous: the Second Letter of Peter.' However, he thought that other writings, e.g. the Pastorals, suffered later interpolations, a hypothesis that in the light of current textual and historical criticism is very improbable. Cf. Ellis, *Making* (note 8), 85f., 296f., 430; K. Aland, 'Neutestamentliche Textkritik und Exegese,' *Wissenschaft und Kirche. FS E. Lohse*, ed. K. Aland, Bielefeld 1989, 142. See below, 68, 139n.

[18] E.g. Harris (note 8); E. Barnikol, *Ferdinand Christian Baur als rationalistisch-kirchlicher Theologe*, Berlin 1970; W. Geiger, *Spekulation und Kritik: Die Geschichtstheologie Ferdinand Christian Baurs*, München 1964; Ellis (note 10), 216–223.

[19] Baur, *Paul* (note 8), II, 110f. = GT: II, 121.

[20] F. C. Baur, 'Abgenöthigte Erklärung,' *TZT* (1836, 3. Heft), 208 = *Werke* (note 8), I, 296.

[21] F. H. Kern, 'Der Charakter und Ursprung des Briefs Jakobi,' *TZT* (1835, 2. Heft), 72, cited in A. Neander, *History of the Planting and Training of the Christian Church*, London [3]1851, 360. He later affirmed that the author was James, the brother of Jesus; F. H. Kern, *Der Brief Jakobi*, Tübingen 1838, 70–73.

false authorship as such.²² Others echoed the same opinion²³ and/or hypothesized Pauline²⁴ and Petrine²⁵ 'disciples' who up-dated and published the apostles' teachings after their deaths. Kurt Aland argued that, since the authors were only instruments of the Holy Spirit, a particular pseudo-authorship was not all that significant.²⁶ Klaus Koch suggested that the heavenly Paul may have been viewed as speaking after his death through his disciple somewhat like God or the heavenly Jesus spoke through his prophets!²⁷ On this approach, of course, one might justify the canonization of all 'orthodox' New Testament apocrypha. To counter this, James Dunn conjectured that there was a radical shift from first-century Jewish Christianity, which accepted pseudepigrapha as an innocent device like the Jews accepted, e.g. I Enoch and IV Ezra, and second-century Gentile Christianity, which excluded such writings from the canon. Unfortunately, since

---

²² Jülicher (note 11), 52 = GT: 38f. Similar, A. T. Lincoln, *Ephesians*, Dallas 1990, lxxi: 'The idea of "intellectual property" basic to... authorship... played little or no role in [antiquity].' More accurately, 'in the Jewish-Hellenistic sphere as contrasted with the Greco-Roman world the consciousness of intellectual property and individual authorship was underdeveloped' (M. Hengel, 'Anonymität, Pseudepigraphie und "literarische Fälschung" in der judisch-hellenistischen Literatur,' in von Fritz [note 1] 283).

²³ E.g. W. H. Simcox, *The Writers of the New Testament*, London ²1902, 38: At that time it was 'as legitimate an artifice to compose a letter as to compose a speech in the name of a great man...;' F. W. Beare, *The First Epistle of Peter*, Oxford ³1970 (1947): To suggest that pseudepigrapha are fraudulent 'is a purely modern prejudice' (48); C. L. Mitton, *The Epistle to the Ephesians*, Oxford 1951, 222: '[P]seudonymity is "the manner approved by ancient literature" [E. F. Scott]..., a judgement in which Moffatt entirely concurs....' Cf. Moffatt (note 13), 40–44; E. F. Scott, *The Literature of the New Testament*, New York 1949 (1932), 179f.

²⁴ E.g. Lincoln (note 22), lxxii, who followed Meade (note 1), 153–157, and Meade's teacher, Dunn (note 14), 344–359, who in turn followed German adherents of the Baur tradition. On the Roman Catholic side cf. P. Trummer, *Die Paulustradition der Pastoralbriefe*, Frankfurt 1978, 241: The [post-Pauline] Pastorals have been consciously constructed on the model of passages in the Pauline letters even though a literary dependence can be shown only in a few places.

²⁵ Cf. L. Goppelt, *Der erste Petrusbrief*, Göttingen 1978, 69f. = ET: 48–53.

²⁶ K. Aland, 'The Problem of Anonymity and Pseudonymity in Christian Literature of the First Two Centuries,' *The Authorship and Integrity of the New Testament*, edd. K. Aland *et al.*, London 1965, 1–13, 7f., critiqued by H. R. Balz, 'Anonymität und Pseudepigraphie im Urchristentum,' *ZTK* 66 (1969), 403–436, 419ff. Cf. A. Meyer, 'Religiöse Pseudepigraphie als ethisch-psychologisches Problem.' *ZNTW* 35 (1936) 262–279 = Brox (note 3), 90–110: If a prophet can speak in the name of God, it is no great step further if one should feel justified to write in the name of a patriarch or of an apostle (107).

²⁷ K. Koch, 'Pseudonymous Writing,' *The Interpreter's Dictionary of the Bible: Supplementary Volume*, ed. K. Crim, Nashville 1976, 713.

the Jews also excluded I Enoch and IV Ezra from their canon, it is difficult to see how Dunn's examples support his hypothesis.[28] In conclusion, these writers, who are representative of a much larger group, offered no historical evidence for their assertions that New Testament pseudepigrapha were recognized as such and were regarded as innocent compositions, and it seems that most of them were chiefly concerned to defend, on Baurian assumptions, the traditional New Testament canon.

ATTITUDES TOWARD PSEUDEPIGRAPHA IN ANTIQUITY

In pagan, Jewish and Christian circles of the Greco-Roman world the use of a false authorship for purposes of fraud and deception was widespread, as Wolfgang Speyer has demonstrated.[29] This fact presupposes a conception of intellectual property that could be violated. Already in 1891 James Candlish concluded that

> in the early Christian centuries, when any work was given out as of ancient or venerable authorship, it was either received as genuine . . . or rejected as an imposture . . . (103).
>
> There would seem to be no external evidence that pseudonymous works were in ancient times composed in perfect good faith, . . . not intended to deceive anyone (262).[30]

Frederik Torm expressed himself similarly:

> The view that religious circles of Greco-Roman antiquity understood pseudonymity as a literary form and straightaway recognized its rightness is a modern invention.[31]

The attitude of early Christian leaders toward pseudepigrapha, especially those in the name of an apostle, supports this view of the

---

[28] J. D. G. Dunn, *The Living Word*, London 1987, 68, 83ff.: 'There was no intention to deceive [by the pseudepigrapher of the Pastorals and of II Peter] and almost certainly the final [sic] readers were not in fact deceived' (84). Cf. B. S. Easton, *The Pastoral Epistles*, New York 1947, 19: '[The author] was in no sense a "forger". . . . The first recipients knew perfectly well who wrote them. . . .' On the Jewish canon see E. E. Ellis, *The Old Testament in Early Christianity*, Tübingen and Grand Rapids 1992, 9, 17, 35, 38, passim; A. E. Steinmann, *The Oracles of God*, St. Louis MO 1999, 83ff.

[29] Speyer (note 6), 5–10, passim. Cf. also Metzger (note 3), 5–11.

[30] Candlish (note 3), 103, 262 = GT: 20, 24.

[31] F. Torm, *Die Psychologie der Pseudonymität im Hinblick auf die Literatur des Urchristentums*, Gütersloh 1932, 19 = Brox (note 3), 119.

matter. It is illustrated by the responses of the Asian elders to the Acts of Paul and of Serapion (†211), bishop of Antioch, to the Gospel of Peter. Presumably, Serapion at first thought that the Gospel of Peter could be genuine but, after noting heretical opinions in it, investigated further and concluded that it was not. In his counsel to the church of Rhossus in Cilicia he states the operative principle:

> For we, brothers, receive both Peter and the other apostles as Christ. But pseudepigrapha in their name we reject, as men of experience, knowing that we did not receive such [from the tradition].[32]

That is, the test for reading in church was apostolicity as determined by received tradition. On examination the bishop discovered apparently that the Gospel of Peter was not a Petrine document heretically doctored, say, like Marcion's Romans, but a pseudepigraphon. As such he excluded it.

Asian elders deposed a colleague from office for authoring, out of 'love for Paul,' an Acts of Paul that included an apostolic pseudepigraphon, III Corinthians. They condemned the man for presuming to write in the name of an apostle and apparently not because, in his story, he allowed a woman to baptize converts. That was Tertullian's later complaint.[33]

Other apostolic pseudepigrapha that raised no doctrinal objections—e.g. the *Preaching of Peter* (c. AD 100–150), *Apocalypse of Peter* (c. AD 140), *Epistle of the Apostles*, the *Correspondence of Paul and Seneca*[34] and probably the *Epistle to the Laodiceans*[35]—were nevertheless excluded

---

[32] *Apud* Eusebius, *HE* 6, 12, 3; cf. 3, 25, 4–7. On doctored apostolic letters cf. E. F. Evans, *Tertullian Adversus Marcionem*, 2 vols., Oxford 1972, II, 644ff. On the uncertainty about or limited circulation of the Petrine writings in Italy in the late second century cf. The Muratorian Canon, which lacks I Peter and mentions the doubts of some either about II Peter or about another 'Apocalypse of Peter' (cf. D. Theron, *Evidence of Tradition*, Grand Rapids 1958, 112). Further, cf. Ellis, *Making* (note 8), 301ff.: In the mid-second century II Peter was recognized as authoritative, i.e. canonical by a number of writers in the East.

[33] Tertullian, *On Baptism* 17.

[34] Cf. 'Kerygma Petri,' 'Epistle to the Laodiceans,' 'Paul and Seneca,' 'Apocalypse of Peter,' *New Testament Apocrypha*, 2 vols., ed. W. Schneemelcher, Cambridge ²1992, II, 34–53, 620–638. On the *Epistle of the Apostles*, cf. B. M. Metzger, *The Canon of the New Testament*, New York 1987, 180ff.

[35] So, J. B. Lightfoot, *Colossians*, London 1875, 347f.; Schneemelcher (note 34), II, 43f. Otherwise: A. Harnack, *Kleine Schriften*, 2 vols., Leipzig 1980, II, 644–654, who argues that the letter had Marcionite tendencies. Cf. *Muratorian Canon* in Theron (note 32), 112: 'forged according to the heresy of Marcion' (*fictae ad haeresem Marcionis*). But see B. F. Westcott, *The History of the Canon of the New Testament*, London ⁵1881, 218: 'bearing on the heresy of Marcion.'

from the church's canon. The exclusion of such documents presupposes, as H. R. Balz has argued,[36] that the 'apostles of Jesus Christ'[37] had a normative authority and that writings authored by others in their names were regarded as deceptive and fraudulent.

Apostolic Authority in the First-Century Church

The unique authority of the apostles, however, was already present in the first-century church, and it underlies Paul's insistence on his own apostolic status. In I Cor 9:1–3 he writes:

> Am I not free? Am I not an apostle? Have I not seen Jesus our Lord? . . . If to others I am not an apostle, I am to you. For in the Lord you are the seal of my apostleship. This[38] is my answer (ἀπολογία) to those who are examining (ἀνακρίνουσιν) me.

Paul here alludes to the spiritual gift and task of the pneumatics to discern, i.e. to examine and give judgment on one another's revelations.[39] In effect he excludes the apostles from such judgments and thus places their gift above that of prophets, i.e. pneumatics.[40] In II Corinthians he contests the questioning of his apostleship and brands his opponents 'pseudo-apostles.'[41] Apparently for similar reasons, in Galatians he underscores his status as 'apostle through Jesus Christ' and his parity with the apostleship of Peter.[42] Such passages reveal the unique significance of apostolic status for the church of the fifties. II Thess 2:2 also probably refers to pseudo-writings in Paul's name that are to be rejected.[43] If so, it shows the authority that an apostle's name carried and the negative verdict on apostolic pseude-

---

[36] Balz (note 26), 403–436, 420.

[37] On the distinction between 'apostles of Jesus Christ' and 'apostles of the churches' = missionaries cf. E. E. Ellis, *Pauline Theology: Ministry and Society*, Lanham MD ⁴1998, 66, 89ff.

[38] Taking the αὕτη to refer, as always in classical Greek, to the preceding matter. Cf. Mt 3:3; 27:58; Acts 8:26; I Cor 6:4; Gal 5:17; Phil 1:22; M. Zerwick, *Biblical Greek*, Rome ⁵1979, 67f. (Section 213); A. T. Robertson, *A Grammar of the Greek New Testament*, London 1914, 697f.

[39] I Cor 2:14f.; cf. 6:5; 14:29 (διακρίνειν). Cf. F. Büchsel, 'ἀνακρίνω,' *TDNT* 3 (1965/1938), 943f.

[40] I Cor 4:3: 'It matters little to me that I should be examined by you or by any human court;' 14:37f.: 'If anyone thinks that he is a prophet or a pneumatic, let him acknowledge that what things I am writing to you are a command of the Lord.'

[41] II Cor 11:13; 12:11f.

[42] Gal 1:1; cf. 1:12, 17; 2:8f.; I Cor 3:22f.; 4:1.

[43] Cf. II Thess 3:17; F. F. Bruce, *1 & 2 Thessalonians*, Waco 1982, 164.

pigrapha at an early time, whether this is Paul's admonition or a pseudo-Paul's contrivance.

The Deceptive Character of Apostolic Pseudepigrapha

Strictly speaking, the only New Testament writings that can be classified as pseudepigrapha are Pauline and Petrine epistles.[44] Do certain of these documents, say, Ephesians, the Pastorals and I–II Peter, if they were not composed under the eye and affirmation of Paul and Peter, also fall under the verdict of fraud and imposture placed against (other) second-century apostolic pseudepigrapha?

To begin with, it should be noted that the early Christians knew how to transmit the teachings of an authority figure without engaging in pseudepigrapha. For example, Mark introduces his work as 'the beginning of the Gospel of Jesus Christ,'[45] and an anonymous author begins his as 'The Teaching of the Lord through the Twelve Apostles.'[46] Luke's Acts gives a third-person narration of apostolic teaching. They deceived no one. Also, unlike these writers, the assumed pseudo-Pauline and pseudo-Petrine authors did not merely create a title but engaged in an elaborate and complex deception to transmit their own ideas under apostolic color.

In II Thessalonians (2:2f.) 'pseudo-Paul,' like the author of the *Preaching of Peter* (*Epistula* 2:4; *Contestatio* 5:2), condemns other forgeries as he creates his own. In Ephesians he not only carefully imitates the introductions[47] and to some degree the conclusions[48] to the Apostle's letters but also fabricates situations in Paul's lifetime and possibly sets up the readers to anticipate another pseudo-Pauline letter:

---

[44] 'Jude... brother of James' (Jude 1), 'James... servant of the Lord Jesus Christ' (Jas 1:1) and 'John, your brother' (Rev 1:9; cf. 1:1, 4; 21:2; 22:8) are less precise and could refer to a number of individuals.

[45] For the possibility that 'gospel' (Mk 1:1) refers to Mark's book cf. R. Guelich, 'The Gospel Genre' and M. Hengel, '... Problems in the Gospel of Mark,' *The Gospel and the Gospels*, Grand Rapids 1991, 197, 246ff. = GT: 208, 260ff. Tertullian (*Against Marcion* 4, 5) says of the Gospels of Mark and of Luke: 'It is permissible for works that disciples [Mark, Luke] publish to be regarded as belonging to their masters [Peter, Paul].' But this comment does not refer to pseudepigrapha, *pace* Lincoln (note 22), lxxii.

[46] J. P. Audet, *La Didachè: instructions des apôtres*, Paris 1958, 187–206, dates it to AD 50–70, others to the second century.

[47] Cf. Eph 1:1 with II Cor 1:1.

[48] Cf. Eph 6:23f. with I Cor 16:23f.; II Cor 13:11, 14; Gal 6:18. Cf. II Tim 4:19–22 with I Cor 16:19f.; Gal 6:18.

26   CHAPTER TWO

> I, Paul, prisoner of Christ Jesus... (3:1).
>
> As I wrote you before in a brief letter, by which, when you read it, you will be able to know my understanding in the mystery of Christ (3:3f.).
>
> For [the gospel] I am an ambassador in chains (6:20).
>
> Tychicus... I have sent to you... that you may know our circumstances... (6:21f.).

Hypocritically, he condemns the very deceit that he is engaged in:

> Putting away all falsehood, let each one speak truth with his neighbor (4:25).

In the Pastorals the fraud is made even more explicit. In the words of R. P. Martin, 'a later writer employed Paul's name to give credibility and authority' to his own writing.[49] L. R. Donelson, who accepts the Baur tradition without question and without argument, expresses this view even more candidly:

> In the interest of deception [the author of the Pastorals] fabricated all the personal notes, all the... commonplaces in the letters.' '[He employs] any device that... might seem necessary to accomplish his deception.[50]

'Pseudo-Paul' chooses to address Timothy and Titus because they are known to be Paul's co-workers[51] and, to further the pretense, he integrates into the letters Pauline idiom, themes and traditions.[52] In I Timothy he writes:

> I commit this charge to you, Timothy my son (1:18).
>
> These things I write to you, hoping to come to you shortly (3:14).
>
> Until I come, give attention to the reading... (4:13).
>
> I desire that the younger [widows] marry... (5:14).
>
> I charge you before God... that you keep the command... (6:13f.).

---

[49] R. P. Martin, '1, 2 Timothy and Titus,' *Harper's Bible Commentary*, ed. J. L. Mays, San Francisco 1988, 1237.

[50] L. R. Donelson, *Pseudepigraphy and Ethical Argument in the Pastoral Epistles*, Tübingen 1986, 24, 55.

[51] Cf. Rom 16:21; I Cor 4:17; 16:10; II Cor 1:1, 19 (Timothy); II Cor 2:13; 8:23; 12:17f.; Gal 2:1 (Titus).

[52] Cf. M. Wolter, *Die Pastoralbriefe als Paulustradition*, Göttingen 1988; P. Trummer (note 24).

He also censures lying even as he practices it:[53]

> Some shall fall away ... through the hypocrisy of lying words ... (4:1f.).

In II Timothy the author enlarges the fictional references to Pauline situations which, even if they contain genuine fragments,[54] are utilized only to give a semblance of genuineness:[55]

> Stir up the charism from God that is in you through the laying on of my hands (1:6).
>
> All those in Asia deserted me.... [But] Onesiphorus..., when he was in Rome, sought me ... (1:15ff.).
>
> [You know] what happened to me in Antioch, Iconium, Lystra... (3:11).
>
> I am already being offered up, and the time of my departure has come (4:6).
>
> [Come] quickly, for Demas has deserted me.... Crescens has gone to Gaul, Titus to Dalmatia. Luke alone is with me. [Bring] Mark... (4:9ff.).

The pseudepigraphers of I–II Peter are quite as brazen. In I Peter one of them writes with double-tongued artistry:

> Putting away ... all guile and hypocrisy..., I beg
> [you to] ... conduct yourselves well among the pagans in order that, seeing your good works, they may glorify God ... (2:1, 11f.).
> I ..., witness of the sufferings of Christ, exhort the elders among you (5:1).[56]
> I have written you briefly through Silvanus.... Mark, my son, greets you (5:12f.).

In II Peter 'pseudo-Peter' writes similarly:

> We [were] eyewitnesses of his majesty.... And we heard this voice from heaven ... when we were with him on the holy mountain (1:16ff.).

---

[53] Cf. also I Tim 1:9f.

[54] Especially II Tim 4. So, P. N. Harrison, *The Problem of the Pastoral Epistles*, Oxford 1921, 115–127; J. D. Miller, *The Pastoral Letters as Composite Documents*, Cambridge UK 1997. But see J. N. D. Kelly, *The Pastoral Epistles*, London 1963, 29f.: The fragments theory 'is a tissue of improbabilities.'

[55] Cf. also II Tim 1:8, 11f., 13.

[56] *Pace* Kümmel (note 11), 421, in I Pet 5:1 the 'I' refers back to 'Peter Apostle of Jesus Christ' (1:1) and his eyewitness to Christ's sufferings. In the same vein I Pet 5:1 speaks of Peter as 'fellow-elder' but not as 'fellow-witness' with his recipients. Cf. L. Goppelt, *A Commentary on I Peter*, Grand Rapids MI 1993, 340f. = GT: 321f.

[The pseudo-teachers] will go after you with forged (πλαστοῖς) words (2:3).⁵⁷

This is a second letter I am writing you... (3:1f.).

'Our beloved brother Paul... wrote you' (3:15).

Given the unique authority of the apostle in the church, these letters display, if they are pseudepigrapha, clear and sufficient evidence of a deceptive intention.

Conclusion

While certain ancient writings were composed—as school exercises and otherwise—in the name and style of an ancient master with no intention to deceive,⁵⁸ apostolic pseudepigrapha are not analogous to them.⁵⁹ For they were produced in a community where the apostles' teaching had a unique 'Word of God' authority⁶⁰ and where its content and even the identity of true apostles were subject to continuing dispute.⁶¹ In this context they inevitably involved a deceptive imposition of apostolic status on a non-apostolic writing. That they may have been written with good intentions or by 'disciples' is irrelevant. As James Packer has well said, 'Frauds are still fraudulent even when perpetrated from noble motives.'⁶²

The role of the apostle in the earliest church, the evidence for literary fraud in Greco-Roman antiquity and the New Testament letters themselves combine to show that apostolic pseudepigrapha were a tainted enterprise from the start. At no point in the church's early history could they avoid the odour of forgery. Only when the decep-

---

⁵⁷ Cf. H. Braun, 'πλαστοῖς,' *TDNT* 6 (1968/1959), 262 = GT: 262f.

⁵⁸ For examples, cf. the articles on 'Letters, Greek,' and 'Pseudepigraphic Literature' in Hammond (note 5), 497, 743; Speyer (note 6), 32–35. For a modern analogy cf. Robert Graves' *I, Claudius*, London 1934.

⁵⁹ Even less analogous to pseudepigrapha are rewritings of Scripture, say, the Targum of Job and the Temple Scroll at Qumran or the Targums of Onkelos and Jonathan. They reflect Jewish hermeneutical practices in which the Scriptures were contemporized and interpreted, and they were recited or read alongside their biblical *Vorlage*.

⁶⁰ I Thess 2:13; I Cor 14:36f.; I Peter 1:23ff. Cf. II Cor 2:15ff.; Col 1:25; II Thess 2:15; Heb 13:7; II Peter 3:2; Jude 17; I Clem 42:1; Ignatius, *ad Rom* 4:3.

⁶¹ See above, notes 39, 40, 41, 42. Cf. II Peter 1:20–2:1; 3:15f. Cf. E. E. Ellis, *Prophecy and Hermeneutic in Early Christianity*, Tübingen 1978, 105–108, 230–235.

⁶² J. I. Packer, *'Fundamentalism' and the Word of God*, London 1958, 184.

tion was successful were they accepted for reading in church, and when they were found out, they were excluded, e.g. II Peter by the minority who regarded it as pseudonymous.[63]

In the light of these factors scholars cannot have it both ways. They cannot identify apostolic letters as pseudepigrapha and at the same time declare them to be innocent products with a right to a place in the canon. Secular scholars for whom the canon is only an antiquarian curiosity will have little concern for what books are in and what are out. However, historians in the Baur tradition who, with the Patristic and Reformation church, recognize the canonical books as an inspired message from God and the basis for Christian doctrine,[64] are presented with a more serious problem. Clearly they may, as Baur suggested, drop and urge the church to drop forged letters from the canon. But they may not, I think, finesse the question with an apologetic fiction about innocent apostolic pseudepigrapha.[65]

---

[63] E.g. the Syrian church. Cf. B. M. Metzger, *The Canon of the New Testament*, New York 1987, 218–223; B. F. Westcott, *A General Survey of the History of the Canon of the New Testament*. Grand Rapids 1980 ([6]1889), 236–247. On the other hand Jerome (*Letters* 120, 11), who doubted on internal evidence that the same man could have written I and II Peter, decided that in II Peter the Apostle employed a disciple as secretary. So also, J. Calvin, *Hebrews, St. Peter*, Grand Rapids 1963 (1551), 325 (Preface).

[64] This distinction is drawn between canonical and apocryphal writings, for example, by Origen (*Commentary in Matthew* 28 [on Matthew 23:37–39]) and by Jerome (*Prologus in Liber Salomonis*, cited in B. Fischer, ed., *Biblia Sacra iuxta Vulgatam Versionem*, 2 vols., Stuttgart 1969, II, 957). Cf. Ellis (note 28), 17, 32; Westcott (note 35), 12f.

[65] Ellis, *Making* (note 8), 322ff. It may be, of course, that the Baur tradition itself is an unhistorical reconstruction based on false assumptions of nineteenth-century scholarship and that, as John Robinson and earlier Theodor Zahn have argued, there are no pseudepigrapha in the New Testament. But that is another topic. Cf. J. A. T. Robinson, *Redating the New Testament*, London 1976; Ellis, *Making* (note 8), 320–329; Zahn (note 17), I, 152–164 (§9), 491–522 (§29); II, 85–133 (§37), 173–293 (§40–44) = GT: I, 108–116, 350–371, 462–495; II, 28–112.

CHAPTER THREE

DATING THE NEW TESTAMENT

In a remote region in the Appalachian mountains a young college graduate applied for a teaching job. The school's board's first question was, 'Do you believe the earth is round or flat?' The applicant knew that in the area opinion was sharply divided, but he was uncertain of the view of the school board. Desperate for a job, he replied, 'I'll be frank with you, gentlemen. I can teach it either way.'

I am told that in some circles applicants for teaching posts in theological faculties have faced something of the same dilemma when queried about the dates of certain New Testament books. In any case the issue is sufficiently important to warrant further inquiry, and departures from traditional orthodoxy or from current critical orthodoxy should at least have a hearing.

The publication of J. A. T. Robinson's *Redating the New Testament* represented such a departure, developing the thesis that all of the New Testament documents were written before AD 70.[1] Highly informed and carefully thought out, it presented in many instances an impressive case, however it may be finally judged. Bishop Robinson addressed himself primarily to a reconstruction of the historical setting of the New Testament books in their relationship to one another and to certain external events. He gave less attention to a second factor, the background and development of the literary criticism of the New Testament. For this reason, among others, his work has been ignored by most scholars since literary criticism was largely responsible for the post-70 dates often assigned to many New Testament writings. It may be worthwhile, then, to explore further the literary question. But first let us review briefly some of the external evidence that influenced Robinson's understanding of the matter, an understanding that for 25 years has stood unrefuted.

---

[1] J. A. T. Robinson, *Redating the New Testament*, London 1976.

CHAPTER THREE

HISTORICAL EVIDENCE FOR DATING NEW TESTAMENT BOOKS

Among the historical events affecting the dating of New Testament books,[2] four have been regarded as especially important: the fall of Jerusalem in AD 70; the persecution of Christians by the Roman emperor Nero in AD 65–68 and, more doubtfully, by the emperor Domitian in c. AD 95; and the synagogue prayer against heretics (the *birkath ha-minim*) that is usually dated about AD 85–90.

1. The fall of Jerusalem was of particular interest to the early Christians since it had been prophesied by Jesus and since, most explicitly in Luke-Acts, it was anticipated (or looked back on) as a judgment of God upon a rejecting nation. Yet the actual event of AD 70 neither colors the synoptic Gospels' wording of Jesus' prophecy[3] nor is the event mentioned or clearly alluded to anywhere in the New Testament.[4]

---

[2] E.g. the proconsulship of Gallio (AD 51–52; cf. Acts 18:12) and the procuratorship of Festus (AD 60–62; Acts 24:27) have an important bearing on the dating of the Pauline literature; the martyrdom of James (†62; Josephus, *Antiquities* 20, 200f.) is significant for the date and authorship of the letters of James and Jude. Cf. E. E. Ellis, *Prophecy and Hermeneutic in Early Christianity*, Grand Rapids ⁴1993, 226–236 (Jude); idem, *The Making of the New Testament Documents*, Leiden 1999, 243ff., 288f. I date the accession of Festus to AD 60 with Lightfoot, Reicke, Schürer, and Zahn (cf. Ellis, *Making*, 241n, 319); for other views cf. R. Riesner, *Paul's Early Period*, Grand Rapids 1998, 3–28 = GT: 2–30. Cf. J. B. Lightfoot, *Biblical Essays*, London 1893, 217–224; B. Reicke, *The New Testament Era*, Philadelphia 1968, 208 = GT: 155; E. Schürer, *The History of the Jewish People in the Age of Jesus Christ*, 3 vols. in 4, Edinburgh ⁴1987, I, 465ff.; T. Zahn, *Einleitung in das Neue Testament*, 2 vols. in 1, Wuppertal ³1994 (1907), II, 647–655 = ET: III, 469–479.

[3] Mt 24:15–22; Mk 13:14–20; Lk 19:42–44; 21:20–24. While the latter Lukan passage clarifies the apocalyptic imagery of Dan 9:27; 12:11 = Mt 24:15; Mk 13:14, it draws its own descriptive phraseology from other Old Testament Septuagint passages (e.g. Hos 14:1; Nah 3:10; Isa 3:25f.; 29:3; Jer 20:4f.; 52:4). This was demonstrated by C. H. Dodd, *More New Testament Studies*, Manchester 1968, 69–83 = *JRS* 37 (1947), 52–54. Further, cf. E. E. Ellis, 'New Directions in the History of Early Christianity,' *Ancient History in a Modern University*, 2 vols., edd. T. W. Hillard *et al.*, Grand Rapids 1998, II, 82–85 = idem, *Christ and the Future in New Testament History*, Leiden 2000, 227–232. Equally, if the source(s) of Eusebius (*HE* 3, 5, 2f.) and of Epiphanius (*Panarion* 29, 7, 8; *Weights and Measures* 15, 2–5) is reliable, the instructions in Jesus' prophecy ('flee to the mountains') are hardly post-70 since they do not accord with what the Jerusalem Christians actually did in c. AD 66. According to this (second-century) source they fled to Pella in the Trans-Jordan valley. On this question cf. Ellis, *Making* (note 2), 25f., 284f. Also, it is not quite correct to say that the Gospels do not, on principle, incorporate historical sequels into the 'kerygmatic' Jesus-story, as Mt 27:8 and 28:15 show. If predictive prophecy is rejected *a priori* then, of course, a post-70 date is required. (A prophecy similar to Lk 21:24 occurs in Rev 11:2).

[4] The passage most often thought to reflect the AD 70 destruction of Jerusalem

This is, of course, an argument from silence. And like the dog that did not bark in the case of Sherlock Holmes,[5] it becomes significant only if the silence itself is contrary to all reasonable expectation. In many writings—ancient and modern—there is no awareness of contemporary events, even earthshaking events, that the author clearly knew of. At the same time in some New Testament books the silence about the destruction of Jerusalem *is* very surprising; that is, in books where Jesus' prophecy of the destruction appears (Matthew, Mark, Luke), where the critique of the Jerusalem temple or its transitory character is a major theme (Acts, Hebrews) and where God's judgments on a disobedient Jewish nation are of particular interest to the writer (Acts, II Peter, Jude).[6] In these cases the absence of any allusion to the destruction would seem to be a fairly strong argument that such books were written before that event took place.[7]

The fall of Jerusalem is important in other respects. It marked not only the catastrophic destruction of a city but also the end of the Jewish world as it had been known. It also was the time when the focus of Christianity shifted to the diaspora and when Jerusalem ceased to be central to the church's concerns. It has become increasingly clear from archaeological remains and from the Qumran library that the Fourth Gospel preserves to a remarkable degree the form of that pre-70 world—the religious divisions, the political temper, the theological issues and idiom, and even topographical details of pre-destruction Jerusalem.[8] However, the Gospel traditionally has

---

is Jesus' parable of the marriage feast in which an offended king 'burned (ἐνέπρησεν) their city' (Mt 22:7; cf. Josephus, *War* 6, 354–364). But as K. H. Rengstorf has shown in *Judentum-Urchristentum-Kirche*, ed. W. Eltester, Berlin 1960, 125ff., burning the enemy's city was an established *topos* and reflects no action peculiar to the events of AD 70. In fact the term 'burned' is found only here in the New Testament and is, like other terms in the apocalyptic discourse (see note 3), probably an allusion to the Old Testament description of the fall of Jerusalem in 586 BC (Jer 52:13, ἐνέπρησεν). Cf. Ellis, *Making* (note 2), 247n.

[5] Robinson's example. It is from the story, *Silver Blaze*. Cf. A. C. Doyle, *The Complete Sherlock Holmes*, 2 vols., Garden City NY c. 1980, I, 335–350, 349.

[6] Acts 7:47–50; 6:13f. (cf. 11:28); Heb 8:4, 13; 9:6f.; 10:1–4. On II Peter cf. Ellis, *Making* (note 2), 299. Cf. also passages where the temple is criticized or where Christ, Christians and/or the Christian community are regarded as God's true temple. They appear in books generally recognized to be pre-70 (I Cor 3:16; II Cor 6:16) and in books whose pre-70 date is disputed (cf. Jn 2:19–22; Acts 7:48; Eph 2:20; Revelation).

[7] For the way in which a Christian writing after AD 70, when speaking of God's true temple, alludes to the fall of Jerusalem, cf. Barn 16:1–5. Cf. also Justin, *Dialogue* 40.

[8] Ellis, *Making* (note 2), 234–237, 402n; J. A. T. Robinson *The Priority of John*,

been datelined at Ephesus in Asia Minor at the end of the first century and, interestingly, it ceases to use the name 'Jerusalem' after Jn 12. Also, Jn 11:48 includes the warning of the ecclesiastical establishment that, if Jesus succeeds, 'the Romans will come and take away our place and our nation.' It may possibly be an ironic allusion to what had in fact occurred. Traditions within John's Gospel (and perhaps a proto-Gospel itself) were formulated and used by congregations of the Johannine mission in pre-70 Palestine, but our canonical Gospel was published (in Greek) only later in Asia.[9]

2. The onslaught of Nero against the Christians, apparently initiated in the winter or spring of AD 65,[10] was remembered in the church as the first of the persecutions by the Roman state. During the course of it both Peter and Paul were executed (Clement) and 'vast multitudes' were torn to death by beasts or fastened to crosses and put to the torch (Tacitus).[11] The charges against the Christians appear to have included 'confessing' the name of Christ[12] and, as both Roman and Christian sources indicate, they involved not only imperial malice but also some kind of legal sanctions.[13] Even without them, the Emperor's actions would have evoked eager imitation from some provincial authorities. In all probability, then, the persecution extended beyond Rome and represented the beginning of an abiding hostility of the state even if the specific sanctions were annulled after the death of Nero.

London 1985, 45–93; idem (note 1), 266–269, 278 = GT: 277–280, 289f. Cf. J. McRay, *Archaeology and the New Testament*, Grand Rapids 1991, 114–119, 186–189; W. F. Albright, 'Recent Discoveries in Palestine and the Gospel of John,' *The Background of the New Testament and its Eschatology. FS C. H. Dodd*, ed. W. D. Davies, Cambridge 1956, 153–171; W. H. Brownlee, 'Whence the Gospel according to John?' *John and Qumran*, ed. J. H. Charlesworth, London 1972, 166–194; C. H. Dodd, *Historical Tradition in the Fourth Gospel*, Cambridge 1963; J. Jeremias, *The Rediscovery of Bethesda: John 5:2*, Louisville 1966.

[9] Cf. Ellis, *Making* (note 2), 164, 234–237, 306f.

[10] So, Robinson (note 1), 145f. = GT: 154f., following G. Edmundson, *The Church in Rome in the First Century*, London 1913, 123–127. The account of Tacitus (*Annals* 15, 44) presupposes some interval between the burning of Rome (July AD 64) and the persecution of the Christians.

[11] I Clement 5:1–7:1; Tacitus, *Annals* 15, 44. Cf. Tertullian, *Apology* 5; cf. Eusebius, *HE* 2, 25, 3ff.

[12] Tacitus, *Annals* 15, 44 (*fateor*); cf. Pliny, *Letters* 10, 96 (*confiteor*); cf. Edmundson (note 10), 131–139; Robinson (note 1), 157 = GT: 166.

[13] Suetonius, *Nero* 16 (*instituta, suppliciis*); Tertullian, *Apology* 5 (*leges*); *To the Pagans* 1, 7 (condemnation of the name); Sulpicius Severus, *Chronicle* II, 29. For a discussion cf. W. H. C. Frend, *Martyrdom and Persecution in the Early Church*, Oxford 1965, 165–169; H. D. Workman, *Persecution in the Early Church*, London 1906, 52–72, 365f.

Nero's attack on the Christians is significant for the present topic in at least two ways. First, it is questionable whether the relatively generous and friendly allusions to the Roman authorities in, say, Acts or I Peter could have been written without some qualification after AD 64.[14] Second, the descriptions in the visions of Revelation, which depict so graphically the abominable acts against God's people, may reflect in some measure the prophet's recent experience of the savagery of the Neronian pogrom.

3. Many scholars point to the persecution of Domitian some 30 years later as the background of John's exile to Patmos and of his revelation there, and they are supported in this view by some fourth-century Christian tradition.[15] However, Domitian's persecution seems to have involved only personal actions against several individual local Christians, a few (Christian) relatives and certain prominent Romans rather than an attack upon the church as such.[16] In the light of this, of some early tradition and of the internal evidence Revelation should probably be dated immediately after the death of Nero, i.e. AD 68–70.[17]

4. The Jewish 'Prayer against Heretics,' is the twelfth of the 'Eighteen Benedictions' used in the synagogue service.[18] In the oldest

---

[14] Acts 13:7; 19:31; 22:25–30; 23:10, 22–33; 25:24–27; 26:30ff.; 28:16; I Pet 2:13–17; 3:13; ct. Acts 16:22, 35–39. Ct. I Clement, where prayer for 'rulers and governors' is offered (60:4; 61:1f.), along with clear allusions to the persecutions suffered at their hands (5:1–7:1).

[15] E.g. Eusebius, *HE* 3,18,1f.; Jerome, *Lives of Illustrious Men* 9 = *NPNF* III, 364. The statements of Irenaeus (*AH* 5, 30, 3, end) and of Victorinus (*On the Apocalypse* 10:11 = *ANF* VIII, 353) are ambiguous. A few sources, also including Jerome (*adv. Jov.* 1, 26), associate the book with Nero, e.g. the title of the Syriac versions (cited in H. B. Swete, *The Apocalypse of St. John*, London ³1909, c). Epiphanius' (*Panarion* 51, 12, 2; 51, 33, 9) reference to the reign of 'Claudius' may, in his source, have read 'Claudius Nero' (so, Hort, note 17, xviii).

[16] Re Domitian's persecution of Christians, Melito (†c. 190, cited in Eusebius, *HE* 4, 26, 9) refers to his 'slander' and 'false accusations;' Tertullian (*Apology* 5) draws a general analogy between Domitian and Nero. Dio Cassius (*Roman History* 67:14) speaks of a charge of 'atheism' against Domitian's kinsman Clemens and his wife Domitilla and against many others who had drifted into 'Jewish customs.' But neither he nor any other Roman writer mentions a persecution of Christians by Domitian; cf. Ellis, *Making* (note 2), 212f. On Clemens and Christianity cf. J. B. Lightfoot, *The Apostolic Fathers*, 3 vols. in 5, London ²1889, I, i, 32–39, and Frend (note 13), 216f.

[17] So, e.g. F. J. A. Hort, *The Apocalypse of Saint John I–III*, London 1908, xxviff.; Edmundson (note 9), 163–179; Robinson (note 1), 221–253 = GT: 232–264; cf. Rev 11:1–3. Further, Ellis, *Making* (note 2), 210–219.

[18] It is also called the Shemoneh Esreh. For the text and English translation cf.

extant text-form, hardly earlier than the ninth century, the prayer reads in part as follows:[19]

> Let Nazarenes and heretics (*minim*)
> perish as in a moment.

The Benedictions were arranged at the rabbinical school at Jamnia under Rabbi Gamaliel II, the grandson of Paul's teacher (cf. Acts 22:3).[20] In the opinion of several writers they display literary parallels with certain passages in Matthew which suggest that the church of St. Matthew was interacting with the rabbis of Jamnia.[21] But the parallels can also be explained—to my mind equally well—by the common background of the two communities in a particular sector of Judaism.

Others suppose that the 'Prayer against Heretics' has influenced the account of the healing of the blind man in Jn 9.[22] Specifically, it is thought to lie behind the man's formal exclusion from the synagogue (Jn 9:22, ἀποσυνάγωγος), which is regarded as incredible during Jesus' preresurrection mission,[23] and thus to predate the Gospel. However, it should be observed that the Prayer can be dated only

---

C. W. Dugmore, *The Influence of the Synagogue upon the Divine Office*, London ²1964, 114–125. He dates the Twelfth Benediction, the *Birkath ha-Minim*, to AD 90–117. The pertinent lines read as follows: '... let the Nazarenes [= Christians] and the Minim [= heretics] perish as in a moment, let them be blotted out of the book of the living and let them not be written with the righteous....'

[19] The oldest text-form was found in the *Geniza* or storage room of a Cairo synagogue established in AD 882. Cf. P. Kahle, *The Cairo Geniza*, London 1947, 1.

[20] Cf. BT Megillah 17b and Berakoth 28b (Baraitha), where the 'Petition against Heretics' apparently is viewed as an annual prayer. In M Berakoth 4:3 it is to be recited daily. For other rabbinic references cf. (H. L. Strack and) P. Billerbeck, *Kommentar zum Neuen Testament aus Talmud und Midrasch*, 4 vols., München 1922–28, IV, 208–249.

[21] E.g. the Matthean form of the Lord's Prayer is thought to be in conscious interaction with the Shemoneh Esreh and other liturgical prayers of the post-70 rabbis. Cf. W. D. Davies, *The Setting of the Sermon on the Mount*, Cambridge 1964, 275–279, 309–313; idem, *The Gospel according to Saint Matthew*, 3 vols., Edinburgh 1997, I, 133–138. But see Ellis, *Christ* (note 3), 15.

[22] E.g. R. E. Brown, *The Gospel according to John*, 2 vols., Garden City NY 1970, I, lxxxv, 380; J. L. Martyn, *History and Theology in the Fourth Gospel*, New York ²1979, 24–62.

[23] This is difficult to accept. Formal exclusion from the community, temporary or permanent, was practiced in pre-Christian Judaism by the Qumran community (1QS 6:25; 7:1f.), and such disciplines were doubtless used by the Pharisees as well. The word used at Qumran (בדל) is sometimes translated in the Septuagint by ἀφορίζειν, a term used in Luke 6:22: 'Blessed are you when they exclude (ἀφορίσωσιν) you ... and cast out (ἐκβάλωσιν) your name as evil ...'. From the beginning Jesus (Luke 4:29), Stephen (Acts 7:58), Paul (II Cor 11:25; cf. Acts 9:23, 29) and others

very loosely, to the late first or second century, and in its original formulation it may not even have been directed specifically against (Jewish) Christians.[24] More significantly, the Prayer is a curse. It is not an excommunication, but at most only presupposes previous actions of that nature. It is difficult to perceive, therefore, how it could have had any bearing on the story in Jn 9 or on the date of the Gospel.

To conclude this brief résumé, the fall of Jerusalem and the persecution of Nero appear to offer, as Robinson argued in much greater detail, significant clues for dating certain New Testament books before AD 70. However, such evidence is not likely, in itself, to be regarded as decisive by most scholars. First, its bearing upon the date of some books may be ambiguous, as in the case of the Gospel of John. More importantly, in modern scholarship's prevalent late dating of the books other factors are given a greater role, factors that Robinson only touched upon or left out of consideration. They are, in a word, the assumptions and results of nineteenth- and early twentieth-century literary criticism that continue to serve many as operating axioms for the analysis of New Testament texts. It is, I think, fair to say that only if these axioms can be demonstrated to be faulty will the criteria underscored by Robinson be accorded sufficient weight to reopen on a broad scale the questions that he raised.

(I Thess 2:14f.; cf. Acts 8:1) were, according to the New Testament evidence, threatened with lynching or were 'reviled' and 'driven out' (ἐξέβαλον, Acts 13:45, 50) by Jewish opponents. If this was so, *a fortiori* some synagogues would certainly have excluded followers of Jesus even from the beginning. But see D. R. A. Hare, *The Theme of Jewish Persecution . . . according to St Matthew*, Cambridge 1967, 48–56.

[24] See above, notes 18, 20. The date of Gamaliel II's death is unknown, but he was the leading member of a delegation to Rome in c. AD 95 (e.g. GenR 20:4). Cf. W. Bacher, *Die Agada der Tannaiten*, 2 vols., Berlin ²1965–66 (1903), I, 79; J. Derenbourg, *Historie de la Palestine*, Farnborough 1971 (1867), 334–340. R. T. Herford's (*Christianity in Talmud and Midrash*, Farnborough UK 1972 [1903], 129–135) dating of the Prayer to c. AD 80, although widely followed, is highly conjectural and is not convincing. Furthermore, in the rabbinic sources the Prayer refers to the 'Minim,' i.e. heretics; the reference to the 'Nazarenes' or Christians in the ninth-century text, therefore, seems to be a later supplement. The Prayer may have been used against Christians, among others, by the mid-second century when Justin (*Dialogue* 16:4; cf. 137:2) speaks of Christians being cursed in the synagogues. But this usage becomes clearly specified only in fourth-century sources, when Epiphanius (*Panarion* 29, 9, 2) and Jerome (on Isa 5:18; 49:7; 52:4) refer to Christians being cursed under the name 'Nazarenes' (as cited in H. L. Strack, *Jesus . . . nach den ältesten jüdischen Angaben*, Leipzig 1910, 66*). Cf. F. Williams, tr. and ed., *The Panarion of Epiphanius of Salamis*, 3 vols., Leiden 1994.

I have addressed elsewhere the general questions of Gospels form-criticism and of the dating of the New Testament documents.[25] But it may be useful to elaborate on three operating axioms that have been determinative for shaping the traditional critical orthodoxy. The axioms may be summarized as follows:

1. Jewish Palestine was a Semitic island in a Greco-Roman sea with sharply distinctive linguistic, cultural and religious thought-patterns and, therefore, New Testament documents reflecting 'Hellenistic' idiom and ideas cannot have been written by Jesus' pupils and belong, not to Christianity's earliest 'Palestinian' form, but to a subsequent stage of its development.
2. The authorship of the New Testament books was an individual enterprise in which the author alone originated and dictated his book and, consequently, genuineness of authorship may be tested in terms of author's style and vocabulary elsewhere or in terms of what is considered possible or appropriate to him. If others wrote in an apostle's name, they probably did so after his death.
3. Early Christian theology underwent a unilinear or dialectical development that may be traced in the New Testament and, therefore, New Testament writings may be progressively dated in terms of their theological divergence from the books among them identified as the earliest.

Before these propositions are considered in detail, it may be appropriate to sketch out the background from which they arose.

Early Literary Criticism

Until the eighteenth century almost all New Testament books were dated, in accordance with the authorship attributed to them, within the first Christian generation. Apart from the Johannine writings this usually meant AD 70 or earlier.[26]

---

[25] Ellis, *Making* (note 2), 19–36, 307–330; idem, *Christ* (note 3), 223–234.
[26] On Revelation see above, note 15; cf. Victorinus, *On the Apocalypse* 10:11: John was on the island of Patmos 'condemned to the labor of the mines by Caesar Domitian.' But see Ellis, *Making* (note 2), 211. M. Luther (*The Catholic Epistles*, St. Louis 1964 [c. 1540], 203, 213) thought on the basis of Jude 17f. that the Epistle

In 1792 Edward Evanson of Mitcham, England, challenged the consensus of the day with a volume that anticipated many arguments which, more thoroughly worked out, were to gain a wide adherence in the following century.[27] Foreshadowing the later 'ultra-Tübingen' school, Evanson regarded Luke-Acts as the most reliable New Testament work and the touchstone by which the others were to be judged. He proceeded to place in the second or third century writings that differed from the historical presentation of Luke-Acts,[28] and also found support for his conclusions in the theological or ecclesiastical situation of specific books. For example, the distinction of 'bishops and deacons' from 'the saints' in Philippians (1:1),[29] the practice of anointing with oil and of 'extreme unction' in James (5:14, 16)[30] and the attack on opponents of clerical power in II Peter and Jude[31] pointed to a church order of the second century or later. Likewise, the false teachers in Titus (3:10),[32] the

---

does 'not seem to have been written by the real apostle, for in it Jude refers to himself as a much later disciple of the apostles.' Also, J. Calvin, *Hebrews and the First and Second Epistles of St. Peter*, Edinburgh 1963 (1562), 325, concluded that Second Peter was written by a disciple at Peter's command. H. Grotius, *Annotationes in Novum Testamentum*, 3 vols., Amsterdam (vol. I) and Paris, 1641–50, III, 38 (cited in W. G. Kümmel, *The New Testament. The History of the Investigation of its Problems*, London 1973, 37 = GT: 34f., but with a mistaken dateline) regarded II Peter as a post-70 writing of Simeon (cf. II Pet 1:1), successor to James as Bishop of Jerusalem.

[27] E. Evanson, *The Dissonance of the Four generally received Evangelists*, Ipswich 1792, in which according to an obituary in *The Gentlemen's Magazine* 75 (1805), 1073, 1233–1236, he 'undertakes to show that a considerable part of the New Testament is a forgery,' e.g. Matthew, Mark, John, Romans, Ephesians, Colossians, Hebrews, the epistles of James, Peter, John and Jude, and the Seven Letters of Revelation. His essay, 'The Doctrines of the Trinity and Incarnation of God examined upon the Principles of Reason and Common Sense' (1772), shows that he was not uninfluenced by the rationalism of his day. Nevertheless, he affirmed both miracles and prophecy. Cf. F. Strachotta, *Edward Evanson (1731–1805): Der Theologe und Bibelkritiker*, Halle 1940. On Luke-Acts as the touchstone cf. Evanson (note 27), 20ff., 111, 258ff. However, Luke-Acts also suffered later interpolations, e.g. Lk 1:5–2:52; 23:43. Interestingly, J. E. C. Schmidt, in his *Einleitung* (260), expressed doubts about I Timothy because of its lack of agreement with Acts (cited in F. D. E. Schleiermacher, *Über den ersten Brief Pauli an Timotheos*, Braunschweig 1896 [1807], 11).

[28] Evanson (note 27), 185, 256–259, 261, 269. Evanson's book, translated into Dutch in 1796, may have had an influence on the rejection of Romans in the following century by the ultra-Tübingen school. Cf. W. C. Van Manen, *Paulus*, 3 vols., Leiden 1890–96, II, 2f., passim; idem, 'Romans,' *EB* IV, 4127–4145, who cites Evanson in both of these writings.

[29] Evanson (note 27), 263f.: Both Philippians and Titus, however, are possibly Pauline letters that have suffered later interpolations.

[30] Idem, 276f.
[31] Idem, 279.
[32] Idem, 261.

anti-Pauline attitude toward the law in Matthew (5:17)[33] and the conception of an incarnate Logos in the Johannine writings[34] all reflected, in the view of Evanson, theological developments long after the time of the apostles.

Although Evanson's criticisms were sometimes not well supported and apparently did not have a great effect on critical developments,[35] they embodied a method and principles that were to shape the future course of biblical criticism. Among other things,[36] Evanson supposed that the New Testament exhibited a long-term theological development and that, by selecting certain New Testament writings as the foundation documents—in his case Luke-Acts—one could determine the authorship and dates of the others. This approach incorporated two specific assumptions. First, it assumed that early Christianity was a unity. Consequently, writings that diverged from the theological or historical views of documents recognized to be from the apostolic period were to be assigned to a later time. This principle, *non hoc ergo post hoc*, came to be a widely accepted and seldom questioned axiom in New Testament studies. A second assumption also became a rather widespread viewpoint, namely that Christology gradually developed from an initial view of Jesus as only a human being to a later, second-century conception of him as the divine Logos. With this approach Evanson concluded that only ten of the New Testament books were authentic witnesses from the apostolic period: Luke-Acts, I–II Corinthians, Galatians, I–II Thessalonians, I–II Timothy and Revelation 4–22.

Early in the nineteenth century a number of German scholars also began to reject the authenticity of certain New Testament books on the basis of literary criticism. Although they cited differences of style and vocabulary, they also based their judgments on theological and

---

[33] Idem, 141.
[34] Idem, 282.
[35] His book did go into a second edition (1805) and prompted a rebuttal by J. Priestley, *Letters to a Young Man*, London 1793; by D. Simpson, *An Essay on the Authenticity of the New Testament*, London 1793; and in the Bampton Lectures for 1810 of T. Falconer, *Certain Principles in Evanson's 'Dissonance...*,' Oxford 1811.
[36] Evanson (note 27) rejected any conception of a canonical unity of the New Testament since he regarded the canon as a fifth-century imposition of an apostate church. Like J. D. Michaelis (*Introduction to the New Testament*, 4 vols. in 6, Cambridge 1793–1801, I, 70; IV, 264, 311), he concluded that if a book was not authentic, it was thereby excluded from the canon. The relevant passages in Michaelis are summarized by Kümmel (note 26), 70ff. = GT: 82–86.

historical criteria, as Evanson had.³⁷ Thus II Thessalonians presents 'non-Pauline' views on the 'Anti-Christ' and on the parousia and, therefore, must have been written by someone other than Paul.³⁸ Since the Gospel of John represents a Christianity different from that of the Synoptics, it cannot be from an eyewitness. I Peter reflects attitudes of a Gentile Christian, incompatible with the thought of the Apostle.³⁹ Ephesians, the Pastorals and II Peter all were suspect because, among other things, their style and language differed from that of the apostles to whom they were traditionally attributed.⁴⁰

It is noteworthy that most of these scholars did not yet focus upon the date of the suspected books⁴¹ and that one or two regarded them as composed or completed soon after the death of those to whom they are attributed.⁴² Also, the possibility was recognized that some of the books may have been written by 'apostolic helpers'⁴³ or what a later generation would call 'secretaries' and 'amanuenses.' All this changes in the writings of Ferdinand Christian Baur.

In his earlier works Christian Baur seldom questioned the apostolic authorship or early dating of New Testament writings.⁴⁴ His

---

³⁷ Evanson's perception of Christology and of New Testament theology generally as a long-term development reappears in F. C. Baur, e.g. *The Church History of the First Three Centuries*, 2 vols., London 1878–79, II, 65f. = GT: 308f. *et passim; Vorlesungen über neutestamentliche Theologie*, Darmstadt 1973 (1864), 38–42, 305f., 351f. Cf. Kümmel (note 26), 140f. = GT: 173f.

³⁸ J. E. C. Schmidt, *Vermutungen über die beiden Briefen der Thessalonicher*, Hadamar 1798, cited in W. G. Kümmel, *Introduction to the New Testament*, Nashville 1975, 264.

³⁹ H. H. Cludius, *Uransichten des Christentums*, Altona 1808, 55ff., 296.

⁴⁰ E.g. W. M. L. de Wette and J. G. Eichhorn, cited in Kümmel (note 26), 86f. = GT: 102f. For the first rejection of the Paulinity of I Timothy on these and other grounds cf. Schleiermacher (note 27).

⁴¹ Schleiermacher (note 27), 101, 114, is an exception. Like Evanson, he interpreted theological differences in terms of a chronological interval. E.g. the absence of the great Pauline themes, the prohibition on second marriages and an established order of widows (I Tim 5:9) disclose 'traces of a later time' (121). But see Acts 10:39.

⁴² E.g. J. G. Eichhorn, *Einleitung in das Neue Testament*, 5 vols., Leipzig 1804–27, III: After Paul's death one of his disciples collected his oral teachings and put them in the form of a letter to Titus (386); since the destruction of Jerusalem is not given as an illustration in the letter of Jude, it was perhaps written in the last years before that event (655). The date of II Peter is uncertain; if Peter had a disciple finish it, it could not have been long after AD 65 (641).

⁴³ Eichhorn (note 42), III, 634, reckons with this possibility in the case of II Peter. It had been advocated earlier by Jerome (*Letters* 120, 11) and by Calvin. Cf. Calvin (note 26), 325.

⁴⁴ E.g. in 1829 Baur, speaking on Acts 7, expresses no doubt about the historicity of Acts. In 'Die Christuspartei . . .' (*TZT* 1831, IV, 61–206 reprinted in *Ausgewählte Werke*, 5 vols., ed. K. Scholder, Stuttgart 1963–75, I, which gives the original page

later dating of many of them coincided with his general reconstruction of early Christian history along the lines of Georg Hegel's philosophy:[45] The Pauline gospel (*thesis*) was opposed by Peter's strict Jewish Christianity (*antithesis*), and the two viewpoints were only gradually brought into reconciliation (*synthesis*) toward the end of the second century. The New Testament documents reflected all stages of this process and were to be dated accordingly. Of course, Baur employed—and employed very acutely—the theological and historical criteria[46] used by earlier critics.[47] But he was also clearly dependent on Hegelian philosophical assumptions which provided the framework and a key for his exegetical interpretations.[48] After Baur completed

numbers) he recognizes Philippians (107f.), James and I Peter (205f.) as authentic even though the last two tend to 'mediate' the quarrel between Paul and his Judaizing opponents (205f.). However, he regards a later date for II Peter (already a traditional option) as confirmed since in it this tendency is carried much further. For an English translation cf. Kümmel (note 26), 129f.; cf. 127. According to E. Zeller (*Erinnerungen eines Neunzigjährigen*, Stuttgart 1904, 93f., cited in H. Harris, *The Tübingen School*, Leicester ²1991, 29), Baur as late as 1834 saw no incompatibility between Acts 15 and Gal 2.

[45] It is unclear when Baur first became a follower of G. W. F. Hegel's thought. By the time of Baur's *Die christliche Gnosis* (Tübingen 1835) and of his *Die sogenannten Pastoralbriefe* (Tübingen 1835) a Hegelian pattern was explicit. But already in his controversy with J. A. Möhler in 1833 he identified his method as Hegelian (*TZT* 1833, IV, 421n), and an even earlier influence of Hegel is evident in *Die Christuspartei* (note 44), 76, 136, 205f. = *Ausgewählte Werke* (note 44), I, 16, 76, 145f. Cf. J. Fitzer, *Möhler and Baur in Controversy*, Tallahassee 1974, 97f.; Harris (note 44), xiif., 26, 33, 155–158. Cf. Kümmel (note 26), 132 = GT: 162f.; Ellis, *Making* (note 2), 440–445. In opposing Peter to Paul he followed J. S. Semler (*ad Galatas*, Halae 1779, 2f.), who followed T. D. Morgan, *The Moral Philosopher*, New York 1977 (1737), 50–80, 362ff.

[46] E.g. on his interpretation of I Cor 1:12, the appeal in I Thess 2:12–14 to the example of Jewish Christians 'has a thoroughly non-Pauline stamp' (F. C. Baur, *Paul*, 2 vols., London 1875–76 (1845), II, 87 = GT²: II, 96). The 'bishops and deacons' in Phil 1:1 reflect a post-Pauline church order (F. C. Baur, 'Ursprung des Episkopats,' *TZT* 1838, III, 141 = *Ausgewählte Werke*, note 44, I, 461).

[47] Like C. C. Tittmann, Baur restricted the influence of Gnosticism on Christianity to the second century; Gnostic echoes and opponents in Ephesians, Colossians, Philippians and the Pastorals pointed, then, to their later origin. Cf. Baur, *Church History* (note 37), I, 127f. = GT²: 121. Like F. D. E. Schleiermacher (note 27), Baur also regarded the attitude toward second marriages and the order of widows in the Pastorals as a sign of a post-apostolic date (*Pastoralbriefe*, note 45, 118ff.; *Paul*, note 46, 103n). But see Ellis, *Prophecy* (note 2), 88; idem, *Making* (note 2), 320–329, 418–422, 440–445.

[48] Even if, as P. C. Hodgson (*The Formation of Historical Theology*, New York 1966, 208) notes, he modified Hegel's scheme as he applied it. From the beginning Baur regarded a philosophical system as an essential precondition for historical investigation. Cf. F. C. Baur, *Symbolik und Mythologie*, 3 vols., Stuttgart 1824–25, I, xi: 'Without philosophy history remains for me (*bleibt mir*) forever dead and mute.'

his critical reconstruction,[49] only five New Testament books remained as apostolic works: four epistles of Paul (Romans, I–II Corinthians, Galatians) and the book of Revelation (AD 70).

Baur differed from Evanson in that he perceived the apostolic community not as a unity but as two parties in conflict. But apart from the book of Revelation this had no practical consequence for his dating of the New Testament. Like Evanson, Baur supposed that the New Testament represented a long development of Christian thought and that theological differences between the various books must be interpreted in terms of a chronological progression. By selecting the right foundation documents—in Baur's case four Pauline letters—one could, more or less, date the rest of the New Testament in terms of them.

Baur's erudition and his acute and systematic argumentation made his views widely influential. Even when his historical reconstruction came to be rejected for its *a priori* and arbitrary elements, it continued, like the smile of the Cheshire cat, to have its effect on the dating of New Testament writings.[50] For many supposed that Baur's exegetical conclusions could be separated from the philosophical commitments that influenced them and often gave rise to them.

In the beginning years of the twentieth century the 'History of Religions School'[51] set forth yet another theory of development. It supposed that early Christian theology progressed in stages from the primitive Palestinian church through 'the Hellenistic communities in Antioch, Damascus and Tarsus' to the Apostle Paul and Gentile Christianity. Within this framework Wilhelm Bousset, in a reconstruction reminiscent of the unitarian Anglican, Edward Evanson, sought to show how a purely human Jesus of Palestine was, under the influence of pagan religious ideas, progressively deified in diaspora Christianity.[52] This school of thought considered not only Paul's

---

[49] Best surveyed in his *Paul* (note 46), in his *Church History* (note 37) and in his *Vorlesungen* (note 37), 39–42.

[50] Cf. E. E. Ellis, 'Foreword' in Harris (note 44), vii–xvi; idem, *Making* (note 2), 440–445; J. Munck, *Paul and the Salvation of Mankind*, Richmond 1959, 69–86.

[51] For a summary and critique of their contributions cf. Kümmel (note 26), 245–280, 309–324 = GT: 310–357, 394–414.

[52] W. Bousset, *Kyrios Christos*, Nashville 1970, 119, 11–21, 317f. = GT: ⁵1964 (1913), 75f., vii–xv, 246f. For Bousset, of course, the miracles and resurrection of Jesus could not have occasioned, at the very beginning, the divine status ascribed to him since, apart from 'the gift of healing' (100 = GT: 59), he rejected them *a priori* on philosophical grounds and regarded them as mythical elaborations. Cf. idem, 98–106 = GT: 57–65, where his philosophical assumptions are clearly evi-

Christology but also his doctrine of the sacraments and his teachings on wisdom and knowledge to be highly influenced by pagan religious antecedents.[53] To be sure, this approach did not necessarily require a 'late' dating of New Testament writings since it considered the development to be virtually in full flower already in the time of Paul. However, it assumed a sharp cultural and religious dichotomy between Palestine and the diaspora, and it assigned most New Testament documents to the latter milieu. Thus, it effectively excluded such books as Matthew, John, James, and I and II Peter from the apostolic associations and/or authorship attributed to them in their text or in early Christian writings and, in fact, also considered them to be from post-apostolic times.[54]

Twentieth-Century Developments and Critique

The above section summarizes some of the results of an earlier literary criticism on which a currently widespread dating of New Testament books has been largely constructed. How reliable are those results and, more importantly, how reliable are the assumptions that made those results persuasive to many scholars? We may address this question in terms of the three axioms mentioned above.

1. First, the sharp separation of Palestine from the Hellenistic world has now been shown to have been mistaken.[55] At the time of Christ

---

dent. Often Bousset appears, like Evanson, to envision a unilinear 'stream of development' (12 = GT: viii). However, he also reflects a Hegelian pattern of thought when he writes that a diaspora Christian 'form of piety, which grew in its own soil, quite early merged with the gospel of Jesus and with the latter entered into a new form...' (19 = GT: xiii). His treatment of the Gospel of John is similar: Taking the Pauline *pneuma* with his own Logos Christology and 'preserving the little bit of humanity in the picture of Jesus that was still to be kept..., [the Fourth Evangelist] has reconciled the myth with history...' (220 = GT: 162).

[53] Bousset (note 52), 157ff., 265–271 = GT: 107ff., 201–206. The interpretation of Pauline 'knowledge' and 'wisdom' in terms of a Gnostic (or Wisdom) mythology was carried out by later 'history of religions' research, e.g. of R. Bultmann and his 'school.' For a critique of this approach cf. O. Betz, 'Der gekreuzigte Christus, unsere Weisheit und Gerechtigkeit,' *Tradition and Interpretation in the New Testament. FS E. E. Ellis*, ed. G. F. Hawthorne with O. Betz, Grand Rapids and Tübingen 1987, 195–215; Ellis, *Prophecy* (note 2), 45–62; M. Hengel, *The Son of God*, Philadelphia 1976; G. Wagner, *Pauline Baptism and the Pagan Mysteries*, Edinburgh 1967.

[54] E.g. Bousset (note 52), 32ff., 358–367 = GT: 2ff., 282–289.

[55] Cf. P. van der Horst, *Ancient Jewish Epitaphs*, Kampen 1991; M. Hengel, *The Pre-Christian Paul*, London 1991, 54–62; idem, *The 'Hellenization' of Judaea in the First Century after Christ*, London 1989; Ellis, *Prophecy* (note 2), 245ff.

Palestine had been a part of that world for over three centuries and had experienced not only the immigration of many Greek-speaking Gentiles but also the resettlement from the diaspora of thoroughly Hellenized Jews. Even those Jews who resisted the foreign culture were not exempt from its influence.[56] The library at Qumran, for example, now provides evidence that the Greek Old Testament was used in first-century Palestine even among very strict Jews. From the same period an inscription has been found in which the dedication of a Jerusalem synagogue is made in Greek,[57] and many ossuary and sepuchral inscriptions show that Greek was widely used by the people. The grave inscriptions are especially significant, for they demonstrate that Greek was not just the language of commerce or of the upper classes but was in many instances the primary or only language of ordinary Jews.[58]

This is the context of the ministry of Jesus and of the earliest church. Much of Jesus' boyhood (and that of his brother James) and of his preresurrection ministry was spent in Galilee, a region long ago recognized by Gustav Dalman as bilingual.[59] Several of Jesus' apostles—Simon Peter, Andrew and Philip, were from Bethsaida (Jn 1:44), a predominantly Greek-speaking city. In that tongue they undoubtedly conducted much of their business, and their Hellenized names suggest that Greek may also have been the language of their homes. In the light of this situation, increasingly illuminated by archaeological discoveries, it is no longer possible to deny apostolic authorship to a New Testament book simply because the book is written in good Greek or reveals a knowledge of Hellenistic ideas or culture. That is, while Semitisms may point to an ultimate background

---

[56] E.g. the Pharisees in their anthropology and in their views of the state after death. Cf. Ellis, *Christ* (note 3), 101n; E. Schürer, *The History of the Jewish People in the Age of Jesus Christ*, 3 vols. in 4, Edinburgh UK ²1987, II, 539–542; R. Meyer, *Hellenistisches in der rabbinischen Anthropologie*, Stuttgart 1937, 11–15; E. R. Goodenough, *By Light, Light*, New Haven 1935, 6; idem, *Jewish Symbols in the Greco-Roman Period*, 12 vols., New York 1953–65, I, 53, 111–115, 264–267.

[57] Cf. E. L. Sukenik, *Ancient Synagogues in Palestine and Greece*, London 1934, 69f. Otherwise: H. C. Kee, 'Defining the First Century CE Synagogue,' *NTS* 41 (1995), 481–500.

[58] Van der Horst (note 55); Ellis, *Prophecy* (note 2), 246; J. A. Fitzmyer, 'The Languages of Palestine in the First Century AD,' *A Wandering Aramean*, Missoula MT 1979, 32–38 = Grand Rapids ²1997; P. E. Hughes, 'The Languages Spoken by Jesus,' *New Dimensions in New Testament Study*, ed. R. N. Longenecker, Grand Rapids 1974, 141ff.; J. N. Sevenster, *Do You Know Greek?* Leiden 1968, 96–175.

[59] Cf. G. Dalman, *Jesus-Jeschua*, Leipzig 1922, 5 = ET: 5; idem, *Orte und Wege Jesu*, Gütersloh ³1924, 177 = ET: 165.

in Palestine (or Syria), correct Greek does not in itself point to a background in the diaspora.

2. The second axiom above is equally open to question. It is the assumption, apparently regarded as self-evident, that the authorship of New Testament books was an individual enterprise and that, therefore, it can be tested by linguistic and/or stylistic analysis. In some instances, e.g. Luke-Acts, a distinctive style can be discerned although it is undoubtedly influenced by the amanuensis (*librarius* or, perhaps, *notarius*) and by the sources that were used. For the Gospels of Matthew and John there is some evidence that prophets and teachers (πνευματικοί) gathered around the particular Apostle and had a share in bringing the Gospels into their present form.[60]

For the letters of Paul a similar situation pertains. It also has become clear, especially since the important investigations of Otto Roller and Randolph Richards into the practice of ancient letter writing,[61] that the Apostle's secretary, i.e. amanuensis participated in the composition of his letters. Roller showed that ancient writers employed a secretary who copied, sometimes onto a wax tablet, and then with a variable degree of freedom transcribed the letter onto papyrus. After reading and correcting it, the author added a closing greeting in his own hand. A few New Testament letters make explicit mention of such an amanuensis:

---

[60] Cf. E. E. Ellis, 'The Date and Provenance of Mark's Gospel,' *The Four Gospels. FS F. Neirynck*, 3 vols., ed. F. Van Segbroeck, Leuven 1992, II, 801–815; idem, 'The Making of Narratives in the Synoptic Gospels,' *Jesus and the Oral Gospel Tradition*, ed. H. Wansbrough, Sheffield UK 1991, 310–333; idem, *Making* (note 2), 333–376. K. Stendahl, *The School of St. Matthew*, Lund ²1969, 34, 190–292, is probably correct in attributing the 'Christianized' interpretations of the Old Testament peculiar to the First Gospel to a Matthean school of exegetes. Re the Fourth Gospel cf. Jn 21:24, which presupposes the participation in some manner of co-workers of the Beloved Disciple in the composition of the Gospel. A somewhat similar tradition is reflected in the Muratorian Canon (9–16): 'The fourth of the Gospels is that of John, [one] of the disciples: When his fellow-disciples and bishops urged him, he said: "Fast with me from today for three days, and what will be revealed to each one let us relate to one another." In the same night it was revealed to Andrew, [one] of the apostles, that while all were to go over [it], John in his own name should write everything down.' Cf. O. Cullmann, *The Johannine Circle*, London 1976, 91–94 = GT: 95–98; Ellis, *Making* (note 2), 36–39.

[61] E. R. Richards, *The Secretary in the Letters of Paul*, Tübingen 1991, 169–201; O. Roller, *Das Formular der paulinischen Briefe*, Stuttgart 1933, 14, 17ff. Given the poor quality of the ink and reed-pen and the rough surface of papyrus, it might take over an hour to write one page of copy. For Greek letters, the use of shorthand by a stenographer (*notarius*) is attested only from later centuries. But in the first century a trusted secretary (*librarius*) might more or less precisely copy and complete a

> I, Tertius, the writer of this letter, greet you in the Lord.
> *Rom 16:22*

> By Silvanus, a faithful brother as I regard him, I have written briefly (δι' ὀλίγων ἔγραψα) to you.[62]
> *I Pet 5:12*

Other letters disclose, in the closing greeting, the use of the same procedure. Even in the brief letter of Philemon Paul has apparently used a secretary:

> I, Paul, write this with my own hand: I will repay it.
> *Plm 19*

> I, Paul, write this greeting with my own hand. This is the mark in every letter of mine. This is the way I write.
> *II Thess 3:17*

> See with what large letters I am writing to you with my own hand.
> *Gal 6:11*

There is also evidence that Paul's co-workers participated in the composition of his letters. That possibility already comes into view with the mention of co-senders at the beginning of some of them. It is strengthened by the fact that all of Paul's letters, with the exception of Philemon, include preformed pieces—hymns,[63] biblical expositions and other literary forms[64]—that are self-contained and that differ from the language, style and theological expression elsewhere in the same and in other letters. This can be demonstrated not only for Paul's letters but also for others.[65] Taken together, these facts show that the current linguistic analysis of New Testament letters is still an over-simplified procedure and that, in spite of the great

---

letter in accordance with oral or written instructions from the author. For Latin letters cf. Cicero, *ad Atticum* 13, 25, 3, where Tiro, the amanuensis, is said to 'take down whole sentences at a breath.' Roller (307) doubts that this refers to stenography; but cf. Richards, 26–43; A. Mentz, *Die Tironischen Noten*, Berlin 1944, 39–50.

[62] The phrase, δι' ὀλίγων ἔγραψα, excludes a metaphorical reference to the carrier of the letter; cf. L. Goppelt, *A Commentary on I Peter*, Grand Rapids MI 1993, 369 = GT: 347.

[63] E.g. Phil 2:6–11; Col 1:12–20; I Tim 3:16. Cf. Ellis, *Making* (note 2), 91ff., 100–109, passim, and the literature cited. See below, 141, 149f.

[64] E.g. expositions: I Cor 2:6–16; cf. I Tim 2:9–3:1a with I Cor 14:34f. and I Pet 3:3–6; cf. Ellis, *Making* (note 2), 78f., 82ff., 156; regulations: ?I Cor 11:3–16; 12:4–11; cf. Ellis, *Making* (note 2), 84–87, 90, 99f., 409, 413ff.; I Tim 3:1b–13, 14; prophecies: II Cor 6:14–7:1; I Tim 4:1–5, 6. See below, 146ff.

[65] E.g. the expositions in Jas 2:20–26; II Pet 3:3–13. Cf. Ellis *Making* (note 2), 117–139.

reliance still placed upon this inheritance from nineteenth-century criticism, any conclusions about the authorship of the letters solely on the basis of their language, style and theological idiom are doubtful.

3. Finally, the axiom, or perhaps one should say the implicit assumption, that early Christian thought developed stage by stage as a block continues to exercise considerable influence, particularly in some German scholarship and in the Hegelian dialectical form popularized by F. C. Baur.[66] This is apparent even when Baur's components have been changed. For example, it appears in the interpretation of early Christian eschatology as a three-step movement: A thoroughgoing apocalypticism (*thesis*) encounters the problem of the delay of the parousia (*antithesis*), and the tension is overcome by a theology of salvation history (*synthesis*).[67] The axiom is also used with a similar pattern to explain ecclesiastical development: The apostle Paul had 'a concept of the church in which, generally speaking, there was no "office" ... Alongside [was] ... the opposite type of congregation, led by presbyters, which was Jewish Christian....' 'The fusion of the two forms' appears in Luke and I Peter and, at a more advanced stage, in the Pastoral Epistles.[68] This is not to say, of course, that such scholars, or Baur for that matter, consciously conformed the historical data to a Hegelian mold. But they do witness to the continuing power of Hegel's thought on the minds of some historians of early Christianity.

One might argue, naturally, that Hegel does provide the key to the development of Christian theology. However, to reconcile his theory with the historical data involves, in several respects, a notable feat of mental gymnastics: (1) When the same concepts[69] and terms[70]

---

[66] E.g. M. D. Goulder, *St. Paul Versus St. Peter: A Tale of Two Missions*, Louisville KY 1995; G. Lüdemann, *Opposition to Paul in Jewish Christianity*, Minneapolis 1989. It is also present, of course, among Anglo-American scholars who follow this heritage of German scholarship. E.g. J. D. G. Dunn, *Unity and Diversity in the New Testament*, London 1977, 345, 356; idem, 'Pseudepigraphy,' *DLNT* 977–984.

[67] E.g. H. Conzelmann, *The Theology of St. Luke*, London 1960, 131–136; idem, 'Luke's Place in the Development of Early Christianity,' *Studies in Luke-Acts*, ed. L. E. Keck, Nashville 1966, 306f.: Luke represents a comprehensive synthesis of components from the earlier period. The same thought-pattern was reflected earlier by R. Bultmann, *Existence and Faith*, New York 1960, 237f. = GT: *TLZ* 73 (1948), 665f.

[68] H. von Campenhausen, *Ecclesiastical Authority and Spiritual Power*, Stanford CA 1969, 296f.; cf. 81–86.

[69] E.g. the 'church order' reflected in I Cor 14:34f. and I Tim 2:11–15.

[70] E.g. ἐπίσκοποι in Phil 1:1 and ἐπίσκοπος/ἐπίσκοποι in I Tim 3:2; Titus 1:7; Acts 20:28.

are used in different books, they are given, often with little or no exegetical basis, strikingly different connotations. (2) Theological differences between New Testament books are ascribed *ipso facto* to different chronological 'stages' in the church's life. (3) Although the New Testament christology has been shown to be in full bloom within two decades after Jesus' resurrection,[71] it is subjected to an elaborate scheme of development under various and sundry religious influences. (4) Documents whose attributions to apostolic figures or associates find a relatively early confirmation and encounter no objection in the ancient writers are reconstructed on doubtful literary or philosophical grounds as fictional productions of a later period. With this kind of record it is hardly too much to say that a unilinear or a dialectical interpretation of historical process in early Christianity is an arbitrary procedure, incapable of providing a satisfactory reconstruction of early Christian history.

Conclusion

This is not the time or place to elaborate an alternative approach to the history of early Christianity,[72] but a few tentative suggestions may not be inappropriate. In research on the Gospels John is now widely recognized to be independent of the Synoptics. This means, among other things, that the origins of its presentation of Jesus' ministry need no longer be viewed as subsequent to theirs.[73] The relationship of Acts to the Pauline literature is probably to be similarly interpreted.[74] For the historical evidence is better served, one would think, by recognizing that Acts, which does not use the Pauline letters, can give a theological and/or historical perspective different from them and, nevertheless, still come from Paul's generation and

---

[71] E.g. Phil 2:6–11; Rom 10:9, 13 = Joel 3:5 MT = 2:32 LXX: κύριος = Yahweh; cf. Ellis, *Christ* (note 3), 38–51, 89–94; D. B. Capes, *Old Testament Yahweh Texts in Paul's Christology*, Tübingen 1992. Cf. M. Hengel, 'Christologie und neutestamentliche Chronologie,' *Neues Testament und Geschichte. FS O. Cullmann zum 70. Geburtstag*, ed. H. Baltensweiler, Tübingen 1972, 43–67 = ET: *Between Jesus and Paul*, London 1983, 30–47; idem (note 53); C. F. D. Moule, *The Origin of Christology*, Cambridge 1977. See below, Chapter Nine, 133–150.
[72] See Ellis, *Making* (note 2), 238–330; idem, *Christ* (note 3), 212–241.
[73] Cf. S. S. Smalley, *John: Evangelist and Interpreter*, Exeter 1978, 9–40; Ellis, *Making* (note 2), 154f., 181ff.; J. A. T. Robinson, *The Priority of John*, London 1985, 1–122.
[74] Cf. E. E. Ellis, *The Gospel of Luke*, Grand Rapids ⁷1996, 4ff., 55–60; J. Jervell, 'Paul in the Acts of the Apostles,' *The Unknown Paul*, Minneapolis 1984, 68–76.

even from his sometime colleague.⁷⁵ In principle the same can be said of the chronological relationship to Paul of the letter of James and of the Gospel of Matthew, even if James and Matthew reflect a tension over against some in the Pauline circle or its predecessors. After all, in the light of the non-Pauline traditions evident within the Apostle's letters, Paul can hardly be regarded as the sole fountainhead even of certain themes for which he is known.

Earliest Christianity appears to have been a unity in diversity, with clusters of prophets and teachers gathering around various apostolic figures. Each group pursued its mission and developed, at varying degrees of rapidity, both common and distinctive theological motifs. These groups have been designated variously as 'the School of St. Matthew,'⁷⁶ 'the Johannine Circle,'⁷⁷ 'Paul and his Co-workers.'⁷⁸ One might equally well speak of a 'Circle of Peter' (I Pet 5:12)⁷⁹ or 'of James' (Acts 12:17).⁸⁰ These different and contemporary apostolic mission-teams combined missionary endeavour with theological reflection and writing. They gave mutual recognition to one another and apparently shared, as the occasion warranted, their oracles, expositions and regulations.⁸¹ This reading of the evidence has much to commend it and, if valid, it undercuts any dating of New Testament books that assumes a unilinear or dialectical development of early Christian thought.

In conclusion, the literary criticism of New Testament literature accepted by most scholars today, and the New Testament chronology based upon it, has underpinnings that are tenuous and that in some

---

⁷⁵ A σίλλυβος with the name 'Luke' was in all likelihood attached to this dedicated work when it was cataloged in Theophilus' library. The early and undisputed identification of this Luke with Paul's sometime colleague is confirmed by the internal evidence and is highly probable. Cf. C. Hemer, *The Book of Acts in the Setting of Hellenistic History*, Tübingen 1989, 308–410; J. A. Fitzmyer, *The Gospel According to Luke*, 2 vols., Garden City NY 1985, I, 47–53; M. Hengel, 'The Titles of the Gospels,' *Studies in the Gospel of Mark*, London 1985, 64–84; idem (note 71), 97–128. Ellis (note 74), 40–50, 64f.; idem, *Making* (note 2), 251–254, 379, 389ff., 397–405.
⁷⁶ Stendahl (note 60).
⁷⁷ Cullmann (note 60). Cf. R. A. Culpepper, *The Johannine School*, Missoula 1975. On the distinction between 'circle' and 'school' cf. Ellis, *Making* (note 2), 150ff.
⁷⁸ Ellis, *Prophecy* (note 2), 3–22. Cf. Acts 13:1f. On 'pseudo-apostolic' groups cf. idem, 13n, 80–115; idem, *Making* (note 2), 314–318; Mt 7:15; II Cor 11:13; I Jn 4:1; Rev 2:2, 6, 14, 210–22.
⁷⁹ Cf. Ellis, 'Date' (note 60), II, 812–815 = *Making* (note 2), 372–376.
⁸⁰ Cf. Ellis, *Prophecy* (note 2), 226–230.
⁸¹ Cf. Rom 1:11f.; 16:3–15; I Cor 16:12; Gal 2:7–9. Re the sharing and application of each other's traditions cf. I Cor 11:16; 14:33b; 15:1ff.; Gal 1:18 (ἱστορῆσαι); I Tim 3:1a *et passim* (πιστὸς ὁ λόγος); II Pet 3:15f.; Ellis, *Making* (note 2), 310–314.

cases can be shown to be historically false. If this is so, the dating of the documents must perforce rely less upon internal literary characteristics and more upon the books' attributions of authorship, upon early patristic tradition and upon historical correlations such as those that J. A. T. Robinson pointed to. That does not mean that his redating of the books is always correct[82] although in some instances he seems to have made important and lasting contributions.

The problem that Robinson's reconstruction faces is not, however, merely a matter of assigning dates. The strong reaction to his proposals in some quarters reminds one of the response Jerome received when he translated the Latin Vulgate directly from the Hebrew rather than from the Greek Septuagint. When one North African bishop, in the Sunday lesson, read from Jerome's version that God prepared an 'ivy' to overshadow Jonah, his congregation, used to the Old Latin version, is said to have indignantly and loudly objected, 'No, gourd! gourd!'[83] But Jerome's translation faced more serious opponents than congregations offended by the alteration of a favorite passage. It also aroused the opposition of theologians and clergy for whom the Septuagint had provided the basis for a considerable package of patristic theology, a package that might prove to be empty if Jerome's version were accepted.

One suspects that proposals for redating the New Testament, like Bishop Robinson's, may pose a similar dilemma for some theologians and historians today. If so, one should not expect immediate applause, and one can even understand the prolonged failure of most scholarship to interact with, much less to respond to his views. But in view of the current state of scholarship in this area, the study of early Christianity and of the New Testament can only be benefited by a full reconsideration of the question.[84]

---

[82] Note the reservations about the Gospel and Letters of John expressed above (33f.) and in Ellis, *Making* (note 2), 199–208, 234–237, 402n, where a post-70 origin of the Johannine Gospel and epistles has been argued. *Pace* Robinson the Pastoral Letters cannot be interspersed among Paul's other letters. When I first reviewed Robinson's *Redating* (note 1), I had not worked enough in II Peter to have a viewpoint although, like him, I was impressed with the arguments of T. Zahn's *Introduction to the New Testament*, 3 vols., Grand Rapids 1953 (1909). I am now convinced that Jude is to be dated AD 55–65 (cf. *Prophecy*, note 2, 226–236) and II Peter AD 60–62. See Ellis, *Making* (note 2), 293–303, 422–425. See below, Chapter Five, 70–73.

[83] Cf. letters 71 and 75 in *The Fathers of the Church*, vol. 12, 'St. Augustine: Letters 1–82,' ed. W. Parsons, New York 1951, 327, 366f.

[84] For the implications of preformed traditions in the New Testament documents for their dating cf. Ellis, *Making* (note 2), 307–319.

CHAPTER FOUR

'THE END OF THE EARTH' (ACTS 1:8)

It has long been recognized that the book of Acts was organized to depict, among other things, the geographical progress of the Christian message from Jerusalem through Judea and Samaria to the lands of Syria, Asia Minor, Greece and to Rome.[1] In this respect it presents the expansion of the Christian witness from the center of Judaism to the center of the Roman Empire, from the mission to Palestinian Jews to the mission to Jews and Gentiles of the diaspora.

THE USE OF THE PHRASE IN ACTS

Luke, the author of Acts and companion and co-worker of Paul,[2] devotes almost all of the latter part of Acts to the Pauline mission. But he pictures Paul's ministry as arising from his teachings in the synagogue and, consequently, as directed to Jews as well as to Gentiles. Even in the last chapter of Acts Luke represents the Apostle's initial preaching at Rome as primarily concerned with his appeal to the Jews, some of whom 'were persuaded... and some disbelieved.'[3]

The book of Acts, then, does not describe a transition of the Christian mission from the Jews to the Gentiles since Jews are recipients

---

[1] Acts 1:1–7:60 (Jerusalem); 8:1–11:18 (Judea and Samaria); 11:19–12:25 (Syria); 13:1–16:10 (Cyprus and Asia Minor); 16:11–19:22 (Greece); 27:1–28:31 (Rome). In an earlier usage of Luke (Lk 3:1; 4:44) and in that of Josephus (*War* 3, 53–58) Judea included Caesarea, the capital of the Roman imperial province of Judea. Cf. B. Reicke, *The New Testament Era*, Philadelphia 1968, 134, 197–200, 339 (map) = GT: 99f., 146–150, 263 (*Tafel* III); H. Conzelmann, *Die Apostelgeschichte*, Tübingen 1963 (*beigelegte Landkarte*). But see M. Hengel, 'Luke the Historian and the Geography of Palestine,' *Between Jesus and Paul*, London 1983, 99 = GT: *ZDPV* 99 (1983) 151.

[2] Col 4:14; 2 Tim 4:11; Plm 24. See the careful case for Lukan authorship developed by C. Hemer, *The Book of Acts in the Setting of Hellenistic History*, Tübingen 1989, 308–364. Cf. Hengel (note 1) 97–128, 121 = GT: 147–183, 175; E. E. Ellis, *The Making of the New Testament Documents*, Leiden 1999, 397–400; idem, *The Gospel of Luke*, Grand Rapids ⁷1996, 40–51. Otherwise: G. Schneider, *Die Apostelgeschichte*, 2 vols., Freiburg 1980, I, 108–111; E. Haenchen, *The Acts of the Apostles*, Philadelphia 1971, 90–116 = GT: ³1959, 81–103.

[3] Acts 28:24; cf. 20:21; Rom 1:16; I Cor 1:23f.; II Cor 11:24.

of the message throughout the book. If Acts, like Paul's letter to the Romans, underscores the rejection of the gospel message by the majority of the Jewish religious leaders and by the nation, it does not omit the continuing positive response of many individual Jews.[4] This fact is important for a proper interpretation of Acts 1:8:

> You shall be my witnesses in Jerusalem and in all Judea and Samaria and to the end of the earth (ἐσχάτου τῆς γῆς).

The Isaian wording of the concluding phrase may reflect a summary of the risen Jesus' commission to his disciples in terms of the Servant of the Lord in Isa 49:6 or it could be Luke's interpretive rendering.[5] In either case it is a conscious allusion by Luke to the verse in Isaiah 49:6 where the phrase has a geographical connotation:

> I will give you as a light to the Gentiles
> That my salvation may reach
> To the end of the earth (ἐσχάτου τῆς γῆς).

The prophecy in Isaiah is not merely that the Servant's mission of salvation will include Gentiles but, much more, that in the course of including Gentiles the mission will extend 'to the end of the earth.'[6] As it is taken up in Acts 13:47, the prophecy retains the same double motif, Gentile inclusion and earth-wide extension. In Acts 1:8 the abbreviated form, 'to the end of the earth,' has only geographical connotations[7] even if there are secondary implications for the inclusion of Gentiles. Therefore, it cannot be equated with the risen

---

[4] Acts 11:19; 13:43; 14:1f.; 16:1; 17:1–4, 10f.; 18:4; 19:10; 20:21; 28:24. Cf. J. Jervell, *Luke and the People of God*, Minneapolis 1972, 63: '[In Acts 28] the Gentile mission is really only beginning.' Cf. Rom 9–11.

[5] Luke also refers to Isa 49:6 in Acts 13:47 and, by allusion, in Lk 2:32. Both passages are probably traditional, but they show in any case Luke's interest in retaining the Isaian reference.

[6] So, A. Motyer, *The Prophecy of Isaiah*, Leicester UK 1993, 388; C. Westermann, *Isaiah 40–66*, Philadelphia 1969, 206, 212: B. Duhm, *Das Buch Jesaja*, Göttingen 1968, 370; already, J. A. Alexander, *Commentary on the Prophecies of Isaiah*, 2 vols., Edinburgh 1865, II, 228; somewhat differently, J. Oswalt, *The Book of Isaiah*, 2 vols., Grand Rapids 1998, II, 294; F. Delitzsch, *Biblical Commentary on the Prophecies of Isaiah*, 2 vols., Grand Rapids 1950, II, 263: Jehovah has set the Servant for a light to the Gentiles 'to become his salvation to the end of the earth' (Isa 49:6). But the Servant of the Lord performs this function whether viewed individually or, as in Acts 13:47f., 14:4, corporately manifested in his apostles, Paul and Barnabas.

[7] Cf. F. F. Bruce, *The Book of Acts. Revised Edition*, Grand Rapids 1989, 37f.; H. Conzelmann, *Acts of the Apostles*, Philadelphia 1987, 7.

Jesus' commission in Matt 28:19 to 'go and make disciples of all nations,' that is, to go to the Gentiles.[8]

If the structure of Acts and the force of the idiom, ἐσχάτου τῆς γῆς, are geographical, what is the location that is in Luke's mind? Since Jerusalem, Judea and Samaria are specific places, probably the 'end of the earth' is also.[9] For two reasons the reference is understood by some scholars to be Rome.[10] (1) It fits the plan of Acts which ends at Rome, and (2) it accords with the (assumed) meaning of the phrase in Pss Sol 8:15 (16) LXX:

> [God] brought someone from the end of the earth....
> He decreed war against Jerusalem.

'The end of the earth' is thought by some writers to refer to Rome, whence Pompey had come to overrun Jerusalem in 63 BC. But for at least three reasons this suggestion is unacceptable. First, in the context the phrase is probably an allusion to Jer 6:22 where 'end of the earth' is used with reference to the Babylonian conquest.[11] That is, the phrase in the Psalms of Solomon alludes to Babylon and at the same time, like the Qumran Commentary on Habakkuk, identifies Babylon, as a type, with Rome or with the Romans.[12] Second, in its application to Pompey the phrase could refer to Spain since Pompey came to the East in 67 BC after a command in Spain (77–71 BC).[13] Third, the phrase 'end(s) of the earth' had a common

---

[8] *Pace* F. J. Foakes Jackson and K. Lake, edd., *The Beginnings of Christianity*, 5 vols., London 1920–33, IV, 9: 'This passage [Acts 1:8] is the Lukan form of the Matthean universal commission' (Lake).

[9] *Pace* H. A. W. Meyer, *The Acts of the Apostles*, New York 1883, 28: '[Acts 1:8] denotes the sphere of the apostles' work ... up to its most general diffusion.' Meyer appears to interpret the phrase as an 'ideal' universal sphere.

[10] E.g. B. Reicke, *The Roots of the Synoptic Gospels*, Philadelphia 1986, 179f.; F. F. Bruce, *Paul*, Grand Rapids 1977, 447f.; Haenchen (note 2) 144n = GT: 112n; R. G. Knowling, 'The Acts of the Apostles,' *The Expositor's Greek Testament*, 5 vols., ed. W. R. Nicoll, Grand Rapids ⁴1974, II, 57; H. J. Holtzmann, *Die Apostelgeschichte*, Tübingen 1901, 25. But see W. C. van Unnik, 'Der Ausdruck ἕως ἐσχάτου τῆς γῆς (Apostelgeschichte i 8),' *Sparsa Collecta*, 3 vols., Leiden 1973–83, I, 386–391.

[11] So, H. E. Ryle and M. R. James, edd., *The Psalms of Solomon*, Cambridge 1891, 80: 'The phrase is used not so much with ... the idea of the remoteness of Italy from Palestine as of reproducing the language of the prophets, in predicting the coming of the Babylonians....'

[12] They make this typological equation fully a century before the Apostles Peter and John do so. Cf. 1QpHab 2:10–6:12; I Pet 5:13; Rev 17:5–10; F. F. Bruce, *New Testament History*, Garden City NY 1972, 11f.

[13] Cf. H. A. Ormond and M. Cary, 'Rome and the East,' *CAH* IX, 321–325,

and apparently fixed meaning that in its westward reference was used of Spain but could by no means apply to the capital city of the Roman Empire.

The Use of the Phrase in Classical Writings

In classical antiquity the inhabited earth was pictured as a disk surrounded by the 'Outer Sea' (ὠκεανός). 'The ends of the earth' (τά ἔσχατα τῆς γῆς) referred, as W. C. van Unnik has shown,[14] to the most distant points on the rim of the disk, for example, the Arctic on the North, India on the East, Ethiopia on the South and Spain on the West.[15] A computer search that I made of the phrase in *Thesaurus Linguae Graecae* fully confirms van Unnik's findings. The expression has that significance in the Septuagint and in the patristic writers (often quoting the Septuagint), where the phrase most often appears in Greek literature. It was used in the same way in the classical writers and apparently retained this geographical meaning from the fifth century BC to the sixth century AD. Thus, Herodotus (†c. 420 BC) speaks of an army going down through Ethiopia to 'the ends of the earth' (τά ἔσχατα γῆς),[16] and a millennium later Procopius (†c. AD 560) speaks of Roman soldiers on the eastern frontier of Persia and India as being 'at the ends of the inhabited world' (ταῖς τῆς οἰκουμένης ἐσχατιαῖς).[17] Writing near the turn of the first century, the geographer Strabo (†c. AD 21) makes this understanding of the phrase very clear:

374–383. Van Unnik (note 10), I, 399, points out that the author of the Psalms of Solomon was well informed about Pompey, at least about his later life. Cf. G. B. Gray, 'The Psalms of Solomon,' *CAP* II, 629f.; R. B. Wright, 'Psalms of Solomon,' *OTP* II, 641.

[14] Van Unnik (note 10), I, 386–401, gives the most thorough analysis, with special attention to the Septuagint (395–399). A. Resch (*Der Paulinismus*, *TU* 27 [1904], 497f.) also surmised that Acts 1:8 alluded to Spain. My computer check of the phrase was from a compact disk of the *TLG* produced at the University of California.

[15] Strabo, *Geography* 1, 1, 6; 1, 2, 31; 2, 3, 5; 2, 4, 2. Cf. Philostratus, *vita Apol.* 6, 1, 1; Philo, *de cher.* 99; idem, *de som.* I, 134; idem, *de migr.* 181.

[16] Herodotus, *History* 3, 25. Cf. the play of Aeschylus († 456 BC), *Prometheus Bound* 665: Io, put out of home and country, to be a wanderer 'at the ends of the earth' (γῆς ἐπ' ἐσχάτοις).

[17] Procopius, *History of the Wars* 2, 3, 52; cf. 6, 30, 9; 2, 22, 7, on the spread of a plague 'right out to the ends of the inhabited world' (τὰς τῆς οἰκουμένης ἐσχατιάς).

> [The] inhabited world is an island. For wherever it has been possible for man to reach the ends of the earth (τὰ ἔσχατα τῆς γῆς), sea has been found. And this sea we call "Oceanus."[18]

Citing Homer, he writes thus of the southern bounds of the earth:

> [The] Ethiopians live at the ends of the earth on the banks of Oceanus' (ἐπὶ τῷ ὠκεανῷ ἔσχατοι).[19]

Concerning the 'end of the earth' westward Strabo is even more specific:

> Gades is situated at the end of the earth (ἐσχάτη τῆς γῆς).[20]

Gades was a prestigious city and the commercial hub of the western reaches of the Roman Empire. It was located west of Gibraltar near the modern Cadiz, Spain, in the area that Strabo had earlier identified with equivalent terminology:

> [The] promontory of Iberia which they call the Sacred Cape is the most westerly point of the inhabited world (δυσμικώτατον τῆς οἰκουμένης).[21]

Diodorus Siculus (†c. 20 BC) described Gades in similar terms:

> The city of Gadeira [Gades] is situated at the end of the inhabited world' (τὰ ἔσχατα τῆς οἰκουμένης).[22]

Pausanius (†c. AD 180) makes a more general allusion to the exile of the Messenians, who returned to Greece after 'fate scattered them to the ends of the earth' (γῆς τὰ ἔσχατα), that is, to Italy, Sicily and western lands (εὐεσπερίτας).[23] The 'western lands' also probably refer to Spain.

In conclusion, the use of the phrase, 'end(s) of the earth,' in Greek literature confirms the initial exegetical impression stated above that the phrase in Acts 1:8 must have a geographical significance. In its westward extent 'the end of the earth' refers generally to Spain and

---

[18] Strabo, *Geography* 1, 1, 8; cf. 1, 2, 31; 1, 4, 6.
[19] Idem, 1, 1, 6; cf. 1, 2, 24.
[20] Idem, 3, 1, 8; cf. 1, 2, 31 (end); 1, 1, 5: 'The Islands of the Blest [Canary Islands] are west of the westward limit (τῆς ἐσχάτης πρὸς δύσιν) of Marousia' [Morocco].
[21] Idem, 2, 5, 14; cf. 3, 1, 4.
[22] Diodorus Siculus, *History* 25, 10, 1.
[23] Pausanius, *Description of Greece* 4, 29, 13; 4, 26, 5.

specifically to the region around Gades, west of Gibraltar. This usage rules out the view that the phrase in Acts alludes to Rome.

A reference to Rome at Acts 1:8 is also excluded by two further considerations. First, Rome does not mark the extent or the completion of the Christian mission in Acts, but only a new base from which the gospel will be taken further 'without hindrance' (Acts 28:31, ἀκωλύτως).[24] Second, if Rome might possibly have been termed the 'end of the earth' by a parochial Psalmist in Jerusalem, it could never have been called that by Luke, who had been in the capital and wrote in the diaspora to Theophilus (Acts 1:1), a cosmopolitan patron who may have resided at Rome and who, in any case, would have thought it absurd to give such a designation to the ruling center of the Empire.

THE CONNOTATION OF THE PHRASE IN ACTS

If 'the end of the earth' in Acts 1:8 refers to a specific place on the rim of the world, only two locations come into serious consideration, Ethiopia on the South and Spain on the West. The former place has been suggested on the basis of the episode of the Ethiopian eunuch in Acts 8:26–40.[25] It is supported by Luke's explicit statement that the eunuch was 'returning' (8:28) to his land, and that after his conversion and baptism he 'was going on his way' (8:39, ἐπορεύετο τὴν ὁδὸν αὐτοῦ).

However, against identifying Ethiopia as the place in mind at Acts 1:8 are the following considerations: (1) At most, Luke portrays only a prospective evangelization of Ethiopia by an otherwise insignificant representative figure. (2) He places the episode in the midst of the Christian missionary enterprise 'in Judea and Samaria' and (3) gives no further attention to the movement of Christianity southward.[26] (4) On the whole he structures the latter half of his work around the mission of Paul and that means, geographically, the movement of Christianity westward. Is there other evidence that may support the view that in Acts 1:8 Luke has in mind the western 'end of the earth,' that is, Spain?

---

[24] Rightly, Schneider (note 2), I, 203n.
[25] So, T. C. G. Thornton, 'To the End of the Earth,' *ET* 89 (1977–78), 374f.
[26] The mentions of Cyrenians (Acts 6:9; 11:20; 13:1) and Alexandrians (Acts 6:9; 18:24) are not really exceptions to this.

It is the Apostle himself who first refers to Spain as the western goal of his mission. Writing to the Christians in Rome, he says:

> When I go to Spain
> I hope to see you in passing.[27]

Clement of Rome, a younger contemporary of Paul, wrote a letter to Paul's church at Corinth a few years (AD 69–70)[28] or, less likely, a few decades (c. AD 95)[29] after the Apostle's martyrdom in Rome (AD 67–68). He offers the earliest and best evidence that Paul did in fact fulfil his intention to undertake a mission to Spain. He summarizes the Apostle's achievements in part as follows:

> Having become a preacher in the East and in the West (τῇ δύσει), [Paul] received the noble (γενναῖον) renown of his faith. Having taught righteousness in the whole world, having reached the limits of the West (τὸ τέρμα τῆς δύσεως) and having witnessed before the governing authorities, thus he departed from the world and went (ἐπορεύθη A) into the holy place. . . .[30]

In writings of the classical period the phrase, τὸ τέρμα τῆς γῆς, was an idiom equivalent to τὰ ἔσχατα τῆς γῆς.[31] Like the latter phrase, such terminology referred in its westward reference most often to Spain (and sometimes to Gaul or Britain) but, for the reasons mentioned above, never to Rome.[32] The following examples may suffice to illustrate this usage:

---

[27] Rom 15:24, 28.
[28] So, Ellis, *Making* (note 2), 280n, 307f.; J. A. T. Robinson, *Redating the New Testament*, London 1976, 327–335 = GT: 323–346; G. Edmundson, *The Church in Rome in the First Century*, London 1913, 187–205; cf. further literature cited by H. E. Lona, *Der erste Clemensbrief*, Göttingen 1998, 75f., although he accepts 'the last decade of the first century' (77) as the date of I Clement. See below, 71f.
[29] So, J. B. Lightfoot, *The Apostolic Fathers*, 3 vols. in 5, London 1890, I, i, 346–358; A. Harnack, *Geschichte der altchristlichen Literatur bis Eusebius II: Die Chronologie*, 2 vols., Leipzig 1958 (1896), I, 255; L. W. Barnard, *The Apostolic Fathers and their Background*, Oxford 1966, 12. L. L. Welborn, 'On the Date of First Clement,' *BR* 29 (1984), 35–54, 37, raises significant objections to the Domitianic date, but he is less persuasive when he limits the 'calamities and reverses' (I Clem 1:1) to internal church quarrels and disconnects the date of the letter (AD 80–140) from external persecutions and problems.
[30] I Clem 5:6f. On AD 67 as the date of Paul's martyrdom cf. Edmundson (note 28), 147–163.
[31] The specific phrase, τὸ τέρμα τῆς δύσεως, is rare if not unique. But cf. the similar τερμάτων γῆς (Philo, *quod Deus immut.* 79; cf. idem, *vita Mos.* 1, 2) and οἰκουμένης τέρματα (Eusebius, *vita Const.* 1, 8, 3f.).
[32] Also, for a writer in Rome 'the West' ordinarily meant Gaul or Spain, but certainly not Rome.

> [Ephorus] imagined that the Iberians, who dwell in such a large part of the western world (ἑσπερίου γῆς), were a single city.[33] The distance from East to West (δύσιν) [is] greater.... From India to Iberia is less than 200,000 stadia....[34]
>
> The first part of Europe is the Western (ἑσπέριον), namely, Iberia.[35]
>
> [The Greeks] say that the Western section [of the world] is from the Gulf of Issus [east of Tarsus] to the capes of Iberia, which are the most westerly parts (δυσμικώτατα).[36]
>
> The regions to the West (δύσιν) of Europe as far as Gades....[37]
>
> The temple of Hercules in Gades [is said to be] ... the end of both earth and sea (γῆς καὶ θαλάττης τὸ πέρας).[38]
>
> The city of Gades is located at the limits of Europe (τὸ τῆς Εὐρώπης τέρμα).[39]
>
> You have come from the Pillars of Hercules [= the straits of Gibraltar],[40] from the Ocean and from the uttermost limits of the earth (*terminisque ultimis terrarum*).[41]

The last four examples show, I believe, that in its specific reference τὸ τέρμα τῆς δύσεως in I Clem 5:7, like the westward reference of ἐσχάτου τῆς γῆς in Acts 1:8, points to the region around Gades, west of Gibraltar.[42]

IMPLICATIONS FOR THE DATING OF ACTS

In view of the meaning of 'end of the earth' in the Greco-Roman literature, the phrase in Acts 1:8 almost certainly alludes to the extension of the gospel to Spain and, more specifically, to the city of Gades. The command is, of course, addressed to the apostles as a whole and not to Paul, and one might argue that it refers to 'the *ends* of the earth,' that is, to the extent of their missions generally,

---

[33] Josephus, *ct. Apion.* 1, 67. Cf. Tacitus, *Histories* 4, 3, middle.
[34] Strabo, *Geography* 1, 4, 6; cf. 1, 2, 31; 2, 1, 1.
[35] Idem, 3, 1, 2.
[36] Idem, 2, 4, 3.
[37] Idem, 2, 4, 4.
[38] Idem, 3, 5, 5.
[39] Philostratus, *vita Apol.* 5, 4; cf. 4, 47; Pliny, *Natural History* 3, 1, 3–7.
[40] Cf. L. Schmitz, 'Heracles,' *DGRBM* II, 393–401, 397.
[41] Livy, *History* 21, 43, 13; cf. 23, 5, 11.
[42] So, already, Lightfoot (note 29), I, ii, 30f.

with the singular ἐσχάτον employed as an allusion to Isa 49:6. In Acts 13:47, however, Luke explicitly applies to the Pauline mission the commission to 'the end of the earth' and thereby specifies the apostle who will be the one to fulfil the command in *his* contribution to the church's expanding mission. Furthermore, he does not hesitate to alter the Old Testament text elsewhere, for example in Acts 2:17–21, to highlight his interpretation or application of it. If he had wished to indicate the spread of the gospel to the bounds of the earth universally, he could easily have utilized the plural ἐσχάτων or ἐσχάτους without foreclosing the allusion to Isaiah, especially at Acts 13:47. In the light of these factors, of the total plan of Acts, and of the equivalent idiom in I Clem 5:7, Luke very probably used the singular intentionally and with contemporary geographical usage in mind, that is, 'the end of the earth' as it was applied to Gades and the adjacent region at the extreme limits of the West.

If the author of Acts is Luke, he doubtless knew of Paul's plans for a Spanish mission. If he wrote before the mission was undertaken, say AD 62–63,[43] or when it was in progress, the open-ended conclusion of Acts would, to some extent, be clarified. In that case Luke did not mention the mission to Gades because, as he finished his volume, it was still outstanding. If he wrote after Paul's mission to Spain but during the Neronian persecution (AD 65–68), he may well have had other reasons for ending his book without explicitly mentioning either Paul's release or a subsequent Spanish mission.[44] If he wrote after AD 68, however, it is more difficult to perceive why he would create or record a preview of the gospel going to Gades and then say nothing more about it.

---

[43] So, Hemer (note 2), 365–410, 408 (AD 62); Reicke (note 10), 174–180, 178 (c. AD 62); A. Harnack, *The Date of Acts and of the Synoptic Gospels*, London 1911, 99 (before the end of Paul's trial). Also advocating an AD 64 or earlier date for Acts, according to Hemer's list (367f.), are the following twentieth-century scholars: P. S. Bihel, E. M. Blaiklock, F. Blass, G. Edmundson, F. V. Filson, J. Finegan, E. R. Goodenough, D. Guthrie, E. F. Harrison, R. N. Longenecker, A. J. Matill, J. Munck, P. Parker, R. B. Rackham, A. T. Robertson, J. A. T. Robinson, C. C. Torrey, V. E. Vine.

[44] Acts 26:32 reflects an optimism that Paul would be (or had been) acquitted but, as I have suggested elsewhere, Luke may have wished not to call attention to Paul's release in order to protect Paul or to protect the Roman magistrate who released him (as he protected Cornelius by omitting 'Caesarea' at Acts 12:17). Cf. E. E. Ellis, *Pauline Theology: Ministry and Society*, Lanham MD ⁴1998, 107–111.

As both J. B. Lightfoot[45] and Adolf Harnack[46] recognized, Paul's release from his first Roman imprisonment is a basic historical fact from which critical reconstructions of early Christian history should proceed. That his release was followed by a journey to Spain is well attested in I Clem 5:7[47] and is entirely in accord with Paul's earlier mission strategy known from the book of Acts and from his letters.

Paul established churches in hub-cities that were centers of trade and transport or on well-travelled arteries of the Roman road and sea-route system—Philippi, Thessalonica, Corinth, Ephesus. Thereby, he was able to evangelize not only the local populace but also merchants, travellers and visitors passing through. In his concern to evangelize Spain he would, following his earlier practice, have considered Gades the prime location for his purposes.

Settled by Phoenicians, Gades in Paul's day was an allied Roman *municipium* that Strabo rated in the density of its populace, in wealth and in prestige as the second city of the Roman world.[48] It was a major commercial center connected to other Spanish cities by 'a splendid road system' (Albertini) and with fishing and merchant ships plying their trade along the western coasts of Europe and Africa and

---

[45] Lightfoot (note 29), I, ii, 30 (on I Clem 5:7): 'This journey of Paul westward [to the pillars of Hercules] supposes that Paul was liberated after the Roman captivity related in the Acts. . . .' Harnack (note 29, I, 239) also considered Paul's mission to Spain to be probable as did T. Zahn and A. Deissmann. Otherwise: Bruce (note 10) and A. Schlatter. Cf. A. Deissmann, *Paul*, New York 1957, 248; A. Schlatter, *The Church in the New Testament Period*, London 1955, 220, 236; T. Zahn, *Introduction to the New Testament*, 3 vols., Grand Rapids 1953, II, 60–67 = GT: I, 443–447.

[46] Harnack (note 29), I, 239f.: 'I hold the release of Paul from his first imprisonment [in Rome] to be a certain fact of history' (*gesicherte Thatsache*, 240n); 'on chronological grounds no objections can be raised against the report that Paul went to the τέρμα τῆς δύσεως, that is, Spain' (239). He gives, among other reasons, the following: I Clem 5:7 and the five years or more between the end of Paul's two-year work in Rome (Acts 28:30) and his execution. Similar, H. W. Tajra, *The Trial of St. Paul*, Tübingen 1989, 196; Hemer (note 2), 390–404; C. Spicq, *Le épîtres pastorales*, 2 vols., Paris ⁴1969, I, 126–146; W. Rordorf, 'Nochmals: Paulusakten und Pastoralbriefe,' *Tradition and Interpretation in the New Testament. FS E. E. Ellis*, ed. G. F. Hawthorne with Otto Betz, Grand Rapids 1987, 322. In addition, Paul's journey to Rome reflected in the Pastoral epistles and in the *Acts of Paul* (c. AD 170–190) is quite different from that in Acts 20–28. Cf. J. Weiss, *The History of Primitive Christianity*, 2 vols., New York 1937, I, 389–392; Rordorf, 324.

[47] Paul's journey to Spain also appears in *Acts of Peter (Vercelli)* 1–3 (AD 160–180) and in the Muratorian Canon (AD 170–190). Cf. Ellis, *Making* (note 2), 278–284.

[48] Strabo, *Geography* 3, 5, 3. Cf. A. N. Sherwin-White, *The Roman Citizenship*, Oxford 1980, 185, 188f., 301–304, 340–343; F. Oertel, 'The Economic Unification of the Mediterranean Region,' *CAH* X, 407f., 415.

as far north as Britain.⁴⁹ It maintained a flourishing sea-traffic with Rome, which in good weather was only a seven-day voyage,⁵⁰ and it may have exported fish as far east as Palestine.⁵¹

There is little evidence for Jewish settlements in Spain in the first century. Josephus states in one place that Antipas was exiled there in AD 39,⁵² and a later rabbinic tradition says that a temple-weaver migrated there after the destruction of Jerusalem in AD 70.⁵³ The best evidence for a Jewish presence in Spain is Paul's stated intention in Rom 15:24, 28 to go there since he customarily preached first to Jews and God-fearers in the synagogue. This is also sufficient answer to the objection that Paul would not have been fluent in the language(s) used at Gades. He would have been able to speak Latin since in Roman colonies, e.g. Philippi and Corinth where Paul established churches, it was 'the language of public business....'⁵⁴

With the phrase, 'the end of the earth,' in Acts 1:8 Luke signals his knowledge of a (prospective) Pauline mission to Spain and his intention to make it a part of his narrative. For reasons that are not altogether clear, he concludes his book without mentioning the Spanish mission. If he wrote before AD 68, the omission can be explained. It is less easy to do so if he wrote after that date. To the various reasons advanced by numerous scholars for an early date for Acts, Acts 1:8 now adds one more. All of the arguments together lead me, after some consideration, to revise my dating of Luke-Acts from a former judgment of 'about 70' AD to a date in the early sixties.⁵⁵

---

⁴⁹ Strabo, *Geography* 3, 2, 1; 3, 4, 3. Cf. E. Albertini, 'The Latin West,' *CAH* XI, 499f.; T. Mommsen, *The Provinces of the Roman Empire*, 2 vols., Chicago 1974, I, 74f.; M. P. Charlesworth, *Trade-Routes and Commerce of the Roman Empire*, Chicago 1974, 141f., 152–157, 163, 208, 235.
⁵⁰ Charlesworth (note 49), 155.
⁵¹ M *Shabbath* 22:2; M *Makshirim* 6:3; cf. S. Applebaum, 'Economic Life in Palestine,' *Compendia* I, 2 (1976), 670.
⁵² Josephus, *War* 2, 183; but see idem, *Antiquities* 18, 252.
⁵³ S. Applebaum, '...Jewish Communities in the Diaspora,' *Compendia* I, 1 (1974), 482. Cf. M *Baba Bathra* 3:2.
⁵⁴ Cf. T. Mommsen, *A History of Rome under the Emperors*, London ²1999, 121. Cf. Acts 16:35–40; 18:12–17; J. Murphy-O'Connor, *St. Paul's Corinth*, Wilmington DE ²1987, 5ff.
⁵⁵ Ellis, *Luke* (note 2), 55–60; idem, *Making* (note 2), 319; idem, *Christ and the Future in New Testament History*, Leiden 2000, 232f.

CHAPTER FIVE

THE ORIGIN AND COMPOSITION OF THE
PASTORAL EPISTLES

I Timothy, II Timothy and Titus, termed the Pastoral Epistles since the eighteenth century, are, with Philemon, letters of the Pauline corpus addressed to individuals. Like other New Testament literature written under Paul's name, they employ the letter-form to convey not just personal communications but primarily teachings and exhortations, some of them preformed traditions already in use in Pauline congregations.[1] In the face of defections and of the depredations of false teachers they emphasize instructions on ministry, church order and related themes in order to protect the Apostle's congregations in Asia Minor and in Greece during the final years of his life.

CANONICITY AND AUTHORSHIP

In the patristic church the reception of the epistles into the New Testament canon was tied to their Pauline authorship for, as Serapion (†c. AD 211) bishop of Antioch put it, 'we receive both Peter and the other apostles as Christ, but pseudepigrapha in their name we reject.'[2] The Pastorals were received almost unanimously. They are explicitly witnessed by the Muratorian Canon and by Irenaeus (c. AD 180),[3] and their canonicity is probably to be inferred from earlier quotations and allusions.[4] They are lacking (along with II Thessalonians and Philemon) only in one manuscript of (some of) Paul's letters (p 46; c. AD 200), which may be a successor to a partial collection of them made during Paul's lifetime.[5] They were rejected

---
[1] Cf. E. E. Ellis, *The Making of the New Testament Documents*, Leiden 1999, 407–417.
[2] Cf. Eusebius, *HE* 6, 12, 3.
[3] Cf. Irenaeus, *AH* 1, 16, 3; 2, 14, 7; 3, 14, 1; Muratorian Canon d, lines 39–68.
[4] Cf. Theophilus, *Autol.* 3:14; Polycarp, *Phil.* 4:1; Ignatius, *ad Eph.* 14:1 (allusion).
[5] Cf. D. Trobisch, *Die Entstehung der Paulusbriefsammlung*, Göttingen 1989, 100–104, 128–132; Ellis (note 1), 86, 132n.

only by certain heretical teachers: I–II Timothy by Tatian and Basilides and all three by Marcion.⁶ They encountered serious objections, however, in the literary criticism of the nineteenth century.

The Baur School

In 1835 F. C. Baur, drawing upon earlier literary questions about the Pastorals, concluded that they reflected a post-Pauline context and identified them, in his Hegelian reconstruction of early Christian history, as second-century forgeries.⁷ His views were elaborated by H. J. Holtzmann, who summed up the objections to Pauline authorship: (1) the historical situation, (2) the gnosticizing false teachers condemned, (3) the stage of church organization, (4) the vocabulary and style, and (5) the theological views and themes.⁸ Baur was ambivalent about the effect of pseudonymity for the canonicity of the Pastorals, but most of his followers thought that it should have no effect. They asserted, against the evidence, that in antiquity pseudonymity was an innocent device.⁹ They often attributed the Pastorals to 'disciples' of Paul and cited as precedents the schools of Pythagoras and of Plato, who wrote letters in the names of those philosophers. There is no evidence, however, that a 'school' of Paul existed after the Apostle's death: The earliest post-apostolic writers such as Clement of Rome, Papias, Ignatius and Polycarp, cite or appeal to various apostles and display no knowledge of any 'school' tendency to transmit only teachings of a particular apostle.¹⁰

The Nineteenth-Century Debate

J. B. Lightfoot and T. Zahn countered the Baur school with the observations that (1) the changed historical circumstances and (2) the more advanced church organization were well accounted for if some years separated Paul's earlier letters, e.g. of I Corinthians (AD 56) from his writing of the Pastorals (AD 64–68), that is, after his release

---

⁶ Cf. Clement, *Strom.* 2, 11, end; Jerome, *Commentary on Titus, Preface*; Tertullian, *adv. Marcion.* 5, 21; Ellis (note 1), 293n.
⁷ Cf. Ellis, 'Ferdinand Christian Baur and his School' (note 1), 440–445.
⁸ F. C. Baur, *Die sogenannten Pastoralbriefe*, Tübingen 1835; H. J. Holtzmann, *Die Pastoralbriefe*, Leipzig 1880, 15–282.
⁹ See above, Chapter Two, 17–29.
¹⁰ Cf. E. E. Ellis, *Christ and the Future in New Testament History*, Leiden 2000, 223f.; idem (note 1), 307–330.

from his first Roman imprisonment, a fact well attested in I Clem 5 (AD 95, Lightfoot; AD 69–70, Edmundson, Robinson) and in second century literature.[11] Anticipating twentieth-century criticism, Lightfoot argued that (3) gnosticizing false teachers were already present during the ministry of Paul, and he also attributed (4) changes in vocabulary, style and (5) in theological emphasis to the origin of the Pastorals in the last years of the Apostle's ministry.[12]

In the nineteenth century both traditional and speculative scholars assumed that Paul himself penned his letters or dictated them verbatim. They consequently supposed that if the major letters were taken as a touchstone, the genuineness of the others could be determined by internal criteria of vocabulary, style and theological motifs. They differed only as to whether such variations were sufficient to exclude Pauline authorship of the Pastorals (the Baur/Holtzmann tradition) or lay within the literary range of a versatile writer like Paul (the Lightfoot/Zahn tradition). The debate, which continued and developed throughout the twentieth century, was something of a standoff.[13] However, the pseudepigraphal viewpoint was undermined by three new insights of twentieth-century criticism: the role of the secretary and of co-senders and the presence of a considerable number of preformed, non-Pauline pieces in almost all of Paul's letters.

Developments in the Twentieth Century

The problem of the Pastorals continued in the minds of many to lie in their vocabulary and style, in their more structured church order, and in the difficulty of 'placing' them within the Pauline missions in Acts.

---

[11] E.g. Muratorian Canon (AD 170–190); *Acts of Peter (Vercelli)* (AD 160–180).

[12] J. B. Lightfoot, 'The Date of the Pastoral Epistles,' 'The Close of Acts,' *Biblical Essays*, London 1893, 399–437; T. Zahn, *Einleitung in das Neue Testament*, 2 vols. in 1, Wuppertal 1994 (^{3}1907), I, 402–495 = ET: II, 1–133. Cf. E. E. Ellis, 'Paul and his Opponents,' *Prophecy and Hermeneutic in Early Christianity*, Tübingen 1978, 89–95. On the date of I Clement cf. Ellis (note 1), 280n; G. Edmundson, *The Church in Rome in the First Century*, London 1913, 187–205; J. A. T. Robinson, *Redating the New Testament*, London 1976, 327–344 = GT: 338–345. Otherwise: J. B. Lightfoot, *The Apostolic Fathers*, 3 vols. in 5, London ^{2}1890, I, i, 346–358.

[13] Cf. M. Prior, *Paul the Letter-Writer and the Second Letter to Timothy*, Sheffield UK 1989, 13–24; E. E. Ellis, *Paul and his Recent Interpreters*, Grand Rapids MI ^{5}1979, 49–57.

With respect to *vocabulary* it was not just the divergence from the terminology of the other Pauline literature but also the absence of many word groups common to Paul (e.g. ἀποκαλύπτειν, ἐνεργεῖν, καυχᾶσθαι, περισσεύειν, ὑπακούειν, φρονεῖν) and the use of different terminology for the same concepts in eschatology (ἐπιφάνεια vis-à-vis παρουσία), church organization (πρεσβύτεροι vis-à-vis προϊστάμενοι and ποιμένες) and soteriology.[14] At the same time many Pauline expressions were evident to all.

Three avenues were taken to resolve this problem. Writers in the Baur/Holtzmann tradition ascribed the Pauline traits to a conscious attempt by the forger to imitate Paul, either to gain apostolic authority for this deception (Donelson) or, reworking certain Pauline traditions, to offer under the Apostle's name what he thought Paul might have taught had he been there (Marshall, Quinn-Wacker, Wolter).[15] Some in the Lightfoot/Zahn tradition contended that the role of the secretary and Paul's use of traditions composed by others accounted for the differences in the Pastorals' style, vocabulary and theological idiom.[16] A few scholars early in the twentieth century argued that the Pastorals were genuine Pauline letters supplemented by second century interpolations, mainly on church order (Harnack), or that they were early second-century products incorporating some genuine Pauline fragments (Harrison; cf. Miller).[17] The fragment-hypothesis failed to convince very many because it could not explain why and how a forger would have used the fragments in such a strange way.[18] The interpolation-hypothesis was a possibility in its day. But with the advances in textual criticism and in the understanding of writing practices of the Greco-Roman world, it lost credibility.

---

[14] M. Dibelius – H. Conzelmann, *The Pastoral Epistles*, Philadelphia 1972, 143–146 = GT: 108ff.

[15] L. R. Donelson, *Pseudepigraphy and Ethical Argument in the Pastoral Epistles*, Tübingen 1986; I. H. Marshall, *The Pastoral Epistles*, Edinburgh 1999, 57–92, 84, 89, 92; J. D. Quinn and W. C. Wacker, *The First and Second Letters to Timothy*, Grand Rapids 1999, 19, 22; M. Wolter, *Die Pastoralbriefe als Paulustradition*, Göttingen 1988.

[16] See below, 79–83.

[17] A. Harnack, *Geschichte der altchristlichen Literatur. Teil II. Chronologie*, 2 vols., Leipzig 1958 (1904), I, 480–485; P. N. Harrison, *The Problem of the Pastoral Epistles*, London 1921; cf. J. D. Miller, *The Pastoral Letters as Composite Documents*, Cambridge 1997.

[18] Dibelius (note 14), 4f. = GT: 4f.; D. Guthrie, 'The Pastoral Epistles,' *Introduction to the New Testament*, Leicester UK ⁴1990, 636–646.

Multiple Copies of Paul's Letters

As was the custom in antiquity,[19] Paul retained a copy of his epistles both for subsequent reference[20] and because of the danger of loss or damage in transit.[21] It is also likely that he allowed the church where he was writing to make a copy of the letter for its own use and that he permitted or instructed the recipients to make copies for themselves or for neighboring congregations.[22] In this way the Apostle himself initiated, virtually at the outset, different textual traditions with inevitable variations in the wording of his correspondence. Therefore, 'it appears to be quite impossible that an interpolator, who anywhere in the stream of tradition arbitrarily inserted three verses, could force under his spell the total textual tradition (which we today have before our eyes in a way quite different from any generation before us)... so that not even one contrary witness remained....'[23] What is said here of Romans applies also to the Pastorals. Any theory that certain verses were later additions must produce some manuscript that lacks the verses, or it will lack all historical probability. The sections that Harnack thought were later interpolations are not absent from any manuscript and were, therefore, in all likelihood a part of the Epistles from the beginning.

Church Organization

The Baur tradition (and also Harnack) supposed that the qualifications demanded for the ministry of 'bishop' or 'overseer' (ἐπίσκοπος) = 'elder' (πρεσβύτερος)[24] reflected a 'developed' church order that was post-Pauline. It rested its case on the twin assumptions that the earliest congregations had no structured ministries and that early Christian (theology and) praxis moved forward gradually and stage-by-stage as a block. These assumptions were deeply embedded in nineteenth-century consciousness from theories of egalitarianism, of historical

---

[19] Cf. Cicero, *To Friends* 7, 25, 1; E. R. Richards, *The Secretary in the Letters of Paul*, Tübingen 1991, 3–7. See Ellis (note 1), 86, 430.
[20] Cf. I Cor 5:9f.; II Cor 7:8; II Thess 2:15; II Tim 4:13.
[21] Cf. Cicero, *To Friends* 16, 18, end.
[22] Cf. II Cor 1:1: 'Achaia;' Gal 1:2; Col 4:16.
[23] K. Aland, 'Neutestamentliche Textkritik und Exegese,' *Wissenshaft und Kirche. FS E. Lohse*, ed. K. Aland, Bielefeld 1989, 132–148, 141.
[24] I Tim 3:2; 5:17; cf. Tit 1:5 with 1:7; J. B. Lightfoot, *Saint Paul's Epistle to the Philippians*, London [18]1913, 95–99; G. W. Knight III, *The Pastoral Epistles*, Grand Rapids MI 1992, 175ff.; I. H. Marshall (note 15), 159f.

and social progress and of biological evolution. But they do not accord either with the variegated church order of the apostolic congregations nor with the present-day recognition that 'development' may be either gradual or extremely rapid.[25]

From the beginning the congregations of all the apostolic missions had some measure of church order. The church at Jerusalem with its leadership of resident apostles, especially Peter (c. AD 33–42)[26] and James (c. AD 42–62),[27] and elders[28] had a more structured organization, probably similar to that of the synagogues and of the Qumran community.[29] According to I Peter (AD 64) and Acts[30] (AD 63–64) certain churches in Asia Minor and Greece founded by the Petrine and Pauline missions also had a recognized church order even if the term, 'elders' (πρεσβύτεροι), in Acts is a Lukan idiom for ministries given different designations in Paul's earlier letters. These letters disclose established ministries of administrative and teaching leadership although they identify them more often as activities[31] than as appointed offices.[32] The Pastorals give more prominence to appointed ministries and to the qualifications for them because, among other things, of the increasing threat to Paul's churches by the (sometimes subtle) infiltration of false teachers.[33] They represent an understandable development of his earlier usage.

Conclusion

The role of the secretary (Richards, Roller)[34] and the use of performed traditions[35] in the composition of the Pastorals cut the ground

---

[25] Cf. Ellis (note 1), 28ff.
[26] Cf. Gal 1:18; Acts 2:14; 3:12; 5:3; 8:14; 9:32; 12:17; Ellis (note 1), 242, 264ff.
[27] Cf. Gal 2:9; Acts 12:17; 15:13; 21:18; Ellis (note 1), 263f., 288–293.
[28] Cf. Acts 11:30; 15:2; 21:18; cf. Jas 5:14.
[29] E.g. Lk 7:3; cf. CD-A 13:7–13; 1 QS 6:14 (הפקיד, overseer), 20 (המבקר, inspector). Cf. E. Schürer, *The History of the Jewish People in the Age of Jesus Christ*, 3 vols. in 4, Edinburgh ²1987, II, 427–439; B. E. Thiering, '*Mebaqqer* and *Episkopos* in the Light of the Temple Scroll,' *JBL* 100 (1981), 59–74; M. Weinfeld, *The Organizational Pattern and the Penal Code of the Qumran Sect*, Göttingen 1988.
[30] I Pet 5:1–3; cf. 1:2. Acts 14:23; 20:17; cf. 20:28.
[31] E.g. Rom 12:8; 1 Cor 12:28; Gal 6:6; I Thess 5:12f.
[32] Phil 1:1.
[33] Cf. Gal 2:4; I Tim 4:1; II Pet 2:1; E. E. Ellis, *Pauline Theology: Ministry and Society*, Lanham MD ⁴1998, 92–107.
[34] Richards (note 19), passim; O. Roller, *Das Formular der paulinischen Briefe*, Stuttgart 1933. Cf. J. Jeremias, *Die Briefe an Timotheus und Titus*, Göttingen ²1981, 9ff.; J. N. D. Kelly, *A Commentary on the Pastoral Epistles*, London 1963, 25ff., 33f.
[35] See below, 79–82, 138–141; for all Paul's letters cf. Ellis (note 1), 116.

from under the pseudepigraphal hypothesis with its mistaken nineteenth-century assumptions about the nature of authorship. They require the critical student to give primary weight to the opening attributions in the letters and to the external historical evidence, both of which solidly support Pauline authorship.

OCCASION AND DATE

Proponents of Paul's authorship of the Pastorals usually, though not always,[36] presuppose the tradition that Paul was released from his first Roman imprisonment (Acts 28), rightly regarded by Harnack as 'a certain fact of history,'[37] and that afterwards he had a second Aegean ministry in which I Timothy and Titus could be placed. The tradition is supported by two considerations: (1) second-century accounts, underlying the *Acts of Paul* (9ff.; c. AD 170–190), of the Apostle's final trip to Rome and martyrdom under Nero on a route different from that in Acts 27–28[38] and (2) very early evidence for a post-Acts 28 Pauline mission to Spain.

Paul's Mission to Spain

The probability of a missionary journey to Spain arises largely (1) from the anticipation of such a task in Rom 15:24; Acts 1:8; 13:47 and (2) from the evidence for it in I Clem 5 (AD 69–70),[39] in the *Acts of Peter* (*Vercelli*) 1–3, 40 (probably Asia Minor, AD 160–180) and in the Muratorian Canon (Rome, AD 170–190). The last two are independent witnesses to a widespread second-century tradition that Paul journeyed from Rome to Spain and, in the apocryphal *Acts of Peter*, that he returned to Rome for martyrdom.

---

[36] B. Reicke, 'Chronologie der Pastoralbriefe,' *TLZ* 101 (1976), 82–94, and J. A. T. Robinson (note 12), 67–85 = GT: 76–94, date I Timothy and Titus preceding, and II Timothy during the Caesarean detention of Paul (AD 58–60).

[37] Harnack (note 17), I, 240n.

[38] So, W. Rordorf, 'Nochmals: Paulusakten und Pastoralbriefe,' *Tradition and Interpretation in the New Testament. FS E. E. Ellis*, ed. G. F. Hawthorne with O. Betz, Grand Rapids and Tübingen 1987, 319–327; Zahn (note 12), I, 461f. = ET: II, 84.

[39] On the date of I Clement cf. Robinson (note 12), 327–335 = GT: 338–346; Edmundson (note 12), 187–205; Ellis (note 1), 280n, 307f. See above, Chapter Four, 59f.

Clement of Rome knows seven imprisonments of Paul, calls Paul and Peter 'our good apostles' (I Clem 5) and, according to Irenaeus (*AH* 3, 3, 3; c. AD 180), sat under their teaching. He speaks of Paul's preaching 'in the West,' which for a writer in Rome would mean Spain or Gaul (cf. II Tim 4:10), and of his reaching 'the extreme limits of the West' (τὸ τέρμα τῆς δύσεως, I Clem 5:6f.). The latter phrase, like 'the end of the earth' (ἐσχάτου τῆς γῆς, Acts 1:8), referred in the usage of the time to the region of Spain around Gades = Cadiz. The Apostle probably sailed from Rome (i.e. Ostia) to Gades, a week's voyage, after he was set free from his first Roman imprisonment.[40] I Clement and the *Acts of Peter* are supported by later traditions of Paul's release and of his post-Acts 28 ministry.[41] Since Paul's Spanish sojourn apparently was unknown to Origen[42] and produced no churches in Spain that claimed Pauline origins, it may have been a brief mission (spring to autumn 63 or AD 63–64), undertaken soon after his release,[43] from which he returned to his churches in the Aegean area.

The Situation of I Timothy and Titus

The situation of I Timothy and Titus differs from that of Paul's earlier Aegean ministry (AD 53–58).[44] His mission had now extended to Gaul[45] and to Spain, and his congregations around the Aegean had multiplied and now encompassed Crete, Miletus, and Nicopolis.[46] They were increasingly endangered by a judaizing-gnosticizing countermission[47] that included church leaders and probably former coworkers.[48] Some house-churches were ravaged and near collapse, as Paul's instructions to Titus (1:5, 10f.) indicate: 'Restore the things

---

[40] See above, Chapter Four, 62f.; cf. *Acts of Peter* (*Vercelli*) 1–3.
[41] Cf. Eusebius, *HE* 2, 22, 1–8: λόγος ἔχει, 2.
[42] Cf. Eusebius, *HE* 3, 1, 3.
[43] See Ellis (note 1), 282f. Cf. Zahn (note 12), I, 445ff. = ET: II, 64–67. *Pace* Zahn (I, 446f. = ET: II, 66), Paul need not have delayed his voyage to Gades after his release in the spring of 63.
[44] Cf. Kelly (note 34), 6–10.
[45] Cf. II Tim 4:10; Zahn (note 12), I, 418f. = ET: II, 25f.
[46] Tit 1:5; 3:12; II Tim 4:20. They may have been founded during the first Aegean mission.
[47] Cf. I Tim 1:3–7, 19f.; 4:1f.; 6:20; II Tim 4:3f.; Tit 1:10–16; cf. Ellis (note 12), 80–115, 133ff.; idem (note 1), 314–318.
[48] Cf. II Tim 1:15–18; 2:16f.; 3:6–9; 4:10; Tit 3:9ff.

that remain, and appoint elders in each city.' 'For many deceivers . . ., especially the circumcision party, . . . are overthrowing whole houses. . . .' This threat to his churches may have occasioned Paul's return from Spain.

To meet the problem, Paul adopted a new strategy for his writing. He ministered as before from a base in a hub-city, perhaps Corinth (cf. II Tim 4:20), with several visits to a number of churches, e.g. in Macedonia (I Tim 1:3), Crete (Tit 1:5), Nicopolis (Tit 3:12), Miletus (II Tim 4:20) and Ephesus.[49] But he could not, as he did earlier,[50] send an epistle to each church or to a group of the many congregations, along with a colleague to explain and apply it. Instead, he sent letters to trusted co-workers, Titus in Crete and Timothy in Ephesus, letters that served both as instruments of personal communication and encouragement and also as vade mecums to give apostolic authorization for the co-workers' teaching.

For the itinerary of his second Aegean ministry one is left largely to conjecture, because Paul's letters and other sources offer little help. The Apostle probably returned there from Spain in late AD 63 or early 64 and labored in Crete (Tit 1:5) and Macedonia (I Tim 1:3) as well as in Achaia for many months, spending the winter of 64–65 at Nicopolis in Epirus.[51] He composed I Timothy and Titus fairly early in this period, probably late in AD 64 (cf. Tit 3:12). In the spring of 67 he visited Miletus, where he left Trophimus (II Tim 4:20), and Troas, where he left his winter coat and a number of books and notebooks (μεμβράνα), which probably included copies of his previous epistles and traditional materials useful for his teaching and for composing letters.[52] From Troas, apparently, he departed for Rome with the intention of returning before winter.

---

[49] I Tim 1:3; 3:14; 4:13; II Tim 1:15–18; 4:19; but see Zahn (note 12), I, 412ff. = ET: II, 17ff.

[50] I Cor 4:17; II Cor 7:6, 12f.; Eph 6:21f.; Col 4:7f.; cf. Phil 2:25.

[51] Cf. Tit 3:12; Zahn (note 12), I, 420–425 = ET: II, 27–35, 66. See above, note 43. Both Titus (3:1) and I Timothy (2:1f.) urge 'submission' and 'thanksgivings' for 'all who are in authority that we may lead a quiet and peaceable life.' They give little or no indication of a current persecution. This is difficult to understand if these two letters were written after the outbreak of the Neronian persecution in the winter or spring of AD 65. Ct. II Tim 1:8; 2:3; 4:16f.

[52] Cf. II Tim 4:13, 20; cf. Richards (note 19), 158ff.

The Situation of II Timothy

Paul took his last missionary journey from the Aegean to Rome, where he was again imprisoned, wrote II Timothy and soon thereafter was beheaded on the Ostian Way.[53] He may possibly have been arrested in Ephesus (Spicq) or Troas (Fee) and taken to Rome a prisoner.[54] More likely, in accordance with second-century traditions used in the *Acts of Paul* (9–10), he returned to Rome a free man[55] to minister to a church that was suffering 'repeated calamities and reverses' (I Clem 1:1) due to the continuing persecution of Nero. He may have traveled by the Egnatian and Appian Ways (Troas—Philippi—Apollonia—Brundisium—Rome), about a four to six week journey or, again following second-century traditions, by a route from Troas via Philippi to Corinth and from there to Italy and Rome (cf. II Tim 4:20).[56]

The Date of II Timothy

According to Eusebius' 'Chronicle' (c. AD 303),[57] Paul was martyred together with Peter in the fourteenth year of Nero, i.e. AD 67–68. However, neither I Clem 5 nor the *Ascension of Isaiah* (4:2ff.; c. AD 150–200) suggests that both apostles died together, and Dionysius bishop of Corinth (c. AD 170)[58] says only that they were executed at about the same time. Probably Peter suffered death near the beginning of the Neronian pogrom in the winter or spring of AD 65 and Paul in late AD 67 or at any rate before the suicide of Nero, 9 June 68.[59] If so, he would have composed II Timothy in the late summer or in the autumn of 67.

---

[53] Cf. II Tim 1:17; 4:6f.; Acts of Paul 11; Eusebius, *HE* 2, 25, 5–8.
[54] C. Spicq, *Les épîtres pastorales*, 2 vols., Paris ⁴1969, I, 141; G. D. Fee, *1 and 2 Timothy, Titus*, Peabody MA ²1988, 244f.
[55] Cf. Rordorf (note 38), 323; Zahn (note 12), I, 437 = ET: II, 67.
[56] Cf. Rordorf (note 38), 323ff. On the travel time between Rome and Greece cf. Ellis (note 1), 276n.
[57] Cf. Jerome, *de viris* 1; 5; 12.
[58] Cf. Eusebius, *HE* 2, 25, 8.
[59] Cf. Zahn (note 12), I, 443–447 = ET: II, 61–67; Edmundson (note 12), 147–152; otherwise: Harnack (note 17), I, 240–243.

The Historical Setting

The Churches

The churches had no separate and distinct buildings in Paul's day, and they usually met in the homes of affluent members. Some of these homes could accommodate a (standing) congregation of between 100 and 200 people in the main room (*atrium*) or in a colonnaded garden (*peristyle*) further back in the house.[60] Paul's Aegean congregations had affluent members, as is evident also in the Pastorals from his comments on slaves and masters and on proper attitudes for wealthy Christians.[61] Such house-churches are probably in view in the references to 'households' (οἶκοι).[62]

Pliny (*Letters* 10, 96, 9f.; c. AD 110), governor of Bithynia-Pontus on the Black Sea northeast of the province of Asia, reported that extensive conversions to Christianity had virtually emptied pagan temples in the province 'for a long time' (? c. AD 100). The Pastorals suggest that conversions around the Aegean, including the province of Asia, had already been extensive in the mid-sixties.[63] Paul's earlier letters disclose that even in the fifties there were at least two house churches in Colossae[64] and two in Ephesus[65] and probably four at Corinth.[66] There were four or five at Rome.[67] When one house church is specified, at least one other in that city is implied. While many numbered their members in the dozens, some probably had congregations of 100 to 150, including the household servants. The size and impact of the church at Ephesus is reflected by the uproar of the silversmiths (Acts 19:23–40), who would hardly have reacted in such a disorderly manner to a minor decline in their sales.

In the mid-sixties the church at Rome suffered the martyrdom of 'a great multitude,'[68] and Paul's churches about the Aegean Sea had

---

[60] Cf. Ellis (note 33), 139–145, 144.
[61] I Tim 6:1f., 17ff.; cf. Rom 16:23; Eph 6:5–9.
[62] I Tim 3:15; II Tim 1:16; 4:19; Tit 1:11; ?I Tim 5:13.
[63] Cf. also Acts 19:10, 26; 20:31; Ellis (note 1) 389ff.; C. Hemer, *The Book of Acts in the Setting of Hellenistic History*, Tübingen 1989, 187; but see B. Witherington, *The Acts of the Apostles*, Grand Rapids 1998, 591f.
[64] Plm 2; Col 4:14. Cf. Ellis (note 33), 139–145.
[65] I Cor 16:19; cf. II Tim 1:16; 4:19.
[66] Rom 16:23; I Cor 1:11; 16:15f.; Acts 18:7f.
[67] Rom 16:5, 10f., 14f.; cf. Phil 4:22. Cf. Ellis (note 33), 139–145.
[68] I Clem 6:1; cf. Tacitus, *Annals* 15, 44.

suffered defections, as the Pastoral Epistles attest. However, in the decade of c. 55–65 the Pauline congregations of Greece, the Greek islands and the province of Asia had greatly increased both in numbers and in area, and their total adherents are probably to be counted in the thousands.

The Co-Workers

The co-workers of Paul include a number who are mentioned in Acts (Trophimus) and in his earlier letters: Apollos, Demas, Erastus, Luke, Mark, Priscilla and Aquila, Timothy, Titus, Tychicus. Others appear only in his letter to Titus (Artemas, Zenas) or in II Timothy: Claudia, Crescens, Eubulus, Linus, Onesiphorus, Pudens, ? Carpus, where they are workers in the church at Rome or participants in Paul's continuing mission outreach.[69]

The Opponents

The opponents represent the same type of opposition throughout the Pastorals[70] that is a more developed form of the false teaching that plagued Paul's and other apostolic missions virtually from the beginning. They originated as a 'judaizing' segment of the ritually strict *Hebraioi*, that is, 'the circumcision party' of the Jerusalem church,[71] that combined a demand for Gentile adherence to the Mosaic regulations and an ascetic ritualism with a zeal for visions of angels and, at least in the diaspora, with gnosticizing tendencies. The latter tendencies promoted an experience of (a distorted) divine wisdom and knowledge and depreciated matter generally and physical resurrection and redemption in particular.[72] At times their vaunted asceticism produced an arrogance primed for a subtle sexual licentiousness.[73] Paul argued that in the messianic age the Old Testament ethical laws abided but its ritual laws were passé[74] and were no

---

[69] See below, Chapter Six, 85–94.
[70] Cf. Kelly (note 34), 10f.; Dibelius (note 14), 65ff. = GT: 52ff.
[71] Cf. Acts 6:1; 11:2f. with Tit 1:10; Ellis (note 1), 314–318; idem (note 12), 80–128.
[72] Cf. I Cor 15:12 with II Tim 2:18.
[73] Cf. Gal 4:9; 5:13–21; Col 2:18, 23 with I Tim 4:3; II Tim 3:6f.; Tit 1:10, 15.
[74] Col. 2:17; cf. Gal 4:9f.; T. R. Schreiner, *The Law and its Fulfillment*, Grand Rapids 1993, 145–178, 171.

longer binding;[75] his gnosticizing-judaizing opponents argued, apparently, that the ritual laws remained in force and that the ethical, i.e. sexual commands were no longer binding.[76]

In the Pastorals the gnosticizing Judaizers were known as 'the circumcision party' (Tit 1:10) and continued their claim to be 'teachers of the law' (I Tim 1:7) although they apparently no longer stressed, as they did in Galatians (5:2ff.), the duty of circumcision. They forbade marriage, promoted food laws and claimed to impart a spiritual 'knowledge' (γνῶσις) whose source was, in the words of an oracle applied to them, demonic spirits (I Tim 4:1ff.; 6:20). They represented one stage of a continuing countermission, which appears in Ignatius (c. AD 110)[77] as a Judaism crossed with gnosticism, a kind of 'Docetic Judaism'[78] that denied not only Christ's resurrection but also his physical incarnation and death, and which later in the second century developed or merged into the full-blown Gnostic heresies. While some of the opponents originated in the mission of 'the circumcision party,' others were teachers in Pauline congregations and defectors from a Pauline theology, including former associates or co-workers.[79]

Composition: Literary Criticism

Literary questions about the Pastorals have addressed their letter-form, the role of the secretary and, perhaps most significant, their use of preformed traditions.[80]

Letter-form

Early in the twentieth century Paul's 'letters,' understood as non-literary products intended solely for the addressees, were distinguished from more formal literary 'epistles' intended for a larger circle (G. A. Deissmann). More recently, they have been the subject of attempts

---

[75] Cf. Rom 10:4; 13:8ff.; Gal 3:24f.
[76] Cf. Ellis (note 12), 36ff., 51f., 61, 80–115, 116–128, 230–236.
[77] Ignatius, *ad Magn.* 8–11; *ad Tral.* 9.
[78] Lightfoot, *Apostolic Fathers* (note 12), II, ii, 103.
[79] I Tim 1:3ff.; II Tim 1:15f.; Tit 1:10f. Cf. Ellis, 'The Circumcision Party and the Early Christian Mission,' *Prophecy* (note 12), 116–128; idem (note 1), 130ff., 202–208, 217ff., 258f., 314–318.
[80] Cf. Ellis (note 1), passim; idem (note 33), 104–107.

to identify the 'letter' as a literary genre. Deissmann's distinctions were at best oversimplified and probably mistaken, and the later attempts at classification were misleading.[81] In fact, in antiquity letters could take virtually any form, as P. L. Schmidt pointed out,[82] and according to Cicero (*To Friends* 2, 4) they were simply 'of many kinds' although he classified his own as newsletters and as the 'familiar and sportive, and the grave and serious.'

The Apostle's letters were intended to be used by others than the immediate addressees[83] and were specifically to be 'read in church.'[84] In the light of his Jewish background, in which not even Targums but only canonical Scripture could be 'read in church,'[85] they were written and received as 'the Word of God,' i.e. as inspired and normative authority for the churches.[86] They were teachings of an apostolic prophet that, unlike other prophetic teaching and writing in the congregations, were not subject to 'testing' or vetting by other prophets.[87] That is, they were teaching pieces clothed in the form of letters. Philemon addresses a specific personal question; others, like I Corinthians, give attention to immediate congregational problems or, like Romans and Ephesians, to more general theological motifs. I Timothy and Titus (and to some extent II Timothy) are virtual manuals of tradition that have genre affinities with Qumran's Manual of Discipline.[88] The Apostle utilizes the letter-form for a number of reasons, not least because by it he can combine personal communication and relationships with his primary purpose of teaching and upbuilding believers in the truth of the gospel of Christ.

---

[81] Cf. G. A. Deissmann, 'Letters and Epistles,' *Bible Studies*, Winona Lake IN 1979 (1901), 3–59 = GT: 189–252; Ellis (note 1), 49ff. But see A. J. Malherbe, 'Hellenistic Moralists and the New Testament,' *ANRW* II, 26, 1 (1992), 292f., 325.

[82] P. L. Schmidt, 'Epistolographie,' *Der Kleine Pauly*, 5 vols., ed. K. Ziegler, Stuttgart 1964–75, II, 324–377, 325.

[83] See above, 69.

[84] Col 4:16; I Thess 5:27; cf. I Cor 7:1, 25; 8:1; 12:1; 16:1, 12.

[85] BT Megillah 32a; cf. P. S. Alexander, 'Jewish Aramaic Translations of Scripture,' *Mikra* (*Compendia* II, 1), edd. M. J. Mulder *et al.*, Leiden 1988, 238f.

[86] Cf. I Thess 2:13 with II Thess 2:15; Ellis (note 10), 237–241.

[87] Cf. I Cor 9:3 (ἀνακρίνειν); 14:29 (διακρίνειν) with 14:37f. See above, 24.

[88] Cf. W. H. Brownlee, *The Meaning of the Qumran Scrolls for the Bible*, New York 1964, 150 (some similarities).

Secretaries

A secretary was a practical necessity in antiquity for all but the briefest letters since the poor quality of pen, ink and paper made writing slow and laborious and could require more than an hour to write a small page.[89] He ordinarily would record first on a waxed wood tablet in shorthand, which was used in first-century Greek and Latin writing,[90] and then would transcribe it in longhand onto papyrus. Such a helper is explicitly mentioned in Rom 16:22 and is implied where Paul, in accordance with the custom, adds a marginal note[91] or an ending[92] to a completed secretarial composition. For the Pastorals a secretary may be inferred from numerous verbal and stylistic peculiarities, and he has been plausibly suggested to be Luke.[93] The secretary's work could range from taking dictation to being a co-author, and in the Pastorals he appears to have had a greater input than in certain other Pauline epistles.[94] However, more significant for the literary form of the Pastorals are the numerous preformed traditions, largely non-Pauline, that are employed in them.

Traditions in the Pastorals

Traditions in the Pastorals have long been recognized in a few passages, e.g. the confession at I Tim 3:16 and the five 'faithful Word' (πιστὸς ὁ λόγος) sayings. In other passages they can also be identified by the use of acceptable criteria. Some preformed pericopes were composed by Paul and some by others that he recognized to be prophetically gifted to mediate divine revelation.

Criteria

Criteria to identify a cited or traditioned piece include (1) a formula that elsewhere introduces or concludes quoted material (e.g. I Tim

---

[89] Cf. Quintilian, *Oratoria*, 10, 3, 31; Roller (note 34), 13f., 6–9.
[90] Richards (note 19), 24–43.
[91] E.g. I Cor 14:34f.; Ellis (note 33), 67f.; idem (note 1), 433f.
[92] E.g. I Cor 16:21–24; Gal 6:11–18; Col 4:18; II Thess 3:17; cf. I Tim 6:20f.; II Tim 4:19–22; Tit 3:15; Plm 19–25.
[93] II Tim 4:11; cf. A. Strobel, 'Schreiben des Lukas? Zum sprachlichen Problem der Pastoralbriefe,' *NTS* 15 (1968–69), 191–210, 209f.; C. F. D. Moule, 'The Problem of the Pastoral Epistles: A Reappraisal,' *BJRL* 47 (1964–65), 434; Spicq (note 54), I, 199; Knight (note 24), 51: perhaps; but see W. Metzger, *Die letzte Reise des Apostels Paulus*, Stuttgart 1976, 10–16.
[94] Cf. Richards (note 19), 23f., 193f.

4:1), (2) the self-contained character of the passage, (3) a relatively large number of *hapax legomena* and an idiom and style that differ from the rest of the letter and from other writings by the same author and (4) a strikingly similar passage in another writing where no literary dependence is probable. One criterion alone may not be significant since, e.g. a different vocabulary or idiom may point only to a change of subject matter, to a different secretary or to a different time of writing. Also, a quotation may not be transmitted tradition (e.g. Tit 1:12), and transmitted traditions may be paraphrased and incorporated without a formula of quotation. Nevertheless, the criteria provide guidelines for measuring probabilities.

The Classification of Traditions

Preformed pieces embrace a variety of topics and literary forms.[95] Among them are doxologies,[96] a vice list,[97] congregational regulations for the conduct of wives[98] and qualifications for ministries,[99] predictive prophecies,[100] confessions that are sometimes hymnic[101] and other hymns.[102] Some of these are in the form of implicit and explicit midrash, that is, commentary on Old Testament texts.[103] One passage combines midrash and a hymnic form,[104] both of which are characteristic of early Christian prophecy.[105]

Some traditions may also be identified and classified in terms of three formulas that introduce or conclude them: 'faithful is the Word' (πιστὸς ὁ λόγος), 'knowing this that' (τοῦτο γινώσκειν/ἰδεῖν ὅτι) and 'these things' (ταῦτα). Such passages are relatively independent of their contexts and are distinguished by other criteria listed above.

---

[95] Cf. Ellis (note 1), 406–417, passim.
[96] I Tim 1:17; 6:15f.
[97] I Tim 1:9f.
[98] I Tim 2:9–3:1a.
[99] I Tim 3:1b–13.
[100] I Tim 4:1–5; II Tim 3:15.
[101] I Tim 2:5f.; 3:16; II Tim 1:9f.; Tit 3:3–7; cf. I Tim 1:15.
[102] I Tim 6:11f., 15f.; II Tim 2:11ff.; Tit 2:11–14.
[103] I Tim 1:9f.; 2:9–3:1a; 5:17f.; II Tim 2:19ff.; cf. Ellis, *Prophecy* (note 12), 188–197, 147–237: 'prophecy as exegesis.'
[104] Tit 3:3–7.
[105] Cf. D. E. Aune, 'The Odes of Solomon and Early Christian Prophecy,' *NTS* 28 (1982), 453ff.: 'the prophetic hymn;' idem, *Revelation*, 3 vols., Nashville 1998, I, xcvii f.

'Faithful is the Word'

This formula introduces[106] or concludes[107] five preformed pieces which, with the exception of I Tim 2:9–3:1a, are confessional statements of Pauline soteriological themes, whose vocabulary is generally Pauline. The formula is absent from Paul's earlier letters[108] and apparently had its origin among Jewish apocalyptic prophets or at Qumran (cf. 1Q27, *Book of Mysteries* 1:8). However, it was used in John's mission (Rev 22:6) and probably came to be used by Paul and his co-workers during his Caesarean or first Roman imprisonment. On the analogy of Ben Sira's use of 'faithful' to designate the prophecies of Samuel and Isaiah,[109] the formula governs a Word that is no mere saying but that is a prophetic Word of God to the hearers. Therefore, the teaching elder = bishop[110] is required to 'hold to the faithful Word' (Tit 1:9), and Timothy in his ministry is said to be nourished on such 'faithful Words' and is urged to mediate them to his congregations (II Tim 2:11ff., 14). Given their Pauline themes and vocabulary, most 'faithful Word' sayings were probably Paul's compositions, but I Tim 2:9–3:1a (and perhaps Tit 3:3–8) is composed by others and is a variant of a tradition used in common with the Petrine mission.[111]

'Knowing this, That'

This and similar phrases do not always have a formulaic significance,[112] but they are sometimes used elsewhere as formulas to introduce a paraphrastic biblical quotation and other cited traditions.[113] In the Pastorals they are used as formulas to introduce a vice list paraphrasing the Fifth to the Ninth Commandments (I Tim 1:9f.) and a transmitted prophecy (II Tim 3:1–5).

---

[106] I Tim 1:15; 4:9f.; II Tim 2:11ff.
[107] I Tim 2:9–3:1a; Tit 3:3–8a.
[108] But see I Cor 10:13. Cf. E. E. Ellis, *The Old Testament in Early Christianity*, Tübingen 1991, 82f.
[109] Sirach = Ecclesiasticus 46:15; 48:22.
[110] See above, note 24.
[111] Cf. I Pet 3:1–6; 1 Cor 14:34f.; Ellis (note 1), 82ff., 407–411, 428f.
[112] E.g. I Thess 1:4f.
[113] Acts 2:3. Cf. Ps 132:11; cf. Polycarp, *ad Phil* 4:1; see Rom 6:6; Eph 5:5; cf. I Cor 6:9f.

'These Things'

This formula is found at the conclusion of cited material and introduces its application to the current situation. It appears at the end of pericopes identified above as traditioned pieces.[114] It also occurs at the end of a regulation on ministry[115] that is distinct from its context[116] and of congregational and household rules,[117] which are probably also preformed traditions incorporated into the Epistles.

Conclusion

A number of other passages are probably reworked traditional material, i.e. hymnic confessions,[118] a doxology,[119] a commission + doxology[120] and other sayings.[121] Together such preformed materials make up about 43% of I Timothy, 16% of II Timothy and 46% of Titus.[122]

THEMES

The teachings of the letters are largely contained in the (reworked and) transmitted traditions and their application. They concern (1) the errors of the false teachers and the proper response to them[123] and (2) the strict qualifications for ministries in the light of the opponents' activities.[124] Not unrelated to this situation are other regulations on church order[125] and on the conduct of believers.[126] As is the case in other Pauline letters, all the teachings are given a christological basis in salvation history,[127] including Christ's identity with

---

[114] I Tim 4:6, 11; II Tim 2:14.
[115] I Tim 3:1b–13, 14; cf. Tit 1:7–9.
[116] Cf. Harnack (note 17), I, 482f.; Kelly (note 34), 231.
[117] I Tim 5:5f., 9f., 17–20; 6:1, 2; Tit 2:2–14, 15.
[118] I Tim 2:5f.; II Tim 1:9f.
[119] I Tim 1:17.
[120] I Tim 6:11–16.
[121] I Tim 6:7f., 10a; II Tim 1:7.
[122] Cf. Ellis (note 1), 417f.
[123] Cf. I Tim 1:3–20; 4:1–10; 6:3–10; Tit 1:10–2:1; 3:9ff.; II Tim 2:14–4:5.
[124] Cf. I Tim 3:1b–13; Tit 1:5–9.
[125] I Tim 2:9–3:1a; 5:3–25; Tit 2:2–14.
[126] I Tim 6:1f.; Tit 3:1–8.
[127] I Tim 3:16; Tit 2:11–14.

God,[128] preexistence,[129] human Davidic descent,[130] faithful ministry,[131] mediatorial work,[132] resurrection[133] and future coming and reign.[134]

---

[128] Tit 2:13. Cf. Ellis (note 10), 77f.; Knight (note 24), 322–326.
[129] I Tim 1:15, ἔρχεσθαι.
[130] II Tim 2:8.
[131] I Tim 6:13.
[132] I Tim 2:5–6a; II Tim 1:9f.
[133] II Tim 2:8.
[134] I Tim 6:14; II Tim 2:11f.; 4:8, 18.

CHAPTER SIX

PAUL AND HIS CO-WORKERS REVISITED*

The present chapter[1] marks a return to a theme addressed earlier, that is, an inquiry into Paul's associates.[2]

In Acts and the Pauline letters some 100 individuals, under a score of titles and activities, are associated with the Apostle at one time or another during his ministry. They are participants both in his preaching and teaching and in his writing, and they define the Apostle's work as a 'collaborative ministry' (Harrington).[3] The total number of Paul's co-workers has been placed at 95 (Redlich) or 81 (Pölzl), depending on how broadly one defines the term.[4] When the names mentioned only in Acts and those with unspecified and general relationships to Paul are eliminated, 36 co-workers under 9 designations can be identified with considerable probability.[5]

Long-Term Co-Workers

A good number of these individuals have a long-term relationship with the Apostle. Barnabas, Mark and Titus are associated with him from his Antiochian ministry (AD 46).[6] The latter two remain in relationship to his mission from time to time until the close of his life in AD 67–68,[7] as do a number who joined him during his mission to Greece: Timothy, Luke, Priscilla = Prisca and Aquila and

---

* Given at Abilene Christian University as one of the 1993 Carmichael-Walling Lectures.
[1] It is a reworking of a longer piece: E. E. Ellis, 'Paul and his Co-Workers,' *DPL* (1993), 183–189.
[2] E. E. Ellis, 'Paul and his Co-Workers,' *NTS* 17 (1970–71), 437–452 = *Prophecy and Hermeneutic in Early Christianity*, Tübingen 1978, 3–22.
[3] D. J. Harrington, 'Paul and Collaborative Ministry,' *NTR* 3 (1990), 62–71.
[4] Cf. F. X. Pölzl, *Die Mitarbeiter des Weltapostels Paulus*, Regensburg 1911; E. B. Redlich, *S. Paul and his Companions*, London 1913.
[5] See the adjoining chart.
[6] Acts 13:1–3, 5; Gal 2:1, 13.
[7] Cf. Ellis, 'Co-Workers' (note 2), 437ff. = idem, *Prophecy* (note 2), 3ff.

	ἀδελφός	ἀπόστολος	διάκονος	(συν)δοῦλος
Achaicus[1]	—	—	(I Cor 16:15ff.)	—
Andronicus[3]	—	Rom 16:7	—	—
Apollos	I Cor 16:12	I Cor 4:9	I Cor 3:5	—
Apphia[1]	(Plm 2)	—	—	—
Aquila and Prisca	—	—	—	—
Archippus	—	—	(Col 4:17)	—
Aristarchus	—	—	—	—
Barnabas	—	(Acts 14:4, 14 (I Cor 9:5f.)	—	—
Clement[1]	—	—	—	—
Demas	—	—	—	—
Epaphras	—	—	Col 1:7	Col 1:7; 4:12
Epaphroditus[(1)]	Phil. 2:25	Phil 2:25	—	—
Erastus	—	—	(Acts 19:22)	—
Euodia and Syntyche[1]	—	—	—	—
Fortunatus[1]	—	—	(I Cor 16:15ff.)	—
Junia[3]	—	Rom 16:7	—	—
Justus[1]	—	—	—	—
Luke	—	—	—	—
Mark	—	—	(II Tim 4:11)	—
Mary[3]	—	—	—	—
Onesimus	Col 4:9	—	—	—
Persis[3]	—	—	—	—
Philemon[1]	(Plm 7)	—	—	—
Phoebe[1]	(Rom 16:1)	—	(Rom 16:1)	—
Quartus[2]	Rom 16:23	—	—	—
Sosthenes[1]	I Cor 1:1	—	—	—
Silas	Acts 15:22 (I Thess 3:2)	I Thess 2:7	—	—
Stephanas[(1)]	—	—	(I Cor 16:15ff.)	—
Timothy	II Cor 1:1 Col 1:1	—	(Acts 19:22) II Cor 3:6; 6:4	—
	I Thess 3:2 Plm 1	(I Thess 2:7)	I Thess 3:2א	Phil 1:1; II Tim 2:24
Titus	II Cor 2:13 (8:16ff.)	—	—	—
Tryphaena and Tryphosa[3]	—	—	—	—
Tychicus	Eph 6:21 Col 4:7	—	Eph 6:21 Col 4:7	— Col 4:7
Urbanus[3]	—	—	—	—
Paul	—	Rom 1:1 passim	I Cor 3:5 passim	Rom 1:1 passim
Christ	Rom 8:29 Heb 2:11f.	Heb 3:1	Gal 2:17; cf. Luke 23:27 Rom 15:8	Phil 2:7
Christians generally	Rom 8:29 I Cor 3:1	—	? Heb 6:10	I Cor 7:22 Eph 6:6

[1] Mentioned in only one passage (one letter). [2] Mentioned only once, with Paul in a greeting.

PAUL AND CO-WORKERS REVISITED

κοινωνός	ὁ κοπιῶν	(συ)στρατιώτης	συναιχμάλωτος	συνεργός
—	(I Cor 16:15ff.)	—	—	(I Cor 16:15ff.)
—	—	—	Rom 16:7	—
—	—	—	—	I Cor 3:9
—	—	—	—	—
—	—	—	—	Rom 16:3ff.
—	—	Plm 2	—	—
—	—	—	Col 4:10	Plm 24 (Col
—	—	(I Cor 9:7)	—	4:10f.)
—	—	—	—	Phil 4:2f.
—	—	—	—	Plm 24 (Col
—	—	—	Plm 23	4:11, 14)
—	—	Phil 2:25	—	Phil 2:25
—	—	—	—	
—	—	—	—	(Phil 4:2f.)
—	(I Cor 16:15ff.)	—	—	(I Cor 16:15ff.)
—	—	—	Rom 16:7	—
—	—	—	—	Col 4:10f.
—	—	—	—	Plm 24 (Col 4:10, 14)
—	—	—	—	Plm 24; (Col
—	Rom 16:6	—	—	4:11)
—	Rom 16:12	—	—	—
Plm 17	—	—	—	Plm 1
—	—	—	—	—
—	—	—	—	—
—	—	—	—	(I Thess 3:2)
—	(I Cor 16:15ff.)	—	—	(I Cor 16:15ff.)
—	II Tim 2:6)	II Tim 2:3	—	Rom 16:21 (I Cor 16:10; I Thess 3:2)
II Cor 8:23	—	—	—	II Cor 8:23
—	Rom 16:12	—	—	—
—	—	—	—	—
—	—	—	—	Rom 16:9
Plm 17	(I Cor 15:10 passim)	(I Cor 9:7)	—	I Cor 3:9
cf. II Cor 1:5–7	—	—	—	—
—	—	—	—	—

[3] Mentioned only once, a recipient of Paul's greeting.

perhaps Erastus (AD 50–53).[8] Similar are certain associates who initially come into view during Paul's first Aegean ministry: Apollos, Trophimus and Tychicus (AD 53–58).[9] On the highly probable Caesarean provenance of three letters from prison—Ephesians, Colossians and Philemon (AD 58–60),[10] the name, Demas, may be added although he abandoned the mission near the end of Paul's life.[11] These ten or so long time co-workers are complemented by many others who are a part of his mission for shorter periods of time.

Of the long-term associates five appear as Paul's subordinates, serving him or being subject to his instructions. They are Erastus, Mark, Timothy, Titus, and Tychicus.[12] Others have a cooperative relationship with Paul but work in relative independence (Apollos, Priscilla = Prisca and Aquila) or join him only on specific missions (Barnabas, Silas = Silvanus, Mark).[13]

Four Frequent Designations

The designations most often given to Paul's fellow workers are in descending frequency as follows: co-worker (συνεργός), brother (ἀδελφός), minister (διάκονος), and apostle (ἀπόστολος).

Co-workers

The first are termed co-workers 'of Paul' 'in Christ' and for the Christian community.[14] They are also co-workers 'with God'[15] in God's work even though they are God's 'servants' (διάκονοι), each of whom 'will receive his own reward according to his own toil' (I Cor 3:8). Co-workers, workers (ἐργάται) and 'those who toil'

---

[8] Acts 16:1ff., 10 ('we'); 18:2; 19:22; Rom 16:3, 21, 23; II Tim 1:2; 4:10f., 19f.; Tit 1:4.
[9] Acts 19:1; 20:4; I Cor 16:12; Eph 6:21; Col 4:7; II Tim 4:12, 20; Tit 3:13.
[10] Cf. E. E. Ellis, *The Making of the New Testament Documents*, Leiden 1999, 266–275.
[11] Cf. Col 4:14; II Tim 4:10; Plm 24.
[12] Cf. Acts 19:22; Phil 2:19; Col 4:7f.; II Tim 4:10ff.; Tit 1:5; 3:12; cf. II Cor 12:18.
[13] Cf. Acts 13:1–5; 15:40f.; I Thess 1:1; Col 4:10; II Tim 4:11; Plm 24.
[14] Rom 16:3, 9, 21; II Cor 8:23; Phil 2:25.
[15] I Cor 3:9; I Thess 3:2 D. So, A. Harnack, 'ΚΟΠΟΣ,' *ZNTW* 27 (1928), 1–10, 7; but see V. P. Furnish, '"Fellow Workers in God's Service,"' *JBL* 80 (1961), 369: 'for God.'

(οἱ κοπιῶντες) usually are virtually equivalent idioms for a specific group or class and are not used of believers generally. The terms are applied to itinerant or local personnel and are connected with the right to pay or support, as Christ ordained,[16] including 'those who toil in word and teaching.'[17] They are entitled to respect and obedience by the congregation[18] and are, at least at times, an appointed group.[19] On the other hand, if they become idlers, they should not receive support, for 'if anyone does not want to work, neither let him eat,' that is, at the community's expense.[20] However, their ministry was a function of their spiritual gifts, and their support and leadership role was apparently unofficial and had no contractual character.

The Brothers

The term 'brothers,' like 'slaves' (δοῦλοι), can refer either to Christians generally or to Christian workers. 'Brothers' often has the latter connotation when it is used with the article. This becomes apparent when 'the brothers' are distinguished from 'the church' (I Cor 16:19f.) or from believers generally.[21] It also probably has this sense in Paul's letter from Antioch to the Galatians: 'Paul ... and all the brothers with me' (1:1f.); co-senders elsewhere are always fellow workers.[22] 'The brothers' may refer to workers in local congregations[23] or to those whose ministry takes on a traveling missionary character.[24]

Ministers

The term, διάκονος, occurs in close connection with the above designations[25] but has a somewhat more specialized meaning. It is probably best rendered 'minister' since it refers to workers with special activities in preaching and teaching, both among Paul and his

---

[16] I Cor 9:14; I Tim 5:18b; cf. Lk 10:7b.
[17] I Tim 5:17; II Tim 2:6.
[18] Cf. I Cor 16:16, 18; I Thess 5:12f.
[19] Cf. Harnack (note 15), 1–10.
[20] II Thess 3:10b. Cf. Ellis, *Prophecy* (note 2), 7, 10f., 20f.
[21] Eph 6:23f.; Phil 4:21f.; Col 4:15; cf. Ellis, *Prophecy* (note 2), 13–17.
[22] Cf. I Cor 1:1; II Cor 1:1; Phil 1:1; Col 1:1; I Thess 1:1; Acts 13:1–3. On the date and provenance of Galatians cf. Ellis (note 10), 255–260; R. N. Longenecker, *Galatians*, Dallas 1990, lxxxviii, and the literature cited.
[23] Phil 1:14; cf. Col 1:2 with 4:15f.; cf. Acts 11:1, 29; 12:17.
[24] II Cor 2:13; 8:18, 22f.; cf. Acts 10:23; 11:12.
[25] I Cor 3:5, 9; II Cor 6:1, 4.

co-workers[26] and among his opponents.[27] Like 'the brothers,' the διάκονοι serve in local congregations[28] as well as on missionary circuits and, as teachers, they are mentioned as deserving of pay.[29]

Apostles of Jesus Christ

As ministers are a special kind of worker, so apostles (ἀπόστολοι) of Jesus Christ are a special kind of minister. In part apostles fulfil the same type of work and can be called ministers.[30] However, in other respects they are a more exclusive category. They are those who have 'seen Jesus our Lord,'[31] that is, those whom the risen Jesus commissioned since his appearances seem always to have been coupled with a commission. In this category of apostles were a large number, including '500 brothers' (I Cor 15:6). This understanding of 'apostles of Christ' is common to the New Testament, also to Luke-Acts.[32] Although the term, apostles, can be used in the New Testament more narrowly to refer to the Twelve,[33] the limitation of apostles of Jesus Christ to the Twelve plus Paul is a creation of the later church.

Apostles of Jesus Christ among Paul's co-workers include Apollos, Barnabas and Silas. Apollos is probably included with Paul and Peter in Paul's phrase 'us apostles'[34] and placed on a par with them. Accordingly, when he is described by Acts[35] as 'instructed in the way of the Lord'[36] and 'knowing only the baptism of John [the Baptist],' it is likely that he is identified as an apostle of the earthly Jesus, who continued his apostleship separate from and without knowledge of Pentecost and of the Jerusalem events (Acts 1–6). He may well have won the converts in Acts 19:1–7. If his fervour 'in spirit' refers

---

[26] I Cor 3:5; II Cor 3:6; 6:4; Eph 3:7f.; Col 1:7, 23; I Tim 4:6; cf. Ellis, *Prophecy* (note 2), 7–13, 102f.
[27] II Cor 11:15, 23. Cf. D. Georgi, *The Opponents of Paul in Second Corinthians*, Philadelphia 1986, 27–32 = GT: 31–38.
[28] Rom 16:1; Phil 1:1; I Tim 3:8.
[29] Gal 6:6. Cf. Longenecker (note 22), 278f.
[30] Cf. I Cor 4:9 with 3:5; Eph 3:5, 7.
[31] I Cor 9:1; cf. 15:5–8.
[32] Cf. E. E. Ellis, *The Gospel of Luke. Revised Edition*, Grand Rapids ⁷1996 (1974), 132–135.
[33] E.g. Acts 4:35ff.; cf. 6:2 with 6:6; 9:27.
[34] I Cor 4:9; cf. 3:22–4:1.
[35] Acts 18:24f.; cf. 19:1–7.
[36] Cf. Lk 3:4; 20:21.

to the Holy Spirit, it could be the same Holy Spirit power that was active in the pre-resurrection apostolic missions.[37] This understanding may explain why in Luke's account Apollos, like the Twelve, remains without a 'Christian' baptism, and it quite likely underlies his later listing as one of the Seventy.[38] His identification as an Alexandrian Jew refers to his birthplace and to his special political and civil rights[39] and probably has no more to do with his Christian background than Tarsus had to do with Paul's.[40] Teaching and preaching in the Aegean area, Apollos remained in occasional association with Paul from the early fifties to the mid-sixties (Tit 3:13).

Barnabas, a native of Cyprus, was a member of the Jerusalem church in its earliest days (Acts 4:36). He introduced the newly converted Paul to the Twelve, invited his participation in the Hellenist mission at Antioch, Syria, and with Paul was numbered among the resident 'prophets and teachers' there.[41] Barnabas and Paul are equated with 'the rest of the apostles' at I Cor 9:5f.; and they are called 'apostles' at Acts 14:4, 14, texts that probably refer to those commissioned by Christ and not to 'apostles of the churches'[42] = commissioned missionaries, a usage that is foreign to Luke-Acts. After working with Paul during the famine-visit to Jerusalem (c. AD 46) and on the Cyprus-Galatian mission, together with his cousin Mark (AD 46–49),[43] and at the council of Jerusalem (AD 49–50),[44] Barnabas returned with Mark to the evangelization of Cyprus.[45] In the fifties he appears to have ministered around the Aegean and in Asia Minor, at times in Pauline congregations, since he is known to Paul's churches at Corinth (AD 56) and at Colossae (AD 58–60).[46] Like Apollos, he is counted by later tradition as one of the Seventy apostles.[47]

---

[37] Cf. Lk 10:9, 17–20; Ellis (note 32), 154–157; idem, *Christ and the Future in New Testament History*, Leiden 2000, 252.
[38] Ps-Hippolytus, *On the Seventy Apostles* 50; cf. *ANF* V (1890), 256.
[39] Cf. Philo, *in Flaccum* 53; *Legatio* 371; A. Kasher, *The Jews in Hellenistic and Roman Egypt*, Tübingen 1985, 261.
[40] Acts 18:24; 22:3.
[41] Acts 9:27; 11:25f.; 13:1.
[42] II Cor 8:23.
[43] Cf. Acts 11:29f.; 13–14; Gal 2:1, 9. Cf. Ellis (note 10), 255–260.
[44] Acts 15:2, 12, 22; cf. Gal 2:13.
[45] Acts 15:39.
[46] Cf. I Cor 9:6; Col 4:10.
[47] Ps-Hippolytus, *On the Seventy Apostles* 24; cf. Clement, *Stromata* = *Miscellanies* 2, 20; Eusebius, *HE* 1, 12, 1; 2, 1, 4.

Silas, a prophet in the Jerusalem church who co-authored and distributed the decree of the Council,[48] joined Paul in his mission to Greece (AD 50–53).[49] According to I Thess 1:1 and II Thess 1:1 he was a co-sender and probably the co-author of these letters.[50] Like Mark,[51] Silas was later a co-worker in the Petrine mission where he also had a writing role as the secretary in composing I Peter (5:12). Both he and Paul are termed Roman citizens (Acts 16:37f.), and in I Thess 2:6 they are jointly referred to as 'apostles of Christ' (Χριστοῦ ἀπόστολοι), an idiom that identifies both as men who were personally commissioned by Christ. With this understanding Silas, like Apollos,[52] is counted as one of the Seventy apostles in church tradition which, in a clear misconception, also makes him a different person from Silvanus. That he, Apollos and Barnabas are called prophets or teachers or ministers does not rule out their apostolic status since Paul can also identify himself with these other ministries.[53]

False 'Apostles'

The larger circle of 'apostles of Christ' included not a few unnamed opponents of Paul who, like Judas, were commissioned by Jesus but turned out to be 'ministers of Satan' (II Cor 11:15). They formed an opposing judaizing-gnosticizing mission that preached 'a different gospel' and were thus 'false apostles.'[54] Or did they only make a false claim to have been commissioned by Jesus? Favoring the former view are Paul's earlier (caustic) recognition of their apostolic status and lettered credentials and the analogy with Satan.[55] In the Judaism of the period Satan was understood to have been originally an angel of God = angel of light[56] who, after his fall,

---

[48] Acts 15:22f.: γράψαντες διὰ χειρὸς αὐτῶν. Cf. T. Zahn, *Die Apostelgeschichte*, 2 vols., Leipzig 1927, I, 534f.; E. G. Selwyn, *The First Epistle of St. Peter*, Grand Rapids 1981 (1946), 12.
[49] Acts 15:40–18:22.
[50] See below, 96.
[51] Cf. Col 4:10; Plm 24; I Pet 5:13; Ellis (note 10), 265, 357–376, 402f.
[52] See above, note 47.
[53] I Cor 3:5; 14:37; 4:17; I Tim 2:7; Col 1:23; cf. Ellis, *Prophecy* (note 2), 132n, 138–142.
[54] II Cor 11:4, 13; cf. Gal 1:6; I Tim 4:1; Ellis (note 10), 314–318.
[55] II Cor 3:2; 11:5, 13ff. Cf. Ellis, *Prophecy* (note 2), 105f.
[56] Cf. Lk 10:18; Jude 8f.; Apcl. Moses 17:1; Job 1:6; Zech 3:1.

was with his angels the invisible power behind earthly rulers[57] and false teachers[58] and who could disguise himself in his former righteousness.[59]

Apostles of the Churches

'Apostles of the churches,' that is, commissioned missionaries are also present among Paul's associates. They involve the unnamed brothers travelling with Titus, including one whose service 'in the gospel' was of high renown;[60] Epaphroditus, the 'apostle' (ἀπόστολος) of the Philippian church to Paul;[61] and Andronicus and Junia, probably a married couple who were kinsmen of Paul and 'outstanding among the apostles' (ἐπίσημοι ἐν τοῖς ἀποστόλοις).[62] Because of this phrase they have sometimes been identified as 'apostles of Christ,' but that meaning is precluded by the descriptions: (1) This otherwise unknown couple could hardly be described, in comparison with Peter, James or even Paul himself, as 'outstanding among the apostles of Christ.' (2) Also, if they were 'apostles of Christ,' the phrase, 'who were in Christ before me,' would be a meaningless redundancy.[63] They are, in fact, identified as commissioned missionaries.

OTHER CATEGORIES OF CO-WORKERS

Paul's Relatives

Near the beginning of his ministry Paul fled from enemies in Jerusalem to Tarsus in Cilicia, the city of his birth, and ministered in that area for about ten years (AD 36–45).[64] That he had relatives there who sheltered him on his arrival is a reasonable surmise. He was later aided by his sister's son after his arrest in Jerusalem during his Collection Visit (AD 58).[65]

---

[57] Cf. I Cor 2:8; cf. Dan 10:13; Ezek 28:12–15; 1QM 1:1; perhaps, Rom 13:1 (ἐξουσίαι); Isa 14:12. Cf. D. Moo, *Romans*, Grand Rapids 1996, 794–798.
[58] CD 12:2f.
[59] II Cor 11:14f.; cf. Mt 12:24.
[60] II Cor 8:16–24, 23.
[61] Phil 2:25.
[62] Rom 16:7.
[63] Cf. I Cor 15:8.
[64] Gal 1:21; Acts 9:30; 11:25; 15:23; 21:39; 22:3.
[65] Acts 23:16.

In Rom 16:7, 11, 21 he mentions six kinsmen, five of whom played a more explicit role in his ministry. The couple mentioned above, Andronicus and Junia, were very early converts, having been won to Christ before the Apostle. Accordingly, they were very likely Jerusalem relatives who were missionaries from that church to Rome. Like Paul, they had suffered imprisonment for the sake of the gospel, although not necessarily at the same time and place (16:7). Jason (16:21) is probably none other than the Jason of Thessalonica who was Paul's host and apparently the patron of a house-church there.[66] Equally probable, Sosipater (16:21) is the fuller name of Sopater, who represented the church of Beroea on the Collection Visit to Jerusalem.[67]

That Lucius of Rom 16:21 is to be identified with Luke, the beloved physician and author of Luke-Acts,[68] is probable although it poses the problem of Paul or his secretary using one form of his name here and another at Col 4:14; Plm 24 and II Tim 4:11. Favoring the identification are the facts that Luke could be an abbreviated form of Lucius and that Acts places Luke with Paul at about this time.[69]

In mentioning these kinsmen co-workers Paul reveals something of the strategy of his mission. He utilized contacts with his relatives in charting the evangelization of Thessalonica and Beroea and, upon their conversion, accepted them as fellow workers in the mission and used their homes as house-churches for his congregations. If Luke was also a kinsman, it would not only put to rest the traditional but mistaken view that Luke was a Gentile[70] but would also explain Paul's mission route to Troas. He travelled there with the intention of adding a confidant to his team who was familiar with the area

---

[66] Acts 17:5–9.
[67] Acts 17:10ff.; 20:4. So, F. Godet, *Epistle to the Romans*, New York 1883, 500 = FT: 614. The out of the way town of Beroea, some 20 miles south of the Via Egnatia, would not, *pace* Bruce and Hemer, be a destination appropriate either to Paul's mission strategy or to his personal circumstances. The presence of Paul's kinsman, Sosipater, however, would readily explain Paul's interest in establishing a church there. Cf. F. F. Bruce, *The Acts of the Apostles*, Leicester UK ³1990, 373; C. Hemer, *The Book of Acts in the Setting of Hellenistic History*, Tübingen 1989, 115f.
[68] So, Origen. Cf. J. D. G. Dunn, *Romans*, Dallas 1988, 909; A. Deissmann, *Light from the Ancient East*, New York ⁴1927, 437f.
[69] Cf. Acts 20:5, 'we.' Cf. W. Schmithals, *Der Römerbrief*, Gütersloh 1988, 564: 'perhaps.'
[70] Cf. Ellis (note 32), 52f.; idem, *Prophecy* (note 2), 116–124, 123n.

and was apparently already ministering in Troas (Acts 16:10, 'we'). In time he also utilized Luke's gifts to provide a Gospel of the words and works of Jesus for reading in his mission congregations.⁷¹

Women Co-workers

A remarkable number of women are mentioned as Paul's associates, both in Acts and in his letters.⁷² Some are called minister (διάκονος) or co-workers (συνεργοί) or missionaries (ἀπόστολοι), and several were engaged in ministries of teaching and preaching.⁷³ Those who 'toiled' and 'labored' were involved in unspecified church work,⁷⁴ and others were members of wealthy families who supported Paul as benefactors and who dedicated their homes for use as house-churches.⁷⁵

The Circumcision Party

Ritually strict 'Hebraists' = 'the circumcision party' and ritually lax 'Hellenists' were in tension within the church virtually from its beginning.⁷⁶ The Hebraists soon divided into two factions, the 'Judaizers' who insisted that Gentile converts be circumcized and keep the Mosaic regulations⁷⁷ and the 'orthodox' Hebraists like James, who were carefully observant of Jewish traditions themselves but who accepted Hellenist and Gentile believers who were not.⁷⁸

Paul firmly opposed the Judaizers,⁷⁹ but he worked in friendly and appreciative cooperation with the 'orthodox' Hebraists and took collections to their (Jacobean) mission based on Jerusalem.⁸⁰ When Hebraist ministers like Silas, a prophet of the Jerusalem church, could

---

⁷¹ Cf. Lk 1:1–4; Ellis (note 10), 251–254, 402–405.
⁷² See the chart above, p. 85ab. Cf. E. S. Fiorenza, 'Missionaries, Apostles, Co-workers,' *WW* 6 (1986), 420–433; K. A. Gerberding, 'Women Who Toil in Ministry, Even as Paul,' *CurTM* 18 (1991), 285–291; P. Trebilco, 'Women as Co-workers and Leaders in Paul's Letters,' *JCBRF* 122 (1990), 27–36 (cited in *NTAb* 35 [1991], 180). For limitations at I Cor 14:34f.; I Tim 2:9–3:13 cf. Ellis (note 86), 53–86.
⁷³ Cf. Rom 16:1, 3, 7; Phil 4:2f.; cf. Acts 18:26.
⁷⁴ Cf. Rom 16:6, 12.
⁷⁵ See Rom 16:15; Col 4:15; Plm 1f.; cf. Rom 16:13, 15f.; Acts 16:14f.
⁷⁶ See Acts 6:1; 11:2f.; 15:1f., 5. Cf. Ellis, *Prophecy* (note 2), 80–128; idem (note 10), 130, 202–208, 217ff., 258f., 314–318.
⁷⁷ See Gal 2:4f., 12ff.; Acts 15:1, 5.
⁷⁸ Gal 2:9f.; Acts 15:19ff.; 21:17; cf. Ellis, *Prophecy* (note 2), 116–128.
⁷⁹ Cf. II Cor 11:22; Tit 1:10; Ellis (note 10), 314–318.
⁸⁰ Cf. Gal 2:10, μνημονεύωμεν ('keep on remembering'); Rom 15:25ff.; I Cor 16:3; II Cor 8–9; Acts 11:29f.; 24:17.

accommodate to a Gentile mission, Paul incorporated them into his ministry-team,[81] and at Caesarea he had among his co-workers two adherents of the circumcision party, Mark and Justus (Col 4:10f.). In this way the Apostle sought to maintain the unity of the church within a diversity of praxis.[82]

THE CLASSIFICATION OF CO-WORKERS' ACTIVITIES

Co-workers are almost always present with Paul, and they participated in his mission in a variety of ways. In his travelling they occasionally conducted him[83] and, more importantly, joined in the task.[84] Some accompanied him on the Collection Visit to Jerusalem as representatives of the various churches.[85]

Affluent believers in various cities, including a number of women (see above), became hosts to Paul, and some opened their homes for the services of a local congregation.[86] Most important were those gifted co-workers who were Paul's associates in preaching and teaching and those who were secretaries, or recipients of or contributors to his letters.

Associates in Preaching and Teaching

In a manner not entirely clear to us the Apostle trained co-workers who were gifted in preaching and teaching[87] not only to learn the basic Christian proclamation and the christological interpretation of Scripture but also to enable them to transmit his and the general apostolic message to new converts. That Paul adhered to an agreed apostolic catechesis is evident in Rom 6:17, 16:17; and when he founded a church, he instructed believers also in his own distinctive Christian doctrines. He admonished his churches to continue in the traditions that he delivered to them and praised them for doing so.[88]

---

[81] Acts 15:40.
[82] Cf. Rom 14; Gal 6:15.
[83] Acts 9:30; 21:16; 27:1, 'we;' 28:15.
[84] Gal 2:1; Acts 11:30; 15:2; 19:29.
[85] II Cor 8:19; Acts 20:4ff.; cf. I Cor 16:3f.
[86] Rom 16:3ff.; I Cor 16:19; Plm 2; Acts 17:5ff.; 18:2f., 7; cf. E. E. Ellis, *Pauline Theology: Ministry and Society*, Grand Rapids 1989, 139–145; Longenecker (note 22), 278f.
[87] Cf. Rom 12:6ff.; I Cor 12:28; Gal 6:6; Eph 4:11.
[88] I Cor 11:2; Col 2:8; II Thess 2:15; 3:6.

To mediate his teachings Paul utilized, probably from the beginning, a number of co-workers, gifted local converts as well as those who accompanied him and who were sent out on certain occasions to establish or to give instruction to his churches.

Stephanus and other *local co-workers* at Corinth had a ministry (διακονία) that probably went beyond practical services to include a ministry of the Word.[89] They and 'the brothers' addressed in II Thess 2:13 B were termed the 'firstfruits' (ἀπαρχή), a concept that referred (also) to the consecrated first-born sons of Israel who were set apart for service to God.[90] (In Israel the tribe of Levi served as substitutes for the first-born of the other tribes, Num 3:11–13). Such local workers, preachers and teachers, most of them trained by Paul himself, are mentioned in a number of his letters.[91] They were at work also in the church at Colossae, which apparently was founded by Paul's 'fellow slave,' Epaphras.[92]

Several co-workers, in particular Timothy, Titus and Tychicus, were *itinerant co-workers*. They accompanied Paul and were on occasion sent to teach his churches in his absence. Timothy had been well instructed by the Apostle and therefore could be dispatched to Thessalonica to 'strengthen and exhort you regarding your faith' and later to Corinth to 'remind you of my ways in Christ just as I teach [them] everywhere in every church.'[93] Sometime later Titus and others were delegated to Corinth on a more difficult mission in the confidence that Titus 'walks in the same Spirit, in the same steps' as Paul himself.[94] Finally, Titus went on a mission to Dalmatia.[95]

Tychicus was sent from Caesarea as a letter-bearer to the Ephesians and others and to the Colossians, not only to add a personal dimension to the correspondence but probably also to explain Paul's teachings as the occasion might require.[96] With similar authority he (or Artemas) was appointed to replace Titus in supervising churches on Crete and to serve as Paul's messenger or perhaps surrogate at Ephesus.[97]

---

[89] I Cor 16:15f.; cf. II Cor 5:18f.
[90] Cf. Exod 22:29 (28); Ellis, *Prophecy* (note 2), 8, 19f.
[91] Gal 6:6; Phil 4:2; cf. 1:1; I Thess 5:12f.; II Thess 3:6–11.
[92] Col 1:7f.; 2:1; 3:16; 4:12, 16.
[93] I Thess 3:2, 6; I Cor 4:17. Later, he served Paul in Ephesus (I Tim 1:3).
[94] II Cor 12:18; cf. 8:16, 23.
[95] II Tim 4:10; cf. Tit 1:5; 3:12.
[96] Cf. Eph 6:21f.; Col 4:7ff.; Ellis (note 10), 266–275.
[97] Cf. Tit 3:12; II Tim 4:12. See above, 71ff.

CHAPTER SIX

As his mission expanded, many co-workers both furthered his evangelistic and teaching ministries and also assisted in his writing.

Associates in Writing

Co-senders—Sosthenes, Timothy, the brothers, Silas—are mentioned in eight of Paul's thirteen epistles, Timothy in six of them. In what ways they contributed is not disclosed, but the mention of them in the greetings is hardly ornamental.[98]

A secretary or *secretaries* are also in evidence in virtually all of the epistles although he is named as such only at Rom 16:22: Tertius. In all likelihood he was selected from among the believers, perhaps from the household of an affluent convert, and was thus a co-worker. The secretary's role in ancient letter-writing could vary from taking dictation to being a co-author. For the Pauline letters it would have varied in accordance with his spiritual gifts, the Apostle's confidence in him and Paul's own situation, e.g. captive or free, traveling or resident in a city. The secretary appears to have had a considerable influence in the composition of the Pastoral Epistles[99] and of a number of other letters.[100]

Probably the secretary in I–II Thessalonians is a co-author and is to be identified with Silas = Silvanus, who also co-authored the Jerusalem decree.[101] But the view that the secretary who wrote Colossians, whether Timothy or another, was also the co-author[102] is more doubtful.

Particular individuals were of necessity the *recipients of Paul's letters*, even those that were addressed and intended for the church as a whole. For churches founded by the Pauline mission, they were doubtless persons whom the Apostle trusted to read the letter to the congregation(s). In the case of Colossians and II Thessalonians the co-workers, that is, 'the brothers' themselves appear to have been the primary recipients of the letters.[103]

---

[98] Cf. S. Byrskog, 'Co-Senders, Co-Authors and Paul's Use of the First Person Plural,' *ZNTW* 87 (1996), 230–250; H. Conzelmann, 'Paulus und die Weisheit,' *NTS* 12 (1965–66), 234f.

[99] See above, 79. Cf. Ellis (note 10), 326f.

[100] Cf. E. R. Richards, *The Secretary in the Letters of Paul*, Tübingen 1991, 128–198.

[101] Acts 15:22f.; see above, note 48; cf. Selwyn (note 48), 9–17; Ellis (note 10), 64n, 115, 134n, 326.

[102] So, W. H. Ollrog, *Paulus und seine Mitarbeiter*, Neukirchen 1979, 241f. Cf. Col 1:1.

[103] Col 1:2; 4:16; II Thess 2:1f.; 3:1–15; Ellis, *Prophecy* (note 2), 17–22.

Although it is difficult to confirm specifically, *a number of the preformed pieces*—confessions, hymns, expositions—that were used by Paul in his letters were very probably created by one or more of the Apostle's co-worker prophets and teachers.[104]

Given the numerous and varied contributions of Paul's fellow ministers to his mission, it is clear that they were an essential factor in its accomplishments and that even Paul's letters were not an individual enterprise. These missioners indeed deserve the considered attention of students of Paul. For it does not detract from his greatness to bring into greater prominence those with whom he served, those he was glad to praise and pleased to call his co-workers.

---

[104] Cf. Ellis (note 10), 327f.

CHAPTER SEVEN

THE INTERPRETATION OF THE BIBLE WITHIN THE BIBLE ITSELF

The Character of New Testament Usage

Old Testament phraseology in the New Testament occurs occasionally as a part of the writer's own patterns of expression that have been influenced by the Scriptures.[1] Most often, however, it appears in the form of preformed traditions, i.e. Old Testament citations or intentional allusions.[2] Professor Lars Hartman[3] suggests three reasons for an author's citation of another: to obtain the support of an authority (Mt 4:14), to call forth a cluster of associations (Mk 12:1f.), and to achieve a literary or stylistic effect (Tit 1:12). He rightly observes that an allusion to the Old Testament sometimes can be discerned only after the total context of a passage has been taken into account.

As might be expected in Greek writings, citations from the Old Testament are frequently in agreement with the Septuagint (= Seventy = LXX), the Greek version commonly used in the first century. But they are not always so, and at times they reflect other Greek versions, Aramaic paraphrases (targums) or independent translations of the Hebrew text.[4] Apart from the use of a different text-form, they may diverge from the LXX because of a lapse of memory. However, this explanation is less probable than has been supposed in the past.[5] More frequently, as will be detailed below, citations diverge from

---

[1] E.g. I Thess 2:4; 4:5. Cf. Jer 11:20; 10:25; Ps 79:6. Cf. F. Johnson, *The Quotations of the New Testament from the Old*, London 1896, passim.
[2] For a somewhat different nuance cf. R. B. Hays, *Echoes of Scripture in the Letters of Paul*, New Haven CT 1989, 21–29, passim.
[3] L. Hartman, 'Scriptural Exegesis in the Gospel of Matthew and the Problem of Communication,' *L'Evangile selon Matthieu*, ed. M. Didier, Gembloux 1972, 134.
[4] For a columnar comparison cf. H. Hübner, *Vetus Testamentum in Novo*, 3 vols., Göttingen 1997–; E. E. Ellis, *Paul's Use of the Old Testament*, Grand Rapids ⁵1991 (¹1957), 150–187; D. M. Turpie, *The Old Testament in the New*, London 1868.
[5] Cf. Ellis (note 4), 10–16, 150ff.; R. N. Longenecker, *Biblical Exegesis in the Apostolic Period*, Grand Rapids ²1999, passim.

the LXX because of deliberate alteration, that is, by a free translation and elaboration or by the use of a different textual tradition, to serve the purpose of the New Testament writer. The textual variations in the quotation, then, become an important clue to discover not only the writer's interpretation of the individual biblical passage but also his perspective on the Old Testament as a whole.

Introductory Formulas

Formulas of quotation, which generally employ verbs of 'saying' or 'writing,' correspond to those found in other Jewish works, such as the Old Testament, the Qumran scrolls, Philo and the rabbis.[6] They locate the citation with reference to the book or the author or less frequently to the biblical episode, such as 'in Elijah' or 'at the bush.'[7] At times they specify a particular prophet (Acts 28:25), a specification that on occasion may be important for the New Testament teaching.[8] When one book is named and another cited, the formula may represent an incidental discrepancy that is no part of the teaching or, more likely, the cited text may be viewed as an interpretation (Mt 27:9) or elaboration (Mk 1:2) of a passage in the book named.

Introductory formulas often underscore the divine authority of the Old Testament, not in the abstract but within the proper interpretation and application of its teaching.[9] Thus, the formula 'Scripture (γραφή) says' can introduce an eschatological, i.e. 'Christianized' summation or elaboration of the Old Testament,[10] and γραφή can be contrasted to traditional interpretations (Mt 22:29). That is, it implies that the revelational, 'Word of God' character of Scripture is present within the current interpretation. In the words of Renée Bloch,[11] Scripture 'always involves a living Word addressed personally to the people of God and to each of its members. . . .' B. B. Warfield puts it similarly:

---

[6] E.g. I Kg 2:27; II Chron 35:12; 1QS 5:15; 8:14; Philo, *de migr.* 118; M Aboth 3:7; Ellis (note 4), 48f.
[7] Rom 11:2; Mk 12:26.
[8] E.g. Mk 12:36; cf. R. T. France, *Jesus and the Old Testament*, London 1971, 101f.
[9] Cf. E. E. Ellis, 'The Role of the Prophet in the Quest for Truth,' *Christ and the Future in New Testament History*, Leiden 2000, 255–278, 272f.
[10] Jn 7:38; Gal 4:30. On the rationale for such freedom cf. Ellis (note 9), 239ff.
[11] R. Bloch, 'Midrash,' *Approaches to Ancient Judaism I*, ed. W. S. Green, Missoula MT 1978, 29–50, 33 = FT: *DBS* 5 (1957), 1263–1281, 1266.

Scripture is thought of as the living voice of God speaking in all its parts directly to the reader.[12]

The formula 'it is written' can also refer to the intended connotation of a specific and right interpretation of Scripture (Rom 9:33; 11:26) even though the connotation may be wrongly applied (Mt 4:6).

Sometimes an explicit distinction between reading Scripture and knowing or hearing Scripture may be drawn. It is present in the story of the Ethiopian eunuch (Acts 8:30) and, implicitly, in Jesus' synagogue exposition at Nazareth (Lk 4:16f., 21). It may be presupposed, as it is in rabbinical writings,[13] in the formula 'have you not (οὐχ) read?' That is, 'you have read but have not understood.' This formula is found in the New Testament only on the lips of Jesus and usually within a scriptural debate or exposition.[14]

A few formulas are associated with specific circles within the Christian community.[15] The nine λέγει κύριος ('says the Lord') quotations probably reflect the activity of Christian prophets. The ἵνα πληρωθῇ ('that it might be fulfilled') quotations, found especially in the Gospels of Matthew and John, may have a similar origin. Both kinds of quotations contain creatively altered text-forms that facilitate an eschatological reapplication of the scriptural passages, similar to the *pesher* midrash found in the Qumran scrolls,[16] to the experiences and understanding of the early church. This is a kind of activity recognized in first century Judaism to be appropriate to prophets as well as to teachers.[17]

Somewhat comparable are the πιστὸς ὁ λόγος ('faithful is the word') passages in the Pastoral letters.[18] They appear to be instructions of Christian prophets[19] and/or inspired teachers, used by Paul in the composition of the letters. Although they do not contain Old Testament quotations, some of these 'faithful sayings' may refer to the exposition

---

[12] B. B. Warfield, *The Inspiration and Authority of the Bible*, Philadelphia 1948, 148.
[13] Cf. D. Daube, *The New Testament and Rabbinic Judaism*, Peabody MA ²1994, 433–436.
[14] E.g. Mt 12:3, 5; 19:4; cf. J. W. Doeve, *Jewish Hermeneutics in the Synoptic Gospels and Acts*, Assen 1954, 105ff.
[15] Cf. E. E. Ellis, *The Old Testament in Early Christianity*, Tübingen 1991, 79–82.
[16] Cf. Ellis (note 4), 139–147; idem, in *NTS* 2 (1955–56), 127–133.
[17] Cf. E. E. Ellis, *Prophecy and Hermeneutic in Early Christianity*, Tübingen 1978, 55–60, 130–132, 182–187.
[18] E.g. I Tim 1:15; 2:9–3:1a; 4:9; see above, 81.
[19] Cf. I Tim 4:1, 6: τοῖς λόγοις τῆς πίστεως.

of the Old Testament.[20] They appear to arise out of a prophetic circle engaged in a ministry of teaching.

Forms and Techniques in Quotation

1. *Combined quotations* of two or more texts appear frequently in a variety of forms: a chain of passages (Rom 15:9–12), a commentary pattern (John 12:38–41; Rom 9–11) and composite or merged citations (Rom 3:10–18; II Cor 6:16–18). With the exception of the last type these patterns were commonly employed in Judaism and in classical writings.[21] They serve to develop a theme and perhaps exemplify the principle in Dt 19:15 that two witnesses establish a matter. Sometimes (e.g. Rom 10:18–21), in the fashion of the rabbis, they bring together citations from the Law, the Prophets and the Writings. Such combinations usually were formed in conjunction with catchwords important for the theme.[22]

2. *Testimonia*. Citations 'testifying' to the messiahship of Jesus were of special interest to the early church. Sometimes they appear as combined quotations (Heb 1), combinations that possibly lie behind other New Testament citations.[23] Such 'testimonies' were primarily thematic combinations for instructional and apologetic purposes and, as the testimonia at Qumran indicate (4QTest), some may have circulated in written form during the apostolic period. However, the hypothesis that they were collected in a precanonical 'testimony book,' used by the church in anti-Jewish apologetic, is less likely.

The 'testimonies' apparently presuppose a worked-out christological understanding of the particular passages and are not simply proof texts randomly selected. The earliest Christians, like twenty-first century Jews, could not, as we do, simply infer from traditional usage the 'Christian' interpretation of a biblical word or passage. Proof texts standing alone, therefore, would have appeared to them quite arbitrary if not meaningless.

According to a thesis of C. H. Dodd[24] the 'testimony' quotations were selected from and served as pointers to larger Old Testament

---

[20] E.g. I Tim 2:9–3:1a; Tit 1:9, 14; 3:3–8; cf. Ellis (note 15), 82f.
[21] Cf. Johnson (note 1), 92–102. For early Judaism cf. C. D. Stanley, *Paul and the Language of Scripture*, Cambridge 1992, 292–337.
[22] E.g. λίθος, ἐκλεκτός in I Pet 2:6–9.
[23] Cf. Ellis (note 15), 70ff., 100f. Otherwise: K. Stendahl, *The School of St. Matthew*, Lund ²1969, 207–217.
[24] C. H. Dodd, *According to the Scriptures*, London 1952, 78–79, 107–108.

contexts that previously and as a whole had been christologically interpreted. For example, Mt 1:23 in citing Isa 7:14 probably has in view the total section, Isa 6:1–9:7, as the additional phrase 'God with us' (Isa 8:8, 10 LXX) and the frequent use of the section elsewhere in the New Testament indicate. Dodd correctly perceived that the *testimonia* were the result of 'a certain method of biblical study.'[25] But what precisely was that method? It may well have included, as Dodd thought, a systematic christological analysis of certain sections of the Old Testament. Beyond this, however, the method probably corresponded to a form and method of scriptural exposition used in contemporary Judaism and known to us as midrash.

Quotation and Midrash

1. The Hebrew term 'midrash' (מדרש) often has the meaning 'commentary,'[26] and in the past it has usually been associated primarily with certain rabbinic commentaries on the Old Testament. Recently it has been used more broadly to designate an activity as well as a literary genre, a way of expounding Scripture as well as the resulting exposition.[27] Thus, 'the house of midrash' (Ben Sira = Sirach 51:23) was a place where such exposition was carried on (and not a library of commentaries). According to Bloch[28] the essence of the midrashic procedure was a contemporization of Scripture in order to apply it to or make it meaningful for the current situation. It can be seen, then, in interpretive renderings of the Hebrew text (= implicit midrash), as in the Greek LXX and in the Aramaic targums.[29] For example, 'Aramaeans and Philistines' in Isa 9:11(12) become in the LXX the contemporary 'Syrians and Greeks.' It appears also in more formal 'text + exposition' patterns (= explicit midrash), for example, the rabbinic commentaries. Both kinds of midrash appear in first-century Judaism in the literature of the Qumran community.

2. *Implicit midrash* appears in double entendre, in interpretive alterations of Old Testament citations and in more elaborate forms.[30]

---

[25] Idem, 126.
[26] Cf. II Chron 13:22; 24:27.
[27] Ellis (note 17), 188–192.
[28] Bloch (note 11), 32–33.
[29] Cf. D. W. Gooding, *Relics of Ancient Exegesis*, Cambridge 1976.
[30] Ellis (note 15), 92–96.

The first type involves a play on words. Thus, Mt 2:23 cites Jesus' residence in Nazareth as a 'fulfilment' of prophecies identifying the Messiah as a Ναζωραῖος (= ?Nazirite), or a נצר (= branch).[31] Possibly the double meaning of ὑψοῦν ('lift up') in John 3:14; 12:32ff., i.e. hang and exalt, alludes to an Aramaic rendering (זקף) of Isa 52:13, which carries both meanings;[32] the terminology is clarified in the Synoptic Gospels where Jesus prophesies that he is to 'be killed and rise' (Mk 8:31; cf. Lk 18:33). A similar double entendre may be present in Acts 3:22–26 where 'raise up' apparently is used both of Messiah's pre-resurrection ministry and of his resurrection.

The second type can be seen in Rom 10:11:

> For the Scripture says, 'Everyone (πᾶς) who
> believes in him shall not be put to shame.'

The word 'everyone' is not in the Old Testament text; it is Paul's interpretation woven into the citation and fitting it better to his argument (Rom 10:12f.). Similarly, in the citation of Gen 21:10 at Gal 4:30 the phrase 'son of the free woman' is substituted for 'my son Isaac' in order to adapt the citation to Paul's application. More elaborate uses of the same principle will be discussed below.

Additional complex forms of implicit midrash occur (1) in making a merged or composite quotation from various Old Testament texts, altered so as to apply them to the current situation, and (2) in the description of a current event in biblical phraseology in order to connect the event with the Old Testament passages. Contemporized composite quotations appear, for example, in I Cor 2:9; II Cor 6:16–18. The use of scriptural phraseology to describe and thus to explain the meaning of current and future events is more subtle and reflects a different focus: The event appears to be of primary interest and the biblical allusions are introduced to illumine or explain it. This kind of midrash occurs, for example, in the Matthean and Lukan infancy narratives, in Jesus' apocalyptic discourse and his response at his trial[33] and in the Revelation of St. John where c. 70% of the verses contain allusions to the Old Testament.

---

[31] Judg 13:5, 7 LXX. On 'branch' see Isa 11:1; cf. 49:6; 60:21; O. Betz, *Jesus der Herr der Kirche*, Tübingen 1990, 399ff.

[32] M. Jastrow, *A Dictionary of the Targumim, the Talmud Babli and Jerushalmi, and the Midrashic Literature*, 2 vols., New York 1903, I, 410. Cf. J. F. Stenning, *The Targum of Isaiah*, Oxford 1949, 178; Ezra 6:13.

[33] Mt 2:1–23; 24:15 parr; 26:64 par; Ellis, *Making* (note 36), 345f.

In the Lukan infancy narratives the Annunciation (Lk 1:26–38) alludes to Isa 6:1–9:7,[34] a section of Isaiah that C. H. Dodd[35] has shown to be a primary source for early Christian exegesis. The Magnificat (1:46–55) and the Benedictus (1:68–79) appear to be formed along the same lines. It is probable that family traditions about the events surrounding Jesus' birth were given this literary formulation by prophets of the primitive Jerusalem church.[36]

The response of our Lord at his trial (Mk 14:62 par) is given by the Gospels in the words of Ps 110:1 and Dan 7:13. It probably represents a summary of Jesus' known response, a summary in biblical words whose 'messianic' exegesis either had been worked out in the Christian community or, more likely, had been taught to the disciples by Jesus. That Jesus made use of both Ps 110:1 and Dan 7:13 during his earthly ministry is highly probable.[37]

The apocalyptic discourse (Mk 13 parr), which also includes the use of Dan 7:13f., consists of a midrash of Jesus on certain passages in Daniel, a midrash that has been supplemented by other sayings of the Lord and reshaped by the Evangelists and their predecessors 'into something of a prophetic tract' linked to the church's experiences. In the course of transmission the midrash 'lost many of its once probably explicit associations with the Old Testament text.'[38] If this reconstruction is correct, it shows not only how teachings of Jesus were contemporized in a manner similar to the New Testament authors' midrashic handling of the biblical texts but also how our Lord's explicit midrash was modified so that the Old Testament references, although not lost, were largely assimilated to the current application. The process is much more thoroughgoing than is the case in the composite quotations cited above.

These examples suggest that implicit midrash sometimes presupposes or develops out of direct commentary on the Old Testament,

---

[34] For example, to Isa 7:13f (Lk 1:27: παρθένος, ἐξ οἴκου Δαυίδ); 7:14 (Lk 1:31); 9:6f. (Lk 1:32, 35). On Mt 2:1–23 as narrative midrash (and not fictional midrash) cf. Ellis (note 15), 93ff.

[35] Dodd (note 24), 78–82. It probably also alludes to Gen 16:11 (Lk 1:31); II Sam 7:12–16 (Lk 1:32, ?35: υἱὸς θεοῦ); Dan 7:14 (Lk 1:33b); and Isa 4:3; 62:12 (Lk 1:35: ἅγιον κληθήσεται).

[36] Cf. E. E. Ellis, *The Gospel of Luke (New Century Bible)*, London ⁷1996, 27ff., 67f.; idem, *The Making of the New Testament Documents*, Leiden 1999, 395.

[37] Cf. France (note 8), 101ff. Further, cf. D. Juel, *Messianic Exegesis: Christological Interpretation of the Old Testament in Early Christianity*, Philadelphia 1988, 151–170.

[38] L. Hartman, *Prophecy Interpreted*, Lund 1966, 242.

i.e. explicit midrash. We may now turn to that form of the early Christian usage.

3. *Explicit midrash* in the New Testament has affinities both with the *pesher* midrash at Qumran and with certain kinds of midrash found in rabbinic expositions, i.e. the proem and *yelammedenu* midrashim. The ancient expositions of the rabbis are preserved in sources that are dated several centuries after the New Testament writings. However, in their general structure they provide significant parallels for early Christian practice since (1) it is unlikely that the rabbis borrowed their methods of exposition from the Christians and (2) similar patterns may be observed in the first-century Jewish writer, Philo.[39] The patterns of exposition probably originated not only as 'sermon' or 'homily' but also as 'commentary,' that is, not only as the complement of the synagogue worship but also as the product of the synagogue school. The type of discourse that finds most affinity with New Testament expositions is the 'proem' midrash. As used in the synagogue, it ordinarily had the following form:

The (Pentateuchal) text for the day.

A second text, the proem or 'opening' for the discourse.

Exposition containing additional Old Testament citations, parables or other commentary and linked to the initial texts by catch-words.

A final text, usually repeating or alluding to the text for the day.

The *New Testament letters* frequently display, with some variation, the general outline of this pattern.[40] The structure appears specifically in Rom 9:6–29:

6f.:	Theme and initial text: Gen 21:12.
9:	A second, supplemental text: Gen 18:10.
10–28:	Exposition containing additional citations (13, 15, 17, 25–28) and linked to the initial texts by the catchwords καλεῖν and υἱός (12, 24ff., 27).
29:	A final text alluding to the initial text with the catchword σπέρμα.

---

[39] E.g. Philo, *de sacrif. Abel.* 76–87; cf. Ellis (note 15), 96–101, 154f.; P. Borgen, *Bread from Heaven*, Leiden 1965, 47–50.
[40] Cf. Ellis (note 17), 155ff.

At Gal 4:21–5:1 the initial text of the commentary is itself a summary of a Genesis passage, an implicit midrash introducing the key word ἐλευθέρα. It is probably Paul's summation, but it might have been drawn from a Genesis midrash similar to Jubilees or to the Qumran Genesis Apocryphon.[41]

21f.: Introduction and initial text. Cf. Gen 21.
23–29: Exposition with an additional citation (27), linked to the initial and final texts by the catchwords ἐλευθέρα (22, 23, 26, 30), παιδίσκη (22, 23, 30, 31) and בן/υἱός = τέκνον (22, 25, 27, 28, 30, 31).
30ff.: Final text and application, referring to the initial text. Cf. Gen 21:10.

The pattern in II Pet 3:3–13 is similar, although less clear.[42] As in Gal 4, the initial 'text' is a selective summary of a section of Scripture.

3f.: Theme: Cited Christian prophecy.
5f.: Initial text (with eschatological application). Cf. Gen 1–7.
7–12: Exposition (with an additional citation: 8) linked to the initial and final texts by the catchwords οὐρανός (5, 7, 10, 12), γῆ (5, 7, 10), ἀπόλλυναι (6, 9, cf. 7). Cf. ἡμέρα (7, 8, 10, 12).
13: Final texts and applications. Cf. Isa 65:17; 66:22.

The above examples show how a composite, interpreted citation and an interpretive summary of a larger section of Scripture may serve as the 'text' in a midrash. The use of short, explicit midrashim as 'texts' in a more elaborate commentary-pattern is only an extension of the same practice.[43] One instance of this appears in I Cor 1:18–3:20, which is composed of the following sections, all linked by catchwords, e.g. σοφία, μωρία:

1:18–31: Initial 'text.'
2:1–5: Exposition/Application
2:6–16: Additional 'text.'

---

[41] Cf. Ellis (note 17), 190f., 224ff.
[42] Cf. Ellis, *Making* (note 36), 125–129.
[43] E.g. Rom 1:17–4:25; cf. Ellis (note 17), 217f.

3:1–17:   Exposition/Application.
3:18–20:   Concluding texts: Job 5:13; Ps 94:11.

The synoptic Gospels also display exegetical patterns similar to those in the rabbis. Mt 21:33–44 T + Q corresponds to the 'proem' form of a synagogue address:[44]

33:         Initial text: Isa 5:1f.
34–41:   Exposition by means of a parable, linked to the initial and final texts by a catchword λίθος (42, 44, cf. 35; Isa 5:2, סקל); cf. οἰκοδομεῖν (33, 42).
42–44:   Concluding texts: Ps 118:22f.; Dan 2:34f., 44f.

In Lk 10:25–37 appears a somewhat different pattern, called in the rabbinic writings the *yelammedenu rabbenu* ('let our master teach us'), in which a question or problem is posed and then answered. Apart from the interrogative opening it follows in general the structure of the proem midrash:

25–27:   Dialogue including a question and initial texts: Dt 6:5; Lev 19:18.
28:         A second text: Lev 18:5.
29–36:   Exposition (by means of a parable) linked to the initial texts by the catchwords πλησίον (27, 29, 36) and ποιεῖν (28, 37a, 37b).
37:         Concluding allusion to the second text (ποιεῖν).

Mt 19:3–9, a summary of a biblical debate on divorce, is similar:

3–5:   Question, answered by the initial texts: Gen 1:27; 2:24.
6:          Exposition linked to the initial text by the catchwords δύο, σὰρξ μία.

---

[44] Cf. Ellis (note 17), 157ff., 247–252; W. D. Davies and D. C. Allison Jr., *The Gospel according to Saint Matthew*, 3 vols., Edinburgh 1997, III, 174f.; C. A. Kimball, *Jesus' Exposition of the Old Testament in Luke's Gospel*, Sheffield UK 1994, 147–196. On the use of the book of Isaiah in the New Testament cf. Ellis (note 9), 52–61; W. H. Bellinger et al., edd., *Jesus and the Suffering Servant: Isaiah 53 and Christian Origins*, Harrisburg PA 1998; R. Schneck, *Isaiah in the Gospel of Mark, I–VIII*, Vallejo CA 1994; D. J. Moo, *The Old Testament in the Gospel Passion Narratives*, Sheffield UK 1983, 79–172.

7–8a: Additional citation (Dt 24:1), posing a problem, with exposition.
8b–9:   Concluding allusion to the (interpolated!) initial text (ἀπ' ἀρχῆς).

As the Gospels uniformly attest, debates with scribes, that is, theologians, about the meaning of Scripture constituted an important part of Jesus' public ministry. They were certainly more extensive than the summarized Gospel accounts although they may have followed the same general arrangement. In any case a *yelammedenu* pattern known and used by the rabbis is the literary form often employed by the Gospel traditioners. In the later rabbinical writings the pattern is usually not a dialogue but the scriptural discourse of one rabbi. In this respect the exegetical structure in Rom 9–11 is closer to the rabbinic model than are the Gospel traditions.[45]

Certain differences between rabbinic and New Testament exegesis should also be noted:

1. The New Testament midrashim often do not have an initial text from the Pentateuch, that is, they do not employ the sabbath text of the synagogue lectionary cycle.
2. They often lack a second, proem text.
3. They often have a final text that does not correspond or allude to the initial text.
4. They have an eschatological orientation.[46]

Nevertheless, in their general structure the New Testament patterns have an affinity with the rabbinic usage that is unmistakable and too close to be coincidental.

4. A kind of exposition known as the *pesher midrash* appears in the Qumran writings, for example, the Commentary on Habakkuk (3:1ff.). It receives its name from the Hebrew word used in the explanatory formula, 'the interpretation (פשר) is.' This formula and its apparent equivalent, 'this is' (הוא), sometimes introduce the Old Testament citation (CD 10:16) or, more characteristically, the commentary

---

[45] E.g. Rom 9:6–29. Cf. Ellis (note 17), 155, 218f. Otherwise: D. A. Koch, *Die Schrift als Zeuge des Evangeliums*, Tübingen 1986, 224–227.
[46] Cf. Ellis (note 17), 163ff.

following the citation. Both formulas occur in the Old Testament, the latter translated in the LXX by the phrase οὗτος (ἐστίν).[47]

Besides the formula, the Qumran *pesher* (פשר) has other characteristics common to midrashic procedure. Like the midrashim discussed above, it apparently uses or creates variant Old Testament text-forms designed to adapt the text to the interpretation in the commentary. It also links text and commentary by catchwords. It is found, moreover, in various kinds of commentary patterns: anthology (4Qflor), single quotations (CD 4:14) and consecutive commentary on an Old Testament book (1QpHab).

More significantly for New Testament studies, the Qumran *pesher*, unlike rabbinic midrash but very much like early Christian practice, is both charismatic and eschatological. As *eschatological exegesis*, it views the Old Testament as promises and prophecies that have their fulfilment within the writer's own time and own Qumran community, a community that inaugurates the 'new covenant' of the 'last (אחרית) days,' and constitutes the 'last (אחרון) generation' before the coming of Messiah and the inbreaking of the kingdom of God.[48]

This characteristic feature, the *pesher* formula combined with an eschatological perspective, appears in a number of New Testament quotations:

> 'In Isaac shall your seed be called' (Gen 21:12). That is (τοῦτ' ἔστιν)... the children of the promise are reckoned for the seed. For this is (οὗτος) the word of promise: '... for Sarah there shall be a son' (Gen 18:10).
> *Rom 9:7–9*

> 'On account of this shall a man leave father and mother and be joined to his wife, and the two shall be one flesh' (Gen 2:24). This is (τοῦτο... ἐστίν) a great mystery... for Christ and the church.
> *Eph 5:31f.*

> It is written, 'Abraham had two sons...' (cf. Gen 21). These are (αὗται... ἐστίν) two covenants....
> *Gal 4:22–24*

> They were all filled with the Holy Spirit and began to speak in other tongues.... This is (τοῦτό ἐστίν) what was spoken by the prophet Joel, 'I will pour out my spirit...' (Joel 2:28).
> *Acts 2:4, 16f.*

---

[47] Cf. Isa 9:14f.; Zech 1:9f.; Dan 5:25f.; 4Qflor 1:2f.; Ellis (note 17), 160, 201–205; Stendahl (note 23), 183–206.

[48] Cf. Jer 31:31; 1QpHab 2:3–7; 7:2.

The *pesher* was regarded at Qumran as *charismatic exegesis* of inspired persons such as the Teacher of Righteousness and other wise teachers, i.e. *maskilim* (מַשְׂכִּילִים). The biblical prophecies were understood, as in the book of Daniel, to be a 'mystery' (רָז) in need of interpretation (פֶּשֶׁר), an interpretation that only the *maskilim* can give[49] or, for the New Testament, that only the pneumatics can give.[50]

5. From midrash to *testimonia*: 'Words lifted from their scriptural context can never be a testimonium to the Jewish mind. The word becomes a testimonium for something or other after one has brought out its meaning with the aid of other parts of Scripture.' With this perceptive observation J. W. Doeve[51] goes beyond the thesis of C. H. Dodd, mentioned above,[52] to contend that 'testimony' citations in the New Testament are derived from midrashim, that is, from expositions of those particular Old Testament passages.

In support of Doeve are several examples of a 'Christian' interpretation of a text which is established by an exposition that is presupposed elsewhere in a 'testimony' citation of the same text:[53]

> 1. The exposition in Acts 2:17–35, 34f. and that underlying Mk 13:5–27, 26 apply Ps 110:1 and Dan 7:13, respectively, to Jesus. This interpretation is presupposed in the use of the same biblical verses at Mk 14:62.
> 2. Heb 2:6–9 establishes by midrashic procedures that Ps 8 is fulfilled in Jesus; in I Cor 15:27 and in Eph 1:20, 22 this understanding of Ps 8 (and Ps 110) is presupposed.
> 3. Acts 13:16–41 is a reworked midrash in which II Sam 7:6–16 is shown to apply to Jesus. This interpretation of II Sam 7 is presupposed in the *testimonia* in Heb 1:5 and in II Cor 6:18.

The midrashic expositions in these examples are not, of course, the immediate antecedents of the cited *testimonia* texts. But they represent the kind of matrix from which the 'testimony' usage appears to be derived. They show, furthermore, that the prophets and teachers

---

[49] Dan 9:2, 22f.; cf. 2:19, 24. Cf. 1QpHab 7:1–8; 1QH 12:11ff. = 20:11ff.
[50] Mt 13:10–13; Lk 21:15; Rom 16:25f.; I Cor 2:6–16; 4:1; Eph 3:3ff.; I Pet 1:11f. Cf. Ellis (note 17), 24–30, 137f., 172; idem (note 15), 116–121.
[51] Doeve (note 14), 116.
[52] Dodd (note 24).
[53] Cf. also I Cor 1:18–31 with II Cor 10:17; Ellis (note 17), 192–197, 213–218.

in the early church were not content merely to cite proof texts but were concerned to establish by exegetical procedures the Christian understanding of the Old Testament.

We may proceed one step further. Rabbinic parables often are found in midrashim as commentary on the Old Testament texts. Christ's parables also occur within an exegetical context, for example, in Mt 21:33–44 and in Lk 10:25–37. Elsewhere, when parables appear independently or in thematic clusters, they sometimes allude to Old Testament passages.[54] Probably such independent and clustered parables originated within an expository context from which they were later detached. If so, their present context represents a stage in the formation of the Gospel traditions secondary to their use within an explicit commentary format.

The Presuppositions of New Testament Interpretation

To many Christian readers, to say nothing of Jewish readers, the New Testament's interpretation of the Old appears to be exceedingly arbitrary. For example, Hos 11:1 ('Out of Egypt I called my son') refers to Israel's experience of the Exodus; how can Mt 2:15 apply it to Jesus' sojourn in Egypt? In Ps 8:4ff. the 'son of man' (בן־אדם) given 'glory' and 'dominion' alludes to Adam or to Israel's king; how can Heb 2:8f.; Eph 1:22 and I Cor 15:27 apply the text to Jesus? If Gen 15:6 and II Sam 7:12–16 are predictions of Israel's future, how can New Testament writers refer them to Jesus and to his followers, who include Gentiles as well as Jews?

As has been shown above, the method used to justify such Christian interpretations of the Old Testament represents a serious and consistent effort to expound the texts. The method itself, of course, may be criticized. But then, our modern historical-critical method also is deficient: Although it can show certain interpretations to be wrong, it cannot achieve an agreed interpretation for any substantive biblical passage. 'Method' is inherently a limited instrumentality and, indeed, a secondary stage in the art of interpretation. More basic are the perspective and presuppositions with which the interpreter approaches the text.[55]

---

[54] E.g. Mk 4:1–20 alludes to Jer 4:3; Lk 15:3–6 to Ezek 34:11.
[55] Cf. Ellis (note 17), 163–172; idem (note 15), 101–121; idem (note 9), 261–278.

The perspective from which the New Testament writers interpret the Old is sometimes stated explicitly, sometimes it can be inferred from their usage. It is derived in part from contemporary Jewish views and in part from the teaching of Jesus and the experience of the reality of his resurrection. Apart from its christological focus, it appears to be governed primarily by four factors: a particular understanding of history, of man, of Israel and of Scripture.

Salvation as History

Jesus and his apostles conceive of history within the framework of two ages, this age (αἰών) and the age to come.[56] This perspective appears to have its earliest background in the Old Testament prophets, who prophesied of 'the last (אחרית) days' and 'the day of the Lord' as the time of an ultimate redemption of God's people and the destruction of their enemies. It becomes more specific in the apocalyptic writers, who underscored the cosmic dimension and (often) the imminence of the redemption and, with the doctrine of two ages, the radical difference between the present time and the time to come.[57] This point of view is clearly present in the message of the Baptist that 'the kingdom of God is at hand' and that the one coming after him, Jesus, would accomplish the final judgment and redemption of the nation (Mt 3:2, 10ff.).

The *two-fold* consummation of judgment and deliverance that characterized the teaching of apocalyptic Judaism becomes, in the teaching of Jesus and his apostles, a *two-stage* consummation. As 'deliverance' the kingdom of God that Judaism expected at the end of this age is regarded as already present within this age in the person and work of Jesus the Messiah.[58] As 'judgment' (and final deliverance) the kingdom awaits the second, glorious appearing of Messiah. This perspective may be contrasted with that of Platonism and of apocalyptic Judaism as follows:

---

[56] E.g. Mt 12:32; Mk 10:30; Lk 20:34f.; Eph 1:21; Heb 9:26.
[57] E.g. Isa 2:2; Dan 10:14; Mic 4:1. Cf. Dan 12:2f.; 1QM; 1Q27 (Mysteries) 1:3–8; 4Q MidrEschat[a, b]; A. Steudel, *Der Midrasch zur Eschatologie aus der Qumrangemeinde*, Leiden 1994, 214f.; M. Black, *The Scrolls and Christian Origins*, London 1961, 135–163; F. F. Bruce, *Biblical Exegesis in the Qumran Texts*, Grand Rapids 1959, 37–65.
[58] Cf. Mt 12:28; Lk 10:9; Rom 14:17; Col 1:13; Ellis (note 9), 116–119, 129–146; idem, *Pauline Theology: Ministry and Society*, Lanham MD [4]1998, 5–17, 56.

CHAPTER SEVEN

Platonism and Gnosticism: Eternity and Spirit

⇑

Time and Matter

Judaism: **C** This Age   **P** Age to Come
⌊↓ _____ | _____ ⇛

New Testament: **C** _ _ _ _ _ **P**
⌊↓ †⇑ _____ ⇓ _ _ _ _ _ _ ⇛

Platonic and later Gnostic thought anticipated a redemption *from* matter and an escape *from* time and history at death. The biblical, Jewish hope was for a bodily resurrection, a redemption *of* matter within time: The present age, from the creation (C) and the Fall (↓) to the coming (*parousia*) of Messiah (P), was to be succeeded by a future age of everlasting life and righteousness under the reign of God. The New Testament's modification of Jewish apocalyptic rested upon the perception that in the mission, death and resurrection of Jesus the Messiah the age to come, the future kingdom of God, had become present in hidden form in the midst of the present evil age, although its public manifestation awaited the parousia (P) of Jesus. Thus, its understanding of the time between Jesus' earthly ministry, death and resurrection and his second coming (P) represents an overlapping of this age and the age to come. In the words of O. Cullmann, for Jesus 'the kingdom of God does not culminate a meaningless history, but a planned divine process.'[59] Equally, for the New Testament writers faith in Jesus means faith in the story of Jesus, the story of God's redemptive activity in the history of Israel that finds its highpoint and fulfilment in Jesus.

For this reason the mission and meaning of Jesus can be expressed in the New Testament in terms of a *salvation history* 'consisting of a sequence of events especially chosen by God, taking place within an historical framework.'[60] Although the concept οἰκονομία ('plan,'

---

[59] O. Cullmann, *Salvation in History*, Philadelphia 1967, 233 = GT: 211.
[60] Cullmann (note 59), 25 = GT: 7.

'arrangement') as used in Eph 1:10 represents this idea, that is, a divinely ordered plan, the term 'salvation history' does not itself occur in the New Testament. The concept is most evident in the way in which the New Testament relates current and future events to events, persons and institutions in the Old Testament. That relationship is usually set forth as a typological correspondence.

Typology

1. Typological interpretation expresses most clearly the basic approach of earliest Christianity toward the Old Testament. It is not so much a system of interpretation as a historical and theological perspective from which the early Christian community viewed itself. As a hermeneutical method it must be distinguished from τύπος ('model,' 'pattern') as it was widely used in the Greek world.

Only occasionally using the term τύπος, typological interpretation appears broadly speaking as *covenant typology* and as *creation typology*. The latter may be observed in Rom 5 where Christ is compared and contrasted with Adam, 'a type (τύπος) of the one who was to come' (5:14). The former appears in I Cor 10:6, 11, where the Exodus events are said to be 'types for us', to have happened 'typologically' (τυπικῶς) and to have been written down 'for our admonition upon whom the ends of the ages have come.' Covenant typology accords with the Jewish conviction that all of God's redemptive acts followed the pattern of the Exodus; it is, then, an appropriate way for Jesus and his apostles to explain the decisive messianic redemption. More generally, covenant typology approaches the whole of the Old Testament as prophecy. Not only persons and events but also its institutions were 'a shadow of the good things to come' (Heb 10:1).

2. New Testament typology is thoroughly christological in its focus. Jesus is the 'prophet like Moses' (Acts 3:22f.) who in his passion and death brings the old covenant (= testament) to its proper goal and end[61] and establishes a new covenant (= testament).[62] As the messianic 'son of David,' that is, 'son of God,' he is the recipient of the promises, titles and ascriptions given to the Davidic kings.[63]

---

[61] Cf. Rom 10:4; Heb 10:9f.; II Cor 3:14: ἡ παλαία διαθήκη.
[62] Lk 22:20, 29; I Cor 11:25: ἡ καινὴ διαθήκη.
[63] E.g. II Sam 7:14; Ps 2:7; Amos 9:11f.; cf. Mt 3:17 parr; Jn 7:42; Acts 13:33; 15:16ff.; II Cor 6:18; Heb 1:5.

Because the new covenant consummated by Jesus' death is the occasion of the new creation initiated by his resurrection, covenant typology may be combined with creation typology: As the 'eschatological Adam' and the 'Son of man,' that is, 'son of Adam,'[64] Jesus stands at the head of a new order of creation that may be compared and contrasted with the present one. This combination in Paul and Hebrews finds its immediate background in the resurrection of Jesus. But it is already implicit in Jesus' own teaching, for example, his self-identification with God's temple,[65] his promise of 'Paradise' to the robber (Lk 23:42f.) and his teaching on divorce based on Genesis 2:24.[66] It is probably implicit also in his self-designation as the Son of man (Mk 14:62), a designation that is derived from Dan 7:13f., 27 with allusions to Ps 8:5f. and Ezek 1:26ff. The Son of man in Ps 8 refers not only to Israel's (messianic-ideal) king but also to Adam; likewise the Son of man in Dan 7:13f. is related not only to national restoration but also to the 'dominion' and 'glory' of a new creation. In apocalyptic Judaism also Israel was associated with Adam and the new covenant with a renewed creation.[67] Jesus and his followers shared these convictions and explained them in terms of the mission and person of Jesus.

3. The Old Testament type not only corresponds to the new-age reality but also stands in antithesis to it. Like Adam, Jesus is the representative headman of the race; but unlike Adam, who brought death, Jesus brings forgiveness and life. Jesus is 'the prophet like Moses' but, unlike Moses' ministry of condemnation, that of Jesus gives justification and righteousness. Similarly, the law as an expression of God's righteousness 'is holy, just and good' and its commandments (Exod 20), actuated by an ethic of love (Lev 19:18), are to be 'fulfilled' by the believer.[68] However, the (works of) law was never intended as a means of man's salvation and, as such, it can only condemn him.

One may speak, then, of 'synthetic' or 'congruous' typology and of 'antithetic' typology to distinguish the way in which a type, to one degree or another, either corresponds to or differs from the real-

---

[64] Ps 8:4, 6ff.; cf. I Cor 15:27, 45.
[65] Mk 14:58; cf. Jn 2:18–22; Ellis (note 9), 44–49, 58–61, 81.
[66] Cf. Mt 19:3–9 par.
[67] E.g. Test. Levi 18; 1QS 4:22f. Cf. Ellis (note 9), 79ff.
[68] E.g. Rom 7:12; 13:8ff.; Gal 5:14; cf. II Cor 3:7f.

ity of the new age. For example, in the New Testament Abraham represents synthetic typology (i.e. his faith)[69] but not antithetic (i.e. his circumcision). Moses and the Exodus can represent both;[70] so can Jerusalem.[71] The old covenant, that is, the (ritual) law, more often represents antithetic typology.

4. Since the history of salvation is also the history of destruction,[72] it includes a *judgment typology*. The flood and Sodom,[73] and probably the prophesied AD 70 destruction of Jerusalem (Mt 24:1ff.), become types of God's eschatological judgment. The faithless Israelite is a type of the faithless Christian;[74] the enemies of Israel a type of the (Jewish) enemies of the Church[75] and, perhaps, a type of Antichrist.[76]

5. In a brilliant and highly significant contribution to New Testament hermeneutics Leonhard Goppelt[77] has set forth the definitive marks of typological interpretation. (1) Unlike allegory, typological exegesis regards the words of Scripture not as metaphors hiding a deeper meaning (ὑπόνοια) but as the record of historical events out of whose literal sense the meaning of the text arises (17f., 201f. = GT: 17ff., 243f.). (2) Unlike the 'history of religions' exegesis, it seeks the meaning of current, New Testament situations from a particular history, the salvation-history of Israel. From past Old Testament events it interprets the meaning of the present time of salvation and, in turn, it sees in present events a typological prophecy of the future consummation (194–205 = GT: 233–249). (3) Like rabbinic midrash, typological exegesis interprets the text in terms of contemporary situations, but it does so with historical distinctions that are lacking in rabbinic interpretation (28–32 = GT: 30–34). (4) It identifies a typology in terms of two basic characteristics, historical correspondence and escalation, in which the divinely ordered prefigurement finds a complement in the subsequent and greater event (202 = GT: 244).

---

[69] Cf. Gal 3:6–14; Rom 4:1–25. See below, 143, note 76.
[70] Cf. Heb 11:28f.; I Cor 10:1–4, 6–10; II Cor 3:9.
[71] Cf. Gal 4:25f.; Rev 11:8; 21:2.
[72] Cullmann (note 59), 123 = GT: 105.
[73] Cf. Lk 17:26–30; II Pet 2:5f.; Jude 7.
[74] Cf. I Cor 10:11f.; Heb 4:11.
[75] E.g. Rev 11:8; Rom 2:24.
[76] Cf. II Thess 2:3f.; Rev 13:1–10.
[77] L. Goppelt, *TYPOS: The Typological Interpretation of the Old Testament in the New*, Grand Rapids 1982.

In a masterly essay[78] Rudolf Bultmann rejected Goppelt's conclusion that salvation history was constitutive for typological exegesis and sought to show that the origin of typology lay rather in a cyclical-repetitive view of history (cf. Barnabas 6:13). Although Judaism had combined the two perspectives, the New Testament, for example, in its Adam/Christ typology, represents a purely cyclical pattern, he argued, parallels between the primal time and the end time.

However, Professor Bultmann, in interpreting the New Testament hermeneutical usage within the context of the traditional Greek conception, did not appear to recognize that the recapitulation element in New Testament typology is never mere repetition but is always combined with a change of key in which some aspects of the type are not carried over and some are intensified.[79] Exegetically Goppelt made the better case and established an important framework for understanding how the New Testament uses the Old.

Corporate Personality

In agreement with the Old Testament conception, the New Testament views *man as both an individual and a corporate being*. It represents the corporate dimension, the aspect most difficult for modern Western man to appreciate, primarily in terms of Jesus and his church.[80] For the New Testament faith in Jesus involves an incorporation into him: It is to eat his flesh (Jn 6:35, 54), to be his body (I Cor 12:27), to be baptized into him (Rom 6:3), or into his name (I Cor 1:13; Acts 8:16), to be identified with him (Acts 9:4f.), to exist in the corporate Christ (II Cor 5:17) who is the 'tent' (Heb 9:11) or 'house' in the heavens (II Cor 5:1), God's eschatological temple.

Corporate existence can also be expressed as baptism 'into Moses' (I Cor 10:2), existence 'in Abraham' (Heb 7:9f.) or 'in Adam' (I Cor 15:22) and, at its most elementary level, the unity of man and wife as 'one flesh' (Mt 19:5; Eph 5:29ff.). It is not merely a metaphor, as we are tempted to interpret it, but an ontological statement about who and what man is. The realism of this conception is well expressed by the term 'corporate personality.'[81]

---

[78] R. Bultmann, *Exegetica*, Tübingen 1967, 369–380.
[79] Idem, 369f.
[80] E.g. Mt 26:26ff. parr; Col 1:24. Cf. S. W. Aaron Son, 'Corporate Elements in Pauline Anthropology,' Dissertation, Fort Worth TX: SWBTS, 1999, 7–44, 92–166, and the literature cited.
[81] Cf. Ellis (note 9), 171–178; idem (note 15), 110ff.; J. S. Kaminsky, *Corporate*

The corporate extension of the person of the leader to include individuals who belong to him illumines the use of a number of Old Testament passages. It explains how the promise given to Solomon (II Sam 7:12–16) can be regarded as fulfilled not only in the Messiah (Heb 1:5) but also in his followers (II Cor 6:18) and, similarly, how the eschatological temple can be identified both with the individual (Mk 14:58; Jn 2:19ff.) and the corporate (I Cor 3:16; I Pet 2:5) Christ. It very probably underlies the conviction of the early Christians that those who belong to Christ, Israel's messianic king, constitute *the true Israel*.[82] Consequently, it explains the Christian application to unbelieving Jews of Scriptures originally directed to Gentiles[83] and, on the other hand, the application to the church of Scriptures originally directed to the Jewish nation.[84]

Corporate personality also offers a rationale whereby individual, existential decision[85] may be understood within the framework of a salvation history of the nation or of the race. These two perspectives are considered by some scholars to be in tension or to be mutually exclusive. However, in the words of Oscar Cullmann,[86] the 'now of decision' in the New Testament is not in conflict with the salvation-historical attitude but subordinate to it: 'Paul's faith in salvation history creates at every moment the existential decision.' For it is precisely within the context of the community that the individual's decision is made: Universal history and individual history cannot be isolated from one another.

The history of salvation often appears in the New Testament as the history of individuals—Adam, Abraham, Moses, David, Jesus; yet they are individuals who also have a corporate dimension embracing the nation or the race. The decision to which the New Testament calls all men relates to these persons both in their corporate and in their individual reality. It is never a decision between the isolated

---

Responsibility in the Hebrew Bible, Sheffield UK 1995, 16–29, passim; A. R. Johnson, *Sacral Kingship in Ancient Israel*, Cardiff ²1967, 2f.; H. W. Robinson, *Corporate Personality in Ancient Israel*, Philadelphia 1964 (1935), a view first expressed in idem, *Deuteronomy, Joshua*, Edinburgh 1907, 266f. Otherwise: A. C. Perriman, 'The Corporate Christ: Re-Assessing the Jewish Background,' *TB* 50 (1999), 241–263; J. W. Rogerson, *Anthropology and the Old Testament*, Oxford 1978, 55–59, answered by A. R. Johnson, *The Cultic Prophet and Israel's Psalmnody*, Cardiff 1979, 10f., passim.

[82] Cf. Ellis (note 4), 136–139.
[83] E.g. Acts 4:25ff.; Rom 11:9f.
[84] E.g. II Cor 6:16ff.; I Pet 2:9f.
[85] E.g. Mk 1:17; II Cor 6:2.
[86] Cullmann (note 59), 248 = GT: 225f.

individual and God but is, rather, a decision to 'put off the old man' Adam and to 'put on the new man' Christ (Eph 4:22ff.). It is to be delivered from the corporeity 'in Moses' and 'in Adam'[87] and to be 'immersed in' and to 'put on' Christ,[88] that is, to be incorporated into the 'prophet like Moses' and into the eschatological Adam of the new creation in whom the history of salvation is to be consummated.[89]

Charismatic Exegesis

The early Christian prophets and teachers explain the Old Testament by what may be called *charismatic exegesis*. Like the teachers of Qumran,[90] they proceed from the conviction that the meaning of the Old Testament is a 'mystery' whose 'interpretation' can be given not by human reason but only by the Holy Spirit.[91] On the basis of revelation from the Spirit they are confident of their ability rightly to interpret the Scriptures.[92] Equally, they conclude that those who are not gifted cannot 'know' the true meaning of the word of God.[93]

This view of their task does not preclude the New Testament writers from using logic or hermeneutical rules and methods. However, it does disclose where the ultimate appeal and authority of their interpretation lie. Correspondingly, an acceptance of their interpretation of Scripture in preference to some other, ancient or modern, also will rest ultimately not on the proved superiority of their logical procedure or exegetical method but rather on the conviction of their prophetic character and role.[94]

---

[87] I Cor 10:2; 15:22.
[88] Gal 3:27; Rom 13:14.
[89] E.g. I Cor 15:45; cf. Acts 3:22ff.
[90] See above, 109ff.
[91] I Cor 2:6–16; cf. Mt 13:11; 16:17. Cf. Ellis (note 9), 273–278.
[92] E.g. Mt 16:17; Mk 4:11; Rom 16:25f.; Eph 3:3ff.; II Pet 3:15f.
[93] E.g. Mt 22:29; II Cor 3:14ff.
[94] Cf. Ellis (note 9), 255–278.

CHAPTER EIGHT

HOW JESUS INTERPRETED HIS BIBLE

Biblical Christians have always taken the Gospels as their trustworthy guide to the teachings of Jesus. There are today strong historical and literary grounds supporting that confessional commitment which enable one with considerable confidence to synthesize from the Gospels Jesus' views and teachings on a number of themes. They include (1) the identification of the books composing our Lord's Bible, (2) his attitude toward these Scriptures and (3) the methods and emphases of his interpretation of them.

THE BIBLE RECEIVED BY JESUS

About a hundred years ago a theory was popularized that the Jewish Bible—our Old Testament—was canonized in three stages: the Pentateuch about 400 BC, the Prophets about 200 BC and the Writings, including the Psalms and wisdom literature, at the Council of Jamnia about AD 90.[1] This theory left the content of the Hebrew Bible in Jesus' day an uncertain quantity as far as its third division was concerned.

While the three-stage canonization theory continues to be widely followed, in the past three decades it has been undermined by the critiques of Jewish and Protestant scholars and, in my view, it has been effectively demolished.[2] The theory failed primarily for three reasons. (1) It was not based on specific evidence but rather on infer-

---

[1] H. E. Ryle, *The Canon of the Old Testament*, London ²1895, 105, 119, 183.
[2] E. E. Ellis, 'The Old Testament Canon in the Early Church,' *The Old Testament in Early Christianity*, Tübingen 1991, 3–50 = *Mikra* (= *Compendia* II, 1), edd. M. J. Mulder *et al.*, Assen and Philadelpia 1988, 653–690. Cf. J. P. Lewis, 'What Do We Mean By Jabneh?' *The Canon and Masorah of the Hebrew Bible*, ed. S. Z. Leiman, New York 1974, 254–261; S. Z. Leiman, *The Canonization of Hebrew Scripture*, Hamden CT 1976, 120–124: The view that the Council of Jamnia 'canonized any books at all is not supported by the evidence...' (124); R. T. Beckwith, *The Old Testament Canon of the New Testament Church*, London 1985; idem, 'Canon of the Bible,' *Dictionary of Biblical Interpretation*, 2 vols., ed. J. H. Hays, Nashville TN 1999, I, 161–164. See above, 22, note 28.

ences, some of which can now be seen to have been clearly mistaken.³ (2) It assumed a late dating for certain Old Testament books, for example, for Ecclesiastes and Daniel, that can no longer be sustained. (3) It assumed without justification that the Council of Jamnia acted to canonize certain books, for the evidence suggests only that it reaffirmed books long received but later disputed by some.⁴

It is significant that the Old Testament apocryphal books, received by Roman Catholics as canonical (or deuterocanonical), were never included in Jewish canonical designations and are never cited in the first century writings of Qumran, Philo or the New Testament. All the Old Testament books appear at Qumran except Esther, a book that also is lacking in one early Christian canonical list, that is not cited in the New Testament and that was questioned by some rabbis and Christian writers.⁵ To summarize briefly, one may say with some confidence that the Bible received and used by our Lord was, with the possible exception of Esther, the Old Testament received today as sacred Scripture by Jews and Protestants.

Jesus' Attitude Toward His Bible

Jesus' use of the Old Testament rests on his conviction that these writings were the revelation of God through faithful prophets, a conviction that is decisive for his interpretation of Scripture and that surfaces explicitly in a number of places in the Gospels. Let us look at four examples of this: Mt 19:4f., Mk 12:24, Mt 5:17f., and Jn 10:35.⁶

Two examples of Jesus' attitude to Scripture appear in his biblical debates with rabbis of other Jewish religious parties. In a question on divorce posed by the Pharisees, Jesus cites Gen 1:27 and 2:24 as the regulative and conclusive texts:

---

³ For example, the testimony of Josephus (c. AD 90; *ct. Apion.* I, 38–42) to a long-settled, universally recognized Jewish canon of Scriptures cannot simply be dismissed as a sectarian viewpoint.

⁴ Cf. Ellis, *Old Testament* (note 2), 37–49; Leiman, *Canonization* (note 2); R. C. Newman, 'The Council of Jamnia and the Old Testament Canon,' *WTJ* 38 (1976) 319–349.

⁵ Lacking Esther is the list of Melito, Bishop of Sardis (c. AD 170), cited in Eusebius, *HE* 4, 26, 13f. For criticisms of Esther among the rabbis cf. BT Megillah 7a; Sanh. 100a; among a few Christian groups, cf. T. Nöldeke, 'Esther,' *EB* II, 1407.

⁶ Cf. also Mt 4:5–7 Q; E. E. Ellis, *Christ and the Future in New Testament History*, Leiden 2000, 266–269.

The one who created them from the beginning
Made them male and female
And said, '... The two shall be one flesh.'
Mt 19:4f.

Noteworthy for our purposes is the fact that, according to Matthew, Jesus identified the editorial comment of the author of Genesis as the utterance of God. That is, the Word of God character of Scripture is not limited to 'thus says the Lord' passages.

In a biblical dispute with the Sadducees on the resurrection[7] Jesus identifies their error thus:

> You err, not knowing the Scriptures nor the power of God.
> *Mt 22:29 = Mk 12:24*

Two points are to be observed here. First, since these trained Scripture-scholars (γραμματεῖς) memorized the Bible by the book, Jesus is not ascribing their theological error to an ignorance of the words of Scripture but to a lack of understanding of its meaning. That is, the 'Word of God' character of Scripture, its divine truth, is not to be found merely by quoting the Bible but by discerning its true significance. Second, the Sadducees' ignorance of the Scripture is tied together with their skepticism about the power of God to raise to life those who have returned to the dust in death. Not unlike some liberal Christians today, they apparently allowed (Epicurean) philosophical dogmas to block their minds from the teaching of the prophets.[8]

In the Sermon on the Mount Jesus contrasts his teaching to what his audience has heard before. For example,[9]

---

[7] Mt 22:23–33 = Mk 12:18–27 = Lk 20:27–40. Assuming Luke's independence of Matthew, those two Gospels rely on a second source, a Q tradition, in addition to their (assumed) use of Mark. This is to be inferred from the agreements of Matthew and Luke against Mark in this episode.

[8] The rabbinic tradition associates the Sadducees' denial of the resurrection with Epicurean philosophy. Cf. M Sanh. 10:1; BT Rosh Hash. 17a; K. G. Kuhn, ed., *Sifre zu Numeri*, Stuttgart 1959, 328 (Section 112 on Num 15:31); J. Neusner, ed., *The Fathers According to Rabbi Nathan*, Atlanta 1986, 47f. (*ARN* 5). Further, cf. M. Hengel, *Judaism and Hellenism*, 2 vols., London 1974, I, 143; (H. L. Strack and) P. Billerbeck, *Kommentar zum Neuen Testament aus Talmud und Midrasch*, 4 vols. in 5, München 1922–28, I, 885; IV, 344. *Pace* E. Schürer, *The History of the Jewish People in the Age of Jesus Christ. New Edition*, 3 vols. in 4, Edinburgh ²1987, II, 391f., the Sadducean denial of resurrection was no mere retention of Old Testament conceptions, not even of Ecclesiastes (cf. Eccl 12:14).

[9] Cf. Mt 5:21, 27, 31, 33, 38, 43.

CHAPTER EIGHT

> You have heard that it was said to those of old
> You shall not commit murder. . . .
> But I say to you that everyone who is angry with his brother shall be liable to the judgment.
> *Mt 5:21f.*

Jesus is thought by some to be setting his authority against that of Scripture,[10] but several considerations exclude this understanding of the matter. First, (1) as we have seen in the illustrations above, Jesus never understands Scripture as words of the Bible in the abstract but as the message in its true meaning and application. Thus, in the biblical debate on divorce (Mt 19:3–9), which is also one of the antitheses in the Sermon (Mt 5:31f.), he counters the Pharisees' appeal to Dt 24:1, 3 by arguing that Gen 1:27 and 2:24 are the governing texts for the principle involved. In doing this, he follows good rabbinic practice, not denying the 'Word of God' character of either passage but arguing against the traditional use of Dt 24 as the regulative passage for the marriage relationship.[11]

So also in the command, 'you shall not commit murder,' Jesus argues not against God's command through Moses but against the traditional limitation of that command to literal murder. If someone objects, 'But the text says "murder,"' one might reply as a certain rabbi once did to his pupil: 'Good, you have learned to read. Now go and learn to interpret.'[12]

A second objection to taking the antitheses in the Sermon to mean that Jesus opposed or transcended the Scripture is (2) the introductory formula used to introduce the biblical texts: 'You have heard that it was said to those of old.' As far as I know, this formula is never used in Christianity or Judaism to introduce Scripture as such, that is, in its true force as the Word of God.[13] The words, 'You have heard,' point to the oral reading and interpretation of Scripture

---

[10] So, apparently, R. A. Guelich, *The Sermon on the Mount*, Waco 1982, 182–185.

[11] It is not that one passage is right and the other wrong but that both are right in different senses. The permission of divorce (Dt 24:1, 3) was God's word to a particularly evil situation, because of 'the hardness of your hearts;' but to employ it as a regulative principle for marriage was a misuse of the text.

[12] Cf. D. Daube, *The New Testament and Rabbinic Judaism*, Peabody MA ²1994, 428ff. He notes a number of rabbinic sayings that are similar to this although not the one that sticks in my memory and that I cannot now locate.

[13] The term, 'it was said' (ἐρρέθη), at Mt 5:31 is so used elsewhere (Rom 9:12) but the preceding clause, 'you have heard that' makes clear that here the word is only an abbreviation for the longer formula. Cf. Daube (note 11), 62.

that the audience of Jesus heard regularly in synagogue,[14] and they show that in the Sermon Jesus is contrasting his teachings with traditional interpretations of the Bible known to his hearers. This is a characteristic feature of our Lord's teachings which perhaps reaches its high-point in his accusation against certain Jewish churchmen and theologians: 'For the sake of your traditions you have made void the Word of God.'[15] This conclusion is reinforced by the fact that the quotations in the Sermon sometimes include an explicit non-biblical interpretation, for example,

> You shall love your neighbor
> And hate your enemy.
> Mt 5:43

The second command is not found in the Old Testament but is part of the interpretation of the Bible at Qumran.[16]

A third and perhaps the most important objection to the proposed interpretation is (3) the passage at Mt 5:17f., which is prefaced to this section of the Sermon:

> Do not suppose that I have come to annul the law and the prophets. I have not come to annul (καταλῦσαι) but to fulfil [them].
> Truly I say to you: Until heaven and earth pass away, not one jot or tittle shall pass from the law until all things be accomplished.

Matthew doubtless knew that some readers could misunderstand the antitheses in the Sermon as setting Jesus over against the holy Scriptures. To preclude that, he includes this explicit declaration of the Lord on the inviolate character of the biblical teaching. This verse is very similar to Christ's word in the exposition at Jn 10:35: 'The Scripture cannot be broken of its force' (λυθῆναι).[17]

---

[14] Cf. Daube (note 11) 55: 'In Rabbinic discussion *shome 'a 'ani*, "I hear," "I understand," or rather "I might understand," introduces an interpretation of Scripture which, though conceivable, yet must be rejected.'

[15] Mt 15:6 = Mk 7:13. Possibly (but not likely) Jesus here also rejects a view expressed by some later rabbis that the oral tradition originated at Sinai and thus was a divinely sanctioned interpretation of Scripture. Cf. W. D. Davies, 'Canon and Christology,' *The Glory of Christ in the New Testament. FS G. B. Caird*, edd. L. D. Hurst *et al.*, Oxford 1987, 19–36, 30f.

[16] 1QS 1:3f., 9ff.

[17] The term 'broken' (λυθῆναι, John 10:35) has this significance. Cf. Billerbeck (note 8), II, 542f.; C. K. Barrett, *The Gospel According to St. John*, London 1956, 319f.; further, cf. D. A. Carson, *John*, Grand Rapids MI 1991, 399.

'The law' and 'the prophets' represent in Mt 5, as elsewhere,[18] the whole Old Testament. Jesus is revealed not only as the proclaimer of God's Word but also as the proclaimer of himself as the one in whom that Old Testament Word is to find fulfilment.

Jesus fulfils the Old Testament in two ways. By his interpretation of it he unveils its true and final (eschatological) meaning. In his person and work he fulfils the true intention of its prophecies and the goal of its history of salvation.

Jesus' Principles of Biblical Interpretation

The great rabbi Hillel (†c. AD 10), who taught Scripture about a generation before our Lord's ministry, is given credit for seven rules or principles for interpreting the Bible although they may be only 'types of argument in use at that time' (Strack-Stemberger). Some of them, for example, interpretation according to context (Rule 7), come down to us today virtually unaltered. They drew inferences and analogies from Scripture, and a number of them were used by Christ in his interpretation of his Bible. Consider the following examples:[19]

> *Rule 1:* קל וחומר, inference from minor and major, *a fortiori*.
>
> Consider the ravens: they neither sow or reap..., and God feeds them (Ps 147:9). Of how much more value are you than the birds.
> *Lk 12:24*
>
> Is it not written in your law: 'I said you are gods' (Ps 82:6). If [God] called 'gods' those to whom the word of God came..., do you say, 'You blaspheme,' because I said, 'I am the Son of God' (Ps 2:7)?
> *Jn 10:34ff.*

---

[18] Cf. Rom 3:21 with 4:7 = Ps 32:1f. The law' can refer to the whole Old Testament (cf. Rom 3:19 with 3:10–18; I Cor 14:21); so also 'the prophets' (cf. Acts 13:27; 26:27).

[19] For Hillel's Rules and their exposition by the rabbis cf. Sifra Lev 2:1ff.; T Sanh. 7:11; *ARN* 37, 10. Cf. *The Tosefta*, ed. J. Neusner, 6 vols., New York 1977–86; Neusner (note 8); M. Mielziner, *Introduction to the Talmud*, New York 1968 ([1]1894), 123–129; H. L. Strack and G. Stemberger, *Introduction to the Talmud and Midrash. Revised Edition*, Edinburgh [6]1991 ([1]1887), 19, 19–23 = GT: 27, 26–30; Schürer (note 8), II, 344. For other New Testament examples, cf. Ellis, 'Biblical Interpretation in the New Testament Church,' *Old Testament* (note 2), 87–91 = *Mikra* (note 2), 700ff.; idem, *Paul's Use of the Old Testament*, Grand Rapids [5]1991, 41f.

From the biblical verse teaching that God cares for the least of his creatures, Jesus infers *a fortiori* that the passage also applies to his disciples. From the verse addressing as 'gods' the whole people of God, he infers *a fortiori* that the title 'Son of God' is appropriate for the One God has sent into the world.[20]

> *Rule 2*: גזירה שוה, an equivalent regulation, an inference drawn from a similar situation (words and phrases) in Scripture.

> On the Sabbath... [Jesus'] disciples plucked and ate grain.... The Pharisees said, 'Why do you do that which is not lawful' (Exod 20:10) ?....
> Jesus said, '... [David] took and ate the bread of the Presence and gave to those with him (I Sam 21:1–6), which is not lawful to eat except for the priests (Lev 24:9)....
> The Son of Man is lord of the Sabbath.'
> *Lk 6:1–5*

David, who received a kingdom from God (I Sam 15:28), was blameless when he and those with him violated the Law in eating the bread of the Presence; the Son of Man, who has also received a kingdom from God (Dan 7:13f.), is equally blameless when those with him violate the Sabbath Law in similar circumstances.

> *Rule 3*: בנין אב מכתוב אחד, constructing a family from one passage, a general principle inferred from the teaching contained in one verse.

> Moses showed that the dead are raised....
> He calls the Lord 'the God of [dead] Abraham'... (Exod 3:6, 15).
> He is not the God of the dead but of the living.
> *Lk 20:37f.*

God is not the God of the dead, yet he affirmed his covenant relationship with the dead Abraham. Therefore, Jesus concludes, he must intend to raise Abraham out of death. From this one passage one

---

[20] That Jesus had (reportedly) identified himself as 'the Son of God,' that is, as the Messiah, is also presupposed by the high priest's question at Mk 14:61f. = Mt 26:63f. Peter's confession (Mt 16:13–20 parr) or some similar teaching of Jesus to disciples had apparently become common knowledge. Cf. S. Kim, *'The "Son of Man"' as the Son of God*, Tübingen 1983, 1–6.

may infer the resurrection of all the dead who have a similar covenantal relationship with God.[21]

Rule 7: דבר הלמד מעניינו, an interpretation of a word or a passage derived from its context.

> He who made them from the beginning
> 'Made them male and female' (Gen 1:27)
> And said,.... '[A man] shall be joined to his wife
> And the two shall be one flesh' (Gen 2:24).
> Therefore, what God has joined let not man separate.
> [The Pharisees said], 'Why then did Moses command
> That he give her a bill of divorce...' (Dt 24:1–4)?
> [Jesus said], 'For the hardness of your hearts....
> But from the beginning it was not so.'
> Mt 19:4–8

At the creation God established marriage as an indissoluble union. This context, Jesus concludes, takes priority over the later provisions for divorce.

We have given no examples of a general principle derived from the teaching of two verses (Rule 4), of an inference drawn from a general principle to a specific example and vice versa (Rule 5) or of an inference drawn from an analogous passage (Rule 6). But the above are sufficient to show how Jesus employed, for the most part implicitly, Hillel's Rules in his exposition of Scripture. Not all of Hillel's Rules are clearly attested in the Gospels and the Rules in Jesus' usage appear less stylized than in the later rabbinic writings. But they are present and do form a part of the hermeneutical framework for our Lord's interpretation of Scripture.

Much of the older form criticism of the Gospels assumed that Jesus uttered pithy pronouncements and that the scriptural references and expositions almost always represented postresurrection creations of the church.[22] In this respect it read the historical development

---

[21] Further, cf. Ellis (note 6), 96–104; idem, *The Gospel of Luke*, Grand Rapids ⁷1996, 234–237.

[22] For example, R. Bultmann, *History of the Synoptic Tradition*, Oxford 1963 (¹1921) 46–50; cf. 16f., 26f., passim = GT: 47–52; cf. 14f., 25f.; M. Dibelius, *From Tradition to Gospel*, London ²1934, 219–222, passim = GT³: 220–224. Cf. J. W. Doeve, *Jewish Hermeneutics in the Synoptic Gospels and Acts*, Assen 1954, 178: '[The] classifications used by Dibelius and Bultmann... are not cognate to the material. For they are derived from the Greek world and not from the Jewish....'

precisely backwards[23] and sometimes gave the impression that the church made Jesus into a Jew. In part this reflected a mistaken dichotomy between Jesus the apocalyptic prophet and Jesus the teacher; in part it simply lacked an understanding of the Jewish context of Jesus' ministry. For example, Jesus' teaching against divorce would have no force with his hearers unless it could be established from Scripture and could thus successfully counter the traditional interpretation of Moses' teaching on the matter. Dt 13:1–3, with its requirement that succeeding prophets agree with Moses' teaching,[24] was too much a part of Jewish consciousness for a prophetic personality to gain a following wandering about the country uttering pronouncements or even quoting isolated biblical texts. What was required was a midrash, an exposition, in which various Scriptures were called upon to aid in understanding a particular text.[25] That Jesus did this and did it with an authority that exceeded the usual scribe, i.e. Scripture scholar, evoked the astonishment of his hearers.[26] Thus, it is, for example, the exposition at Mt 19:3–9 that represents the authoritative foundation of Jesus' teaching on divorce which the pronouncement at Mt 5:31f. summarizes and depends on. The biblical expositions of Jesus elsewhere are likewise the bedrock of his teaching and of the Synoptic tradition,[27] and from a critical perspective they cannot be regarded as creations of the Gospel traditioners.

---

[23] Cf. E. E. Ellis, *The Making of the New Testament Documents*, Leiden 1999, 19–27, 30-33, 333–354; idem, *Prophecy and Hermeneutic in Early Christianity*, Tübingen 1978, 247–253; idem (note 6), 246–251.

[24] Dt 13:1–5 and the judgment on false prophets invoked there is reproduced in the Temple Scroll (11QTemple 54:8–18) and referred to in CD 12:2f.; M Sanh. 7:4 and applied to Jesus in BT Sanh. 43a; cf. Justin, *Dialogue* 69. Cf. Billerbeck (note 8), I, 1023f.; A. Strobel, *Die Stunde der Wahrheit*, Tübingen 1980, 81–94; W. A. Meeks, *The Prophet-King*, Leiden 1967, 47–57. The demand by the Jewish churchmen for 'a sign' from Jesus (Mk 8:11) also presupposes a suspicion or conviction that he is a false prophet and his miracles the work of demons (Mk 3:22). Cf. W. L. Lane, *The Gospel According to Mark*, Grand Rapids 1974, 277f.; O. Betz, *Jesus der Messias Israels*, Tübingen 1987, 73f.

[25] Cf. Doeve (note 21), 115f.: To the Jewish mind it 'is not the detached passage, the separate text, that has weight, that proves something....' 'The word becomes a testimonium for something or other after one has brought out its meaning with the aid of other parts of Scripture.'

[26] Cf. Mt 7:28f. par; 13:54 parr; 22:33; Daube, 'Rabbinic Authority' (note 12), 212–223.

[27] A number of Christ's expositions are found both in Mark and in Q traditions, for example, Mk 4:10–12; 12:1–12; 12:18–27; 12:28–34; 12:35–37. See above, note

Two commentary patterns found in rabbinic writings also appear in expositions of Jesus that are, in fact, among the earliest extant examples of this form of exegetical discourse. They are the *proem* midrash and the *yelammedenu* midrash.[28] An example of the former type appears at Mt 21:33–44:[29]

33: Initial text: Isa 5:1f.
34–41: Exposition by means of a parable, linked to the initial and final texts by the catchword λίθος (42, 44, cf. 35; Isa 5:2, סקל); cf. οἰκοδομεῖν (33, 42).
42–44: Concluding texts: Ps 118:22f.; Dan 2:34f., 44f.

The opening (= proem) text has been reduced to an allusion and a key word ('stone,' Isa 5:2) omitted, but the reference to Isa 5 is clear. In Mark one of the concluding texts[30] has been omitted, but it is retained by Matthew and Luke from the Q *Vorlage* as an allusion. The pattern is looser than that in the later, more stylized proem midrashim in the rabbinic writings, but the common root of the two patterns is clearly evident.

The *yelammedenu rabbenu*[31] midrash is similar to the proem pattern except that the opening is formed by a question and a counter-question. An example is found in Mt 12:1–8:[32]

---

[7]. Further, cf. Ellis (note 2), 97f.; on Mt 19:3–9 and 12:1–8, P. Sigal, *The Halakah of Jesus of Nazareth according to the Gospel of Matthew*, Lanham MD 1986, 83–159; M. Bockmuehl, 'Halakhah... in the Jesus Tradition,' *Early Christian Thought in its Jewish Context*, ed. J. Barclay *et al.*, Cambridge 1996, 264–278.

[28] See above, 108n.; below, 134n. For rabbinic examples of these two types of midrash, see *Pesikta de-Rab Kahana*, edd. W. G. Braude *et al.*, Philadelphia 1975, xf., xxviii–xxxvii, xlix, passim; *Pesikta Rabbati*, ed. W. G. Braude, 2 vols., New Haven CT 1968, I, 3–5, 17, 26, passim. Although collected later, these midrashim are largely the work of third and fourth-century Palestinian rabbis. Cf. S. Maybaum, *Die ältesten Phasen der Entwicklung der jüdischen Predigt*, Berlin 1901, 1–27; E. E. Ellis, "Quotations in the New Testament," *ISBE*² IV (1988), 18–25. For an example in Philo, see above, 106n.

[29] Matthew and Luke (20:9–19) utilize both Mk 12:1–12 and a Q tradition, as their agreements against Mark show. On Lk 20:9–19 cf. C. A. Kimball, *Jesus' Exposition of the Old Testament in Luke's Gospel*, Sheffield UK 1994, 147–164.

[30] Dan 2:34f., 44f.

[31] ילמדנו רבנו, 'let our rabbi teach us.' For a discussion of the origin of the pattern cf. J. W. Bowker, 'Speeches in Acts: A Study in Proem and Yelammedenu Form,' *NTS* 14 (1967–68) 96–111.

[32] The parallels at Mk 2:23–28 and Lk 6:1–5 have lost a part of the commentary pattern, indicating that Matthew is (or has retained) the earliest form of the tradition. For further examples cf. Mt 15:1–9; 19:3–9; Lk 10:25–37; Ellis, *Prophecy* (note 23), 158f. For rabbinical examples cf. Braude, *Pesikta Rabbati* (note 28), I, 3,

1: Theme.
2: Pharisees' biblical question: Exod 20:10, allusion.
3f.: Jesus' counter-question (I Sam 21:6) and commentary.
5f.: Jesus' second counter-question (Num 28:9) and commentary.
7a: Concluding text: Hos 6:6.
7b–8: Application.

Summarized here, using the *yelammedenu* commentary pattern, is a complex debate on Sabbath Law between Jesus and other Jewish churchmen about the true meaning of Scripture for present conduct. Although it cannot now be elaborated, (1) the eschatological and christological hermeneutic of Jesus (Mt 12:6, 8) is at the center of the conflict between his views and the traditional interpretation of Scripture by the Pharisees. At the same time (2) Jesus defeats the Pharisees on their own ground by showing, exegetically, that the subordination and relativising of ritual laws vis-à-vis the moral law were recognized by Scripture even for the Old Testament time.[33]

CONCLUSION

Jesus' interpretation of his Bible proceeds from his recognition of the canon of sacred books accepted by the main-stream Judaism of his day and from his settled conviction that these writings, rightly understood, were the expression of the mind of God through faithful prophets. The exposition of the received Scripture is, then, the sum and substance of Jesus' message, both in teaching his followers and in debating his opponents. This is true even when the Gospel traditioners and Evangelists—because of, among other things, the limits of space—have summarized, compacted or omitted the express biblical references that originally formed the basis of Jesus' teachings.

Contrary to some misguided modern interpreters, there is never any suggestion in the Gospels of Jesus opposing the Torah, the Law of God, the Old Testament. It is always a matter of Jesus' true exposition of Scripture against the misunderstanding and/or misapplication of it by the dominant Scripture-scholars of his day. This becomes

---

and the Piskas cited. In the Gospels the pattern is usually employed in Jesus' debates with opponents, but it can also be used, as in the rabbinic writings, to summarize Jesus' instruction of his hearers; cf. Mt 11:2–6; 11:7–15.

[33] Mt 12:4f., 7. Cf. Ellis, (note 6), 16–19, 31f., 227f.

apparent in Jesus' encounters with such rabbis in numerous debates, a number of which the Evangelists are careful to retain.

The Judaism of Jesus' day was a Torah-centric religion. To gain any hearing among his people, Jesus' teaching also had to be Torah-centric. Thus it was necessary, not only from his own conviction that the Law is the Word of God and that he himself is the fulfilment of that Law but also from practical considerations, that our Lord show by his teachings as well as by his acts that his message and his messianic person stood in continuity with and in fulfilment of Israel's ancient Word from God. It is in this frame of reference that one finds the meaning of Jesus' interpretation of his Bible.

CHAPTER NINE

PREFORMED TRADITIONS AND THEIR IMPLICATIONS
FOR THE ORIGINS OF PAULINE CHRISTOLOGY

My examination of preformed traditions in the New Testament began with an M.A. thesis,[1] followed by a doctoral dissertation on *Paul's Use of the Old Testament*.[2] This interest broadened, sparked by John Bowker's essay on the 'Proem and Yelammedenu Form,'[3] into studies of Old Testament expositions (midrashim) in Acts, the New Testament letters[4] and the Gospels.[5] In the mid-seventies initial work on a commentary on I Corinthians required an inquiry into various other kinds of preformed traditions in that letter[6] and in other Pauline literature.

The same period marked the beginnings of the study recently published, *The Making of the New Testament Documents*,[7] a full investigation of literary traditions and their implications for the authorship and dating of the Gospels and of the letters. The present chapter can only briefly sketch the more comprehensive study with its new paradigm of the history of early Christianity. It seeks to show the

---

[1] E. E. Ellis, 'The Nature and Significance of Old Testament Quotations in the Gospel of Mark,' M.A. Thesis, Wheaton (IL) College Graduate School, 1953.

[2] E. E. Ellis, *Paul's Use of the Old Testament*, Edinburgh 1957; cf. idem, 'A Note on Pauline Hermeneutics,' *NTS* 2 (1955–56), 127–133.

[3] J. W. Bowker, 'Speeches in Acts: A Study in Proem and Yelammedenu Form,' *NTS* 14 (1967–68), 96–111.

[4] E. E. Ellis, 'Midrash, Targum and New Testament Quotations' (1969); 'Midrashic Features in Acts' (1970); 'Exegetical Patterns in I Corinthians and Romans' (1975); 'How the New Testament Uses the Old' (1977); 'Prophecy and Hermeneutic in Jude' (1978), *Prophecy and Hermeneutic in Early Christianity* (*WUNT* 18), Tübingen 1978, 147–172, 188–208, 213–236. The essay on Jude was given, if I recall correctly, as a paper at an SBL seminar on midrash led by Nils Dahl and Wayne Meeks in New York 1970.

[5] E. E. Ellis, 'New Directions in Form Criticism,' *Jesus Christus in Historie und Theologie. FS H. Conzelmann*, ed. G. Strecker, Tübingen 1975, 299–315 = Ellis, *Prophecy* (note 4), 237–253.

[6] Given as a paper in an SNTS seminar led by Peter Stuhlmacher and myself, and published later as E. E. Ellis, 'Traditions in I Corinthians,' *NTS* 32 (1986), 481–502.

[7] E. E. Ellis, *The Making of the New Testament Documents*, Leiden 1999.

implications of certain preformed traditions in Paul's letters for the origins of the Apostle's christology.

THE MAKING OF THE NEW TESTAMENT DOCUMENTS

From Traditions to Gospels

For the Synoptic Gospels the study of expository forms discloses one clear dominical proem midrash[8] and numerous *yelammedenu rabbenu* type midrashim.[9] An examination of Gospel narratives reveals two stock patterns on which the large majority were constructed.[10] The first pattern, used mainly for healing episodes, has the following structure: Setting + Appeal to Jesus + Jesus' Response + Reactions.[11] It is highly christological and designed to serve as a teaching by narration as much as Jesus' parables (*meshalim*) were a teaching by illustrative story.[12] With a shift of emphasis the pattern can be structured as a narrative proper,[13] as a pronouncement story (apothegm),[14] or as a more extended saying, discourse or dialogue.[15]

The second pattern uses biblical quotations and allusions to frame the narrative, e.g. in the stories of Jesus and the Baptist,[16] of the

---

[8] Mt 21:33–44 T + Q. Cf. Ellis (note 4), 251ff.; idem, in Strecker (note 5), 313ff. So also, W. D. Davies and D. C. Allison, Jr., *The Gospel According to Saint Matthew*, 3 vols., Edinburgh 1997, III, 174f.: 'While ... we have reservations about ascribing the pattern to Jesus himself, it does appear that Matthew's text in its current shape corresponds to an old form of synagogue address' (175). But the pattern is present in parallel passages found in all three Synoptic Gospels (T) and apparently in a tradition used by Matthew and Luke that differs from Mark (Q). See above, 130f.

[9] Mt 11:7–15 Q; 12:1–8 T + Q; 15:1–9 par; 19:3–9 par; 22:23–33 T + Q; 24:4–31 ? T + Q; Lk 10:25–37; cf. Mt 21:15f. Cf. Ellis (note 7) 175n, 249n, 350; idem, *The Old Testament in Early Christianity*, Tübingen 1991, 97f., 103n, 134–138 = IT (Brescia 1999): 129ff., 138n, 174–179. In these passages Jesus responds to biblical questions in the form of a (summarized) biblical commentary.

[10] Cf. Ellis (note 7), 333–356, 349ff.

[11] E.g. Exorcisms: Mk 1:21–28 par (unclean spirit); Mt 8:28–34 T (Gadarene); 12:22–32 T + Q (deaf mute); healings: Mt 8:1–4 T + Q (leper); Mk 5:21–43 T + Q (Jarius' daughter).

[12] Cf. B. Gerhardsson, 'Illuminating the Kingdom,' *Jesus and the Oral Gospel Tradition*, ed. H. Wansbrough, Sheffield UK 1991, 266–304.

[13] E.g. Leper (Mt 8:1–4 T + Q). Cf. Ellis (note 7), 341ff.

[14] E.g. Paralytic (Mt 9:1–8 T + Q).

[15] E.g. Jarius' daughter (Mk 5:21–43 T + Q).

[16] Mt 3:1–17 T + Q. Cf. Ellis (note 7), 345–348.

Magi and Flight,[17] and of the Entry and the Cleansing of the Temple.[18] It may be termed a narrative midrash in that the story about Jesus is presented as an interpretation or fulfilment of the biblical texts that frame it. And it may be derived from the 'text + exposition' midrashic patterns which Jesus, in my judgment, had taught his pupils to use to summarize his teaching.[19] Since the biblical texts in the narrative midrashim presuppose their messianic understanding, they, like other 'testimony' texts, were probably detached from antecedent dominical expositions (midrashim) in which the christological meaning had been exegetically established.[20] So also certain clustered parables[21] or sayings of Jesus[22] appear to be detached expository pieces from similar 'text + exposition' episodes.

To communicate with and to persuade the Torah-centric Judaism of his day, Jesus of necessity had to justify his acts and teachings from the Scriptures.[23] In antithesis to the classical form criticism,[24] the Gospel traditions at root set forth a high christology designed to present Jesus as the fulfilment of Old Testament promises. And, as J. W. Doeve, Birger Gerhardsson, Rainer Riesner and others have argued,[25] they were composed by apostles and transmitted in a carefully cultivated and controlled manner from their creation to their incorporation into the four Gospels.[26]

As I understand the history, the Gospels are the products, respectively, of four apostolic missions,[27] whose leaders can be identified

---

[17] Mt 2:1-23.
[18] Mt 21:1-16 T + Q + John.
[19] Cf. E. E. Ellis, *Christ and the Future in New Testament History*, Leiden 2000, 25-31, 242-254.
[20] Cf. Ellis (note 4), 252f.; idem (note 9), 100f., 130-138 = IT: 133ff., 163-180.
[21] E.g. Mt 13; Lk 15-16, i.e. those with biblical allusions (above, 112).
[22] Cf. Mt 5:31f. with Mt 19:3-9; Mt 5:21f. with Mk 9:41-48.
[23] Cf. J. Jeremias, *New Testament Theology I*, London 1971, 205: 'Jesus lived in the Old Testament;' Ellis (note 19), 17ff.
[24] For a critique cf. Ellis (note 7), 19-27; idem (note 19), 20-29, 246-254; idem (note 4), 237-253.
[25] J. W. Doeve, *Jewish Hermeneutics in the Synoptic Gospels and Acts*, Assen 1954; B. Gerhardsson, *Memory and Manuscript*, Grand Rapids ²1998; R. Riesner, *Jesus als Lehrer*, Tübingen ³1988. Cf. also E. Güttgemanns, *Candid Questions Concerning Gospel Form Criticism*, Pittsburgh PA 1979.
[26] Cf. Ellis, 'From Traditions to the New Testament,' 'Traditions in John's Gospel' (note 7) 1-47, 154-183; idem (note 19), 14ff.
[27] Cf. Clement, *Stromata* 1, 1, 11: Clement's mentors, whom he carefully sought

in Gal 2. The Jacobean mission, centered on Jerusalem, produced the Gospel of Matthew.²⁸ The Petrine mission, following Peter's departure from Jerusalem (Acts 12:17), was based for a time at Caesarea Palestine where Mark composed his Gospel.²⁹ The Johannine mission was located in Palestine until a few years before the Jewish revolt³⁰ where it produced and used traditions and perhaps an Aramaic proto-Gospel.³¹ Afterward it was active at Ephesus where John composed our canonical Gospel.³² The Pauline mission, for whom Luke wrote his Gospel, was based initially at Antioch. But it ranged across the breadth of the Roman world and was situated successively at Ephesus, Caesarea Palestine, Rome and Spain.³³

---

out, 'preserved the true tradition (παράδοσιν) of the blessed teaching directly from Peter and James and John and Paul.'

²⁸ See above, 61, note 44. Cf. Ellis (note 7), 251n, 290f. Jesus traditions in James are closest in form and substance to the Gospel of Matthew. Peter is given more prominence in Matthew (esp. 10:2 ('first'); 15:15; 16:17–19; 17:24–27; 18:21; cf. Davies [note 8], II, 647–652) than in Mark, reflective of James' desire to give Peter full credit for his important role in the church. Probably also, in Mark, the Gospel initially of the Petrine mission, Peter would not wish to have his own role overly emphasized.

²⁹ Cf. Ellis, 'The Date and Provenance of Mark's Gospel' (note 7), 357–376, 369–372: Irenaeus (AH 3, 1, 1), commonly misread on this point, says only that Mark 'delivered' (παραδέδωκεν) his Gospel to Rome after Peter and Paul's departure' (ἔξοδον) to ministries elsewhere (360f.). The request by Roman Christians for a document of Jesus' word and work (Clement of Alexandria apud Eusebius HE 2, 15, 1) came during Peter's initial visit to Rome during Claudius' reign, probably in AD 53–54 (Hippolytus, Ref. 6, 20 = 6, 15; cf. Manson; Lietzmann). Mark returned to Caesarea and composed his Gospel in AD 55–58 from traditions then being read in congregations of the Petrine mission (cf. Mk 13:14). Cf. Ellis (note 7), 265, 357–372; T. W. Manson, Studies in the Gospels and Epistles, Manchester UK 1962, 39; H. Lietzmann, A History of the Early Church, 4 vols., Cleveland OH 1961 (1944), I, 111 = GT: I, 110.

³⁰ Ellis (note 7), 152, 234–237, 402; cf. J. B. Lightfoot, 'St. Paul and the Three,' St. Paul's Epistle to the Galatians, Peabody MA 1993 (¹⁰1892), 360; C. H. Dodd, Historical Traditions in the Fourth Gospel, Cambridge 1965, 245; M. Hengel, The Johannine Question, London 1989, 110–134 = GT: 276–325.

³¹ Cf. C. F. Burney, The Aramaic Origin of the Fourth Gospel, Oxford 1922, 27; C. C. Torrey, Our Translated Gospels, New York 1936, passim; W. H. Brownlee, 'Whence the Gospel According to John?' John and Qumran, ed. J. H. Charlesworth, London 1972, 185ff.; Ellis (note 7), 386n.

³² John's Gospel was composed 'at Ephesus in Asia' (Irenaeus), 'last of all' (Clement), 'in his old age' (Epiphanius); cf. Irenaeus, AH 3, 1, 1 = Eusebius HE 5, 8, 4; Clement Al. apud Eusebius, HE 6, 14, 5ff.; Epiphanius, Panarion 51, 12, 2; 51, 33, 7ff. Cf. Ellis (note 7), 152, 213f., 234–237.

³³ Cf. Ellis (note 7), 256–263, 266–284, 391n, 422–425. Re Paul's mission to Spain cf. Rom 15:24, 28; Acts 1:8; 13:47 (ἐσχάτου τῆς γῆς); I Clem 5:7 (τὸ τέρμα τῆς δύσεως); Muratorian Canon c; Acts of Peter (Vercelli) 1–3, 40; Epiphanius, Panarion 26, 6, 5. See above, Chapter Four, 53–63.

Luke's Gospel[34] best explains the historical relationship between the four canonical Gospels.[35] It alone contains such a variety of sources, encompassing the Gospel of Mark (or proto-Mark), traditions in common with the Gospel of Matthew (Q), traditions in common with the Gospel of John and traditions of the Jerusalem church.[36] Luke could have obtained access to all these sources on one occasion, and probably only one, that is, during his time in Palestine at Paul's collection visit, arrest and subsequent detention in Caesarea for trial, spring 58 to autumn 60.[37]

At that time the three other missions were active in the area. The fact that Luke utilized Mark's Gospel, along with other evidence, datelines Mark at Caesarea between AD 55–58.[38] In my judgment Luke employed only traditions from the Matthean and Johannine missions and not the Gospels of those missions; this dates the first and fourth Gospels later, at least in their Greek dress: Matthew in the early sixties[39] and John about AD 85–95.[40] John's Gospel incorporates some ten oral or written traditions that are Synoptic-like[41]

---

[34] On the date and authorship cf. Ellis (note 7), 389ff., 397–405.

[35] Cf. Ellis (note 7), 251f., 400–405; E. E. Ellis, *The Gospel of Luke*, Grand Rapids ⁷1996, 21–29, 67, 271f. On Luke's knowledge of Jerusalem cf. M. Hengel, *Between Jesus and Paul*, London 1983, 101, 109, 126ff.

[36] E.g. Lk 1–2; 24. Cf. Ellis, 'Luke-Acts: A Key to the History of Earliest Christianity' (note 7), 251–254; cf. 154–164, 181ff., 195–199, 389ff., 400–403.

[37] Cf. Acts 20:16; 27:12. The 'we' sections of Acts (16:10–17; 20:5–21:19; 27:1–28:16; cf. 1:1; Lk 1:2f.) in all probability refer to the author and thus place Luke with Paul at this time, whether or not he remained in Palestine during the whole two years. Cf. Ellis (note 7), 397f.; B. Witherington III, *The Acts of the Apostles*, Grand Rapids 1998, 53f.; C. J. Hemer, *The Book of Acts in the Setting of Hellenistic History*, Tübingen 1989, 312–334.

[38] See above, note 29. Mark composed his gospel in Caesarea after his visit to Rome with Peter during the reign of the emperor Claudius (†13 October 54) but before Luke's use of that Gospel between AD 58–60.

[39] None of the Synoptic Gospels display any knowledge of the fulfilment of Jesus' prediction of the AD 70 destruction of Jerusalem, and they present it totally in terms of Old Testament judgments, especially that of 586 BC (Dodd, Reicke). Equally, they know nothing of the Jerusalem Christians' flight to Pella about AD 66. Cf. C. H. Dodd, 'The Fall of Jerusalem and the "Abomination of Desolation,"' *More New Testament Studies*, Manchester UK 1968, 69–83; B. Reicke, 'Synoptic Prophecies on the Destruction of Jerusalem,' *Studies in New Testament and Early Christian Literature. FS A. P. Wingren*, ed. D. E. Aune, Leiden 1972, 125f.; Ellis (note 7), 288–292, 319, 375, 389ff.; idem (note 19), 227–233.

[40] See above, notes 31 and 32; Ellis (note 7), 16f., 289–292, 393f., 401f.

[41] I.e. Jn 1:19–34 (the Baptist); 2:13–22 (temple cleansing); 4:46–54 (healing official's son); 5:1–9 (healing at Bethesda); 6:1–15, 16–21 (feeding and walking on water); 9:1–7 (healing blind man); 12:1–8 (anointing); 12:12–19 (entry to Jerusalem); 18–20 (passion and resurrection narrative). Cf. Ellis (note 7), 154–162.

in substance or in form, but he probably did not use the Synoptic Gospels themselves[42] although he may have known them.

The Gospel authors' names (and the book titles) were probably attached only when more than one Gospel was being read in congregational worship, about the turn of the second century according to Bo Reicke.[43] Luke's name, however, would have been tagged to his work from the beginning when it was cataloged in the library of his patron, Theophilus.[44] In all probability the responsible authors are accurately identified by the Gospels. But in the composition of their Gospels all had secretarial help and, for Matthew and John at least, other co-worker assistants.[45] That no author's name was given in the Gospel text may point to the corporate nature of the authorship, or it may reflect only the Oriental custom of writing anonymously[46] and of giving priority to title over authorship.[47]

Traditions in the Letters

The New Testament letters were produced by the same four apostolic missions. But preformed pieces in them are less easy to recog-

---

[42] So, P. Gardner-Smith, *Saint John and the Synoptic Gospels*, Cambridge 1938, 31 (from the perspective of the classical form criticism); P. Borgen, 'The Independence of the Gospel of John,' *Early Christianity and Hellenistic Judaism*, Edinburgh 1996, 203f. (from the perspective of current form criticism). Cf. also B. Lindars, *Essays on John*, Leuven 1992, 92f.; G. Beasley-Murray, *John*, Waco TX 1987, xxxvii; S. S. Smalley, 'St. John's Gospel' *ET* 97 (1985–86), 103; D. M. Smith, *Johannine Christianity*, Columbia SC 1984, 170f.; E. Haenchen, *John*, 2 vols., Philadelphia 1984, I, 75f.; L. Morris, *Studies in the Fourth Gospel*, Grand Rapids 1969, 15–63. Otherwise: C. K. Barrett, *The Gospel According to John*, London ²1978, 45; F. Neirynck, *Evangelica II*, Leuven 1991, 571.

[43] B. Reicke, *The Roots of the Synoptic Gospels*, Philadelphia 1986, 150–155. M. Hengel (*Studies in the Gospel of Mark*, London 1985, 83f.; idem, *The Johannine Question*, London 1989, 74ff., 193 note 3) apparently places the titles at the Gospels' initial composition and use in worship.

[44] Ruth F. Strout ('The Development of the Catalog and Cataloging Codes,' *The Library Quarterly* 26 (1956), 254–275, 257) points out that the Greeks introduced cataloging by author. The Oriental practice was to catalog by subject or title. Cf. Ellis (note 7), 379; idem (note 35), 64f. See below, note 46.

[45] Cf. Mt 13:52 with 23:34; Jn 21:24 ('brothers'); Ellis (note 7), 36–39.

[46] Cf. M. Smith, 'Pseudepigraphy in Ancient Israelite Tradition,' *Pseudepigrapha I*, ed. K. von Fritz, Geneve 1972, 191–215 = idem, *The Cult of Yahweh*, 2 vols., Leiden 1996, I, 55–72: 'Israelite literature was originally and customarily anonymous,' including Ecclesiastes and the Wisdom of Solomon (210 = 68), and later misattributed to a famous name. Only under Greek influence did pseudepigrapha appear, apparently as the product of related sectarian groups (215 = 71f.).

[47] See above, note 44.

nize because, apart from Old Testament quotations, no antecedent forms or multiple uses of the same traditional pieces are extant.[48] However, following the pioneering work of Ernst Lohmeyer and Martin Dibelius,[49] many preformed pieces may be identified with a considerable degree of probability by the careful use of a number of criteria.

The task is to show that an episode or an underlying tradition was used in catechesis, sermons, liturgy and the like before it was incorporated into a New Testament letter. Significant criteria to do so are

1. the presence of formulas indicating that an antecedent tradition is being cited;[50]
2. the self-contained character of the passage vis-à-vis its context;[51]
3. the relative frequency of vocabulary, idiom, style or theological expression that differs both from the rest of the letter and from other letters of the same author;[52]
4. the presence of a highly similar piece in another contemporary writing by a different author with which no direct literary dependence is probable.[53]

---

[48] The closest is the common use of a pre-existing tradition in the 'rejected stone' theme in Rom 9:30–10:21 and in I Pet 2:4–8, expounding Isa 8:14; 28:16 (Ps 118:22). Cf. Ellis (note 7), 60, 136ff., 312f.; idem (note 2), 89f.; C. H. Dodd, *According to the Scriptures*, London 1952, 35f., 41f. See also Ellis (note 7), 82ff., on I Cor 14:34f.

[49] E. Lohmeyer (1890–1946), *Kurios Jesus*, Heidelburg ²1961 (1928); M. Dibelius (1883–1947) in his various commentaries.

[50] A number have the same introductory formulas that elsewhere introduce Old Testament quotations; cf., e.g. II Cor 1:7b; Eph 5:5; Jas 1:3; I Pet 1:18; II Pet 1:20; 3:3 with Jude 5 and Acts 2:30 (I Tim 1:9f.). Further, cf. Ellis (note 7), 64n, 99n, 119, 121, 135, 407–416; idem (note 4), 222ff.

[51] E.g. I Cor 13; II Cor 6:14–7:1.

[52] A striking example is τὸ πνεῦμα τὸ ἐκ τοῦ θεοῦ in the pericope I Cor 2:6–16; cf. Ellis (note 4), 25f., 156, 213–216; idem (note 7), 78f. Since the letters were composed in multiple copies—one retained by the author (Ellis) and probably one for the church from which the author wrote—and since transmission of the letter to other churches began almost immediately (Aland), theories of later interpolation (O'Neill, Walker) are without merit unless there is an extant manuscript lacking the passage in question. Cf. Ellis (note 7), 85f., 430; K. Aland, 'Neutestamentliche Textkritik und Exegese,' *Wissenschaft und Kirche. FS E. Löhse*, ed. K. Aland, Bielefeld 1989, 142; cf. Col 4:16. Cf. W. O. Walker, Jr., 'Romans 1.18–2.29: A Non-Pauline Interpolation?' *NTS* 45 (1999), 533–552, and the literature cited; J. C. O'Neill, *Paul's Letter to the Romans*, Baltimore MD 1975, passim; idem, *The Recovery of Paul's Letter to the Galatians*, London 1972, 6–15, passim.

[53] Cf., e.g. the arguments of Dodd (note 48) regarding the midrash on the rejected stone at Rom 9:33 and I Pet 2:6ff.; admonitions on true and false wisdom in I Cor 2:6–16 and in Jas 3:13–18; cf. Ellis (note 7), 67; the commonality (40%–80%

Of course, not all criteria will be present in a given case, and different New Testament authors may reshape a tradition to their particular interests and emphasis. But the criteria provide guidelines that serve as a check on subjective judgments.

The percentage of probable or highly possible preformed traditions in New Testament letters range from zero in Philemon to 72% in Jude.[54] Interestingly, almost all letters considered pseudo-Pauline or pseudo-Petrine by scholars in the Baur tradition[55] evidence a large percentage of preformed material: Ephesians 54%; Colossians 42%; I Timothy 43%; Titus 46%; I Peter 39%; II Peter 33% or 55%.[56] Exceptions are II Thessalonians (24%) and II Timothy (16%). Of course, the percentages are approximate, and conclusions may differ in the analysis of other literary critics. But it is fair to say, I think, that most New Testament letters contain a substantial amount of preformed traditions, a number of them not composed by the letter's author.

Such traditions include Old Testament expositions (midrashim),[57] household[58] and congregational[59] regulations, paraenesis,[60] catechesis,[61]

---

of the same terms or cognates) in vice lists in the Pauline, Petrine, Jacobean and Johannine missions; cf. Ellis (note 7), 59–69. See below, note 66.

[54] Cf. Ellis (note 7), 49–142, 139. Others are Romans, 27%; I Corinthians, 17%; II Corinthians, 11%; Galatians, 32%; Philippians, 7%; I Thessalonians, 37%; Hebrews, 37%; James, 12%. On I–III John cf. Ellis (note 7), 189–200.

[55] Cf. F. C. Baur, *Paul*, 2 vols., London 1875–76, I, 246–249; II, 106–111, passim = GT: I, 276–279; II, 116–122; A. Hilgenfeld, *Historisch—Kritische Einleitung in das Neue Testament*, Leipzig 1875, 246f., 328–348. Baur found genuine only Romans, I–II Corinthians, Galatians and Revelation. His associate, Hilgenfeld, added Philippians, I Thessalonians and Philemon. For a critique cf. Ellis, 'Ferdinand Christian Baur and his School' (note 7), 440–445; idem, 'Toward a History of Early Christianity' (note 19), 216–223.

[56] Depending on whether the two extensive midrashim, II Pet 1:20–2:22 and II Peter 3:3–13, are preformed pieces *en bloc* (= 55% of the letter) or whether they only made use of traditions, identifiable by formulas (= 33% of the letter), and were composed as a whole when the secretary prepared the epistle.

[57] E.g. Rom 4:1–25; I Cor 10:1–13; Gal 4:21c–5:1; cf. Ellis (note 7), 79ff., 96, 101f.; further, 117, 119, 120–130, 136ff. C. H. Dodd, *The Epistle of Paul to the Romans*, London ²1959, 161ff., was probably right in regarding the whole of Rom 9–11 as a preformed sermon [or sermons] of Paul 'incorporated here wholesale' (163).

[58] E.g. Eph 5:22–6:9; Col 3:18–4:1; I Pet 2:18f., 21b–25; 3:1–7.

[59] E.g. I Cor 11:3–16. Cf. I Thess 5:20f. with I Jn 4:1; I Cor 14:34f. with I Tim 2:9–12; I Pet 3:3–6; Ellis (note 7), 66ff, 82f.

[60] E.g. Gal 5:25–6:10; Eph 4:25–5:14. Cf. I Pet 2:18–3:7. Further, cf. Jas 1:3f. with Rom 5:3ff.; I Pet 1:6f.; Ellis (note 7), 102f., 119, 135.

[61] E.g. I Cor 8:6; Rom 5:12–21 (perhaps). Cf. Ellis (note 7), 96.

confessions,[62] hymns,[63] vice and virtue lists.[64] Ordinarily composed and originally utilized by and for the congregations of one mission (cf. Acts 13:1–3), they were, like Gospel traditions, shared at times with apostolic leaders of the other missions,[65] who (reworked and) used them and sometimes incorporated them or their motifs[66] into letters to their congregations. For example, the hymn to Christ in Phil 2:6–11 was probably created in Palestine, judging from the incarnation/exaltation, descent/ascent theme reminiscent of the theology of the Johannine mission and from stylistic and other features pointing to an Aramaic or Semitic-Greek background.[67] Paul founded no churches in Palestine, and the hymn is very likely non-Pauline.[68] It was obtained by Paul, probably in Caesarea, and later incorporated into his letter.

---

[62] E.g. I Cor 8:6; 12:4–11; 15:3–7; Eph 4:4a, 5f.; I Tim 2:5f.; 3:16; I Jn 3:2b; 4:2f. Confessions, hymns and catechesis overlap, and it is often uncertain just how a particular piece may have been used in the congregations.

[63] E.g. Phil 2:6–11; 3:20f.; Eph 1:3–14; Rev 4:8b; 5:9. Cf. I Tim 3:16 with I Pet 3:18, 22; Ellis (note 7), 68, 135f.

[64] E.g. Gal 5:19–23; Col 3:5–15; Jas 3:13–18. For vice lists only cf. Rom 1:29ff.; I Cor 6:9f.; I Tim 1:9f.; I Pet 4:3f.; Rev 9:20; 21:8; 22:15. Cf. Jude 8–13; Ellis (note 7), 61–64, 95, 106f., 109f., 232, 313, 407, 412.

[65] Cf. Ellis (note 7), 60–69, 310–314. See above, notes 53, 58, 59, 63.

[66] On a common response to antecedent motifs see above, note 53. Further, on suffering and vindication cf. Rom 5:3; 8:17; II Cor 1:7 with I Pet 1:6f.; 4:13; on the support of Christian workers cf. Mt 10:10 Q with I Pet 5:2; I Cor 9:9–14; Gal 6:6; I Tim 5:17f.

[67] John's mission was based in Palestine before c. AD 66; cf. Ellis (note 7), 164, 234–237. Cf. J. A. Fitzmyer, 'The Aramaic Background of Phil 2:6–11,' *CBQ* 50 (1988), 470–483; R. P. Martin, *Carmen Christi*, Cambridge 1967, 38–41. Lohmeyer (note 49), 73, concludes that the origin of the hymn is to be sought 'in circles of the oldest primitive Christian congregations,' not excluding Jerusalem. Otherwise: G. Strecker, *Theologie des Neuen Testaments*, Berlin 1996, 78: 'The hymn apparently originates in a prePauline hellenistic Jewish Christianity.' For Johannine affinities cf. Jn 1:14; 3:13; 6:38, 42, 62; Rev 1:17f. Also favoring the preformed character of the hymn is the fact that it goes far beyond the needs of the present context, i.e. Christ's servant attitude as an example for Christian conduct and disposition, to include also an incarnation/exaltation christology. See below, 149f.

[68] Cf. O. Hofius, *Die Christushymnus Philipper 2.6–11*, Tübingen ²1991, 1; M. Silva, *Philippians*, Chicago 1988, 105. Otherwise: M. Dibelius, *An die Thessalonischer I, II. An die Philipper*, Tübingen ³1937, 73 (preformed, Pauline).

CHAPTER NINE

IMPLICATIONS OF PREFORMED TRADITIONS FOR THE AUTHORSHIPS AND DATES OF THE LETTERS

The Nature of Authorship

Numerous preformed traditions in New Testament letters, many non-authorial,[69] raise doubts about the adequacy of internal literary criteria to test their authorship. The influence of the secretary[70] and sometimes of co-senders,[71] difficult matters to measure, make such internal criteria more doubtful. These factors require the historian to give more weight to the authorships stated in the letters and to second-century external evidence. They are also significant for the nature of authorship.

It has been traditionally assumed that the author penned the letter himself or dictated it verbatim. The literary and historical evidence shows, however, that authorship was more a corporate enterprise in which the author employed co-worker secretaries and pieces composed by others in the letter that went out over his name.[72]

Dating the Documents

Preformed traditions, particularly the biblical expositions and the vice lists, also have implications for the dating of the New Testament documents. Biblical expositions, using patterns similar to the proem and *yelammedenu rabbenu* midrashim found in the rabbis,[73] appear both in Gospel traditions[74] and in the epistolary traditions of three apos-

---

[69] E.g. I Cor 2:6–16; II Cor 6:14–7:1; Phil 2:6–11. Cf. Ellis (note 4), 25f.; idem (note 7), 78f., 99f. See above, notes 65 and 66.

[70] Quintilian (*Orat.* 10, 3, 19), who states that he rejects the 'fashionable' use of a secretary, reveals what the common practice was. Indeed, the use of a secretary was a virtual necessity in ancient letter writing, and his role could vary from taking dictation to being a co-author. Cf. E. R. Richards, *The Secretary in the Letters of Paul*, Tübingen 1991, 23–67; O. Roller, *Das Formular der paulinischen Briefe*, Stuttgart 1933, 17–20, who estimates that, because of the poor quality of writing materials—reed pen, poor ink, rough-surface papyrus, a skilled secretary could compose less than one page per hour (13f.).

[71] Cf. I Cor 1:1; II Cor 1:1; Gal 1:1f.; Phil 1:1; Col 1:1; I Thess 1:1; II Thess 1:1; Plm 1; Ellis (note 7), 39, 245; S. Byrskog, 'Co-Senders, Co-Authors and Paul's Use of the First Person Plural,' *ZNTW* 87 (1996), 230–250.

[72] Cf. Ellis (note 7), 39–42.

[73] Cf. W. G. Braude, *Pesikta Rabbati*, 2 vols., New Haven CT 1968, I, 3ff.

[74] See above, 108f., 130f., 134.

tolic missions—Jacobean,[75] Pauline[76] and Petrine.[77] But in Christian documents that can be clearly dated after AD 70, e.g. the Epistle of Barnabas,[78] the Old Testament expositions, while employing certain Jewish techniques, do not appear to use such midrashic patterns.

Traditioned vice lists in all four missions,[79] based on the Ten Commandments and apparently with one root in a dominical teaching,[80] emphasize vices of sexual immorality and/or of idolatry, and they are sometimes directed against the teaching of opponents. They point to the broader question of the nature of the opposition or false teaching reflected in the letters of the four apostolic missions.

The New Testament letters do not picture the errors of the false teachers in precisely the same terms or as involving the same individuals. But they describe them with sufficient similarity to make probable that the same type of opposition is in view. The opponents can rightly be called gnosticizing Judaizers,[81] who were not isolated

---

[75] Jas 2:20–26; cf. Jude 5b–19; Ellis (note 7), 119, 258f.; idem (note 4), 221–236.

[76] E.g. Rom 4:1–25; I Cor 2:6–16; 10:1–13; Gal 3:6–14; 4:21–5:1. Cf. Ellis (note 7), 96, 78–81, 103, 101f.; idem (note 4), 217f.; idem (note 9), 98f.

[77] II Pet 1:20–2:22 and 3:3–13 are similar to the proem midrash in that they open (2:1ff.; 3:3f.) and close (2:22; 3:13) with cited sacred texts and contain supporting biblical texts and commentary joined by catch-words. But the opening texts, introduced by formulas, appear to be cited Christian prophecy. The Johannine letters and Revelation have 'midrash pesher' formulas and other Jewish exegetical terminology, but they do not use the proem or *yelammedenu rabbenu* patterns. Cf. Ellis (note 7), 54–57, 120–133, 189f., 193ff. See above, 106–111.

[78] The Epistle of Barnabas (16:3f.; c. AD 70–79) clearly refers to the destruction of Jerusalem and cites the Old Testament frequently. He uses some Jewish techniques of quotation but does not employ the proem, *yelammedenu* or similar midrashic patterns, nor do other diaspora Christian writings such as the Didaché (AD 60–90), I Clement (AD 68–70) or the letters of Ignatius (c. AD 110) or of Polycarp (c. AD 110). A midrashic pattern of exegesis was used by the Christian Persian sage, Aphraates (c. AD 300–350), who was apparently trained in exegetical method to some degree by a Jewish sage. Cf. L. Ginsberg, 'Aphraates, The Persian Sage' *JE* 1 (1901), 663ff.; G. Weil and M. Plessner, 'Afraates,' *EJ* I (1928), 932f. But see J. Neusner, *Aphrahat and Judaism*, Atlanta GA 1999 (1971), 6, 150–158, 187ff. Cf. P. Schaff *et al.*, edd., *The Nicene and Post-Nicene Fathers. Second Series*, 14 vols., Grand Rapids 1961 (1890–1900), 13 (1898), 345–412. Cf. Ellis (note 7), 182n.

[79] See above, note 64.

[80] Mk 7:20ff. = Mt 15:18ff. Similar lists are present at Qumran (IQS 10:21–26) and in Philo (*de sacrif. Abel.* 22, 27 = 77f., 88ff.; ? *de confus. Ling.* 24 = 117f.). Cf. Ellis (note 7), 232f.

[81] By gnosticizing I mean their claims and evident experience of extraordinary powers—visions, miracle working, ecstasies, that made them impressive promoters of their claim to have and to convey a divine gift of γνῶσις. Cf. I Cor 12:8: 'word

teachers but who formed a fifth mission,⁸² that also claimed apostolic credentials,⁸³ in opposition to the allied missions of James, John, Paul and Peter. The common opposition reflected in the various New Testament letters strongly suggests that this literature was produced in the same general chronological period. But for a more specific dating of the documents, other evidence would have to be considered.⁸⁴

IMPLICATIONS OF PREFORMED TRADITIONS FOR PAULINE CHRISTOLOGY

The Body of Christ and the Temple of God

Traditioned pieces used in the expression of Paul's christology may be classified as (1) those from the earthly Jesus and (2) other preformed christological concepts. An explicit reference to Jesus' christological teachings concerns the Last Supper. At that event Jesus symbolically identified his body and his covenant blood with the bread and wine that he directs his disciples to partake.⁸⁵ In I Cor 11:23–26, Paul both cites this tradition and defines it as a proclamation of 'the Lord's death until he comes' (11:26). In I Cor 10:16f.

---

of knowledge;' II Cor 11:3–6, 12–15; 12:1, 11f.; I Tim 6:20: 'knowledge falsely so called.' By Judaizers I refer to that wing of the ritually strict Jewish Christians who insisted that Gentile Christians must follow the ritual law of Moses. Cf. Ellis, 'The Circumcision Party and the Early Christian Mission' (note 4), 116–128. For similarities between the opponents of Paul and of Peter; of Paul and of James; of Paul and of John cf. Ellis (note 7), 130ff., 316ff.; 130, 258f., 316ff.; 202–208, 217ff., 315–318. On their character as an opposing mission and not as isolated teachers cf. Ellis (note 7), 314–318; idem (note 4), 101–115.
⁸² See above, note 81.
⁸³ In II Cor 10–13 Paul calls the opponents 'pseudo-apostles' (11:13), but he does not deny that they had been commissioned by Jesus. They are 'Hebraists' with roots in strict Palestinian Judaism (11:22). Probably they were apostles of Jesus Christ who, like Judas, perverted their calling. Cf. Ellis, 'Paul and His Opponents' (note 4), 80–115, 89–95, 102–115.
⁸⁴ E.g. the stated authorships, supported by some early patristic witnesses, and the absence of any references to the AD 70 destruction of Jerusalem in letters stressing divine judgment on ungodliness, e.g. Hebrews, II Peter, Jude, suggest a pre-70 date for them. Cf. Ellis (note 7), 307–319.
⁸⁵ Cf. Mt 26:26ff.; Mk 14:22ff.; Lk 22:19f. Paul and Luke are closer to one another and may represent the independent use of the same traditional piece. Cf. W. Schrage, *Die erste Brief an die Korinther*, 4 vols., Neukirchen 1991–, III (1999), 9; G. D. Fee, *The First Epistle to the Corinthians*, Grand Rapids 1987, 546f.; Ellis (note 35), 249–252, 254ff.; J. Jeremias, *The Eucharistic Words of Jesus*, Philadelphia ⁴1977, 96–105, 111–114 = GT: 90–99, 105–108.

he explains theologically the actions of blessing the cup and breaking the bread at the Lord's Supper (and the subsequent common partaking) as a participation in the shed blood[86] and in the crucified body of Christ. The Apostle later identifies a participation in the Lord's Supper without discerning 'the body' makes one liable for the body and the blood, i.e. the death of the Lord.[87]

The body here refers to the 'body of Christ' manifest in the congregation, in agreement with Paul's admonitions in the context and with his teachings elsewhere that believers are 'the body of Christ.'[88] Paul's teaching on the church as the corporate body of Christ is an important theme in his letters, and it is once introduced as a tradition that he had taught the congregation previously.[89] It has its roots not only in the general Old Testament background of corporate personality[90] but more specifically in the traditioned teaching of Jesus at the Last Supper.[91]

A second christological theme that is rooted in the teaching of Jesus is Paul's temple typology. It is expressed in two somewhat different images. The first is Christ as the rejected temple stone, a conception found in a tradition underlying Rom 9:32f. and I Pet 2:4–8[92] and derived to some degree from Jesus' exposition of Isa 5 (Mt 21:33–44 T + Q).[93] The second and more complex image appears in traditioned pieces that identify (the corporate) Christ and Christians as the eschatological temple of God. Both themes are introduced with formulas that point to previously traditioned teaching.[94]

---

[86] A. M. Stibbs in his *The Meaning of the Word 'Blood' in Scripture* (London 1962, 29–32) rightly argues that 'blood' in this context is that which is poured out in death and refers to the sacrifice of Christ that pays for sin and secures the forgiveness of God.

[87] I Cor 11:27–34, 27.

[88] I Cor 11:20ff.; 12:27; Eph 1:22f.; 4:7–16, 12, 16; 5:29–32; Col 3:15; cf. Rom 12:4f.; I Cor 6:15. Cf. Ellis (note 7), 72ff.; idem (note 19), 174f.; Schrage (note 85), III (1999), 5–107, 51; Fee (note 85), 562ff. and the literature cited.

[89] Cf. I Cor 6:15f.: οὐκ οἴδατε ὅτι. Cf. Rom 11:2; Ellis (note 7), 73.

[90] Cf. S. W. Aaron Son, 'Corporate Elements in Pauline Anthropology,' Ph.D. Diss., Ft. Worth TX: Southwestern Seminary, 1999, 133–136; J. S. Kaminsky, *Corporate Responsibility in the Hebrew Bible*, Sheffield UK 1995, 16–29, passim, and the literature cited. See above, 118, notes 80 and 81.

[91] Cf. Lk 22:19f. with 22:28: μετ' ἐμοῦ; Ellis, 'Jesus' Use of the Old Testament and the Genesis of New Testament Theology;' 'Eschatology in Luke Revisited;' 'Present and Future Eschatology in Luke' (note 19), 29ff., 119n, 126n, 123n, 144n.

[92] See above, note 48; cf. Ellis (note 7), 74–77.

[93] Cf. Mt 21:42 (Ps 118:22f.), 44 (Dan 2:34f., 44f.). See above, note 8.

[94] See above, note 89. E.g. II Cor 5:1: οἴδαμεν ὅτι; I Cor 3:16: οὐκ οἴδατε ὅτι.

Jesus' identification of himself as God's temple, i.e. the locus of God's self-manifestation,[95] occurred during his teachings at Jerusalem with the enigmatic words, 'Destroy this temple and in three days I will raise it up.'[96] This saying, understood by all hearers to refer to the Jerusalem temple, became the grounds for a charge against Jesus at his trial.[97] According to Jn 2:21f. only after his resurrection did his disciples, his pupils, realize that he spoke of his body as God's temple. It was apparently Stephen, the Hellenist prophet and forerunner of that mission, who first saw the broader implication of this aspect of Jesus' teaching. He contrasts in Acts 7 the temple of the old covenant with the new creation that is 'not made with hands' in which God dwells with the one who is 'humble and contrite in spirit.'[98] Both Paul and Peter, and their respective missions, express and elaborate this thought to affirm that the church is not only Christ's corporate body but also the eschatological temple of God.

Several preformed christological traditions in Paul's letters appear to have no antecedent, at least no direct antecedent, in Jesus' teachings. A number may be mentioned here: I Cor 8:6; 10:1–13; Phil 2:6–11; Col 1:15–20;[99] I Tim 3:16. We shall look in more detail at the first three.

I Cor 8:6

Of three traditioned christological pieces in I Corinthians (8:6; 12:4–11;[100] 15:3–7)[101] I Cor 8:6 is notable for its *Deus/Christus Creator*

Cf. Ellis, 'The Structure of Pauline Eschatology' (note 19), 147–164; idem, 'Isaiah and the Eschatological Temple' (note 19), 52–61.

[95] Traditionally Judaism identified this locus as the holy of holies in the Jerusalem temple. Cf. Exod 25:22; Lev 16:2; A. Edersheim, *The Temple*, Grand Rapids 1950, 313f.

[96] Jn 2:19. Bultmann regarded this form of the saying as the relatively more original. Cf. R. Bultmann, *The Gospel of John*, London 1971, 126 = GT: 89.

[97] Mk 14:58 par. Cf. D. Catchpole, *The Trial of Jesus*, Leiden 1971, 126–130; Ellis, 'Deity Christology in Mark 14:58' (note 19), 44–51.

[98] Isa 66:1f.; Acts 7:47–50; cf. Mk 14:58 and II Cor 5:1: ἀχειροποίητον; I Pet 2:5. Cf. Ellis, 'Isaiah and the Eschatological Temple' (note 19), 56–61.

[99] Cf. E. E. Ellis, '*Christus Creator, Christus Salvator*: Expounding Colossians 1:12–20,' *Textbook on Exegetical Method. FS H. Hoehner*, edd. B. Fanning and D. Bock, Wheaton IL 2006, forthcoming.

[100] Cf. Ellis (note 7), 90; Schrage (note 85), III, 136f.

[101] Cf. Ellis (note 7), 90f.; P. Stuhlmacher, *Das paulinische Evangelium*, Göttingen 1968, 266–276; but see Fee (note 85), 722–731.

theme.¹⁰² Introduced by a brief formulaic ἀλλά,¹⁰³ it has a balanced parallelism that breaks the flow of Paul's argument and is similar in form and idiom to traditioned pericopes elsewhere, e.g. Rom 11:36; Eph 4:4ff. and Col 1:15–20. It also goes beyond the theme of the context to include *Deus/Christus Salvator*: 'we for him;' 'we through him.'

The formulation of I Cor 8:6 is similar to the Stoic affirmation about the Logos or Cosmic Soul: 'From (ἐκ) you are all things (πάντα), in you are all things, for (εἰς) you are all things.'¹⁰⁴ It is even closer in Jewish writers. Philo apparently took over the phraseology from the Stoics.¹⁰⁵ And the Wisdom of Solomon (9:1f.) speaks of God, 'who made all things by your Word (τὰ πάντα ἐν λόγῳ σου) and by your wisdom (σοφίᾳ) formed man.' Paul's usage probably arises (1) from this Jewish background, (2) from Jesus' teachings that associate or identify him with divine wisdom,¹⁰⁶ (3) from Paul's and his co-workers' christological exegesis, and (4) from the Apostle's Damascus-road experience.¹⁰⁷

The wider use in Paul's letters of traditioned pieces with similar expressions,¹⁰⁸ together with the background, literary form and context of the present passage, argue that I Cor 8:6 is a preformed confession incorporated at this point in the epistle both to underscore the supremacy of God the Father and of the Lord Jesus Christ over idols and over any demonic powers behind them and also to assert that Christ is the mediator of and thus the Lord over the present Genesis creation. The latter has been questioned in recent christological studies.¹⁰⁹ But the whole point of Paul's argument concerns

---

¹⁰² Cf. Ellis (note 7), 87–90.

¹⁰³ The term is also an introductory formula for Old Testament citations at Rom 9:7; 12:20; Gal 3:12, 16. Cf. Ellis, *Paul's Use* (note 2), 160, 180, 182.

¹⁰⁴ Marcus Aurelius, *Meditations* 4, 23; Chrysippos in Stobaeus, *Eklogai* 1, 1, 26, cited in E. Norden, *Agnostos Theos*, Darmstadt 1956 (1913), 240, 241f.

¹⁰⁵ Cf. Philo, *quod deterius potiori insidiari soleat* 54; *de cherubim* 127; *de sacrif. Abel.* 8 (III).

¹⁰⁶ Lk 7:35 Q; Mt 12:42 Q; S. Kim, '*The "Son of Man"' as the Son of God*, Tübingen 1983, 90ff.; idem, *The Origin of Paul's Gospel*, Tübingen ²1984, 219ff., 245f.

¹⁰⁷ Kim, *Origin* (note 106), 223–233, 225: 'this understanding [by Paul] of Jesus Christ really took place at the Damascus christophany (or shortly thereafter, but, in any case, in the light of it), ...'

¹⁰⁸ E.g. Rom 11:33–36; Col 1:16; Eph 4:5f.; cf. Heb 2:10; Rom 3:30.

¹⁰⁹ E.g. J. D. G. Dunn, *Christology in the Making*, Grand Rapids ³1996, 179–183; idem, *The Theology of Paul*, Grand Rapids 1998, 272–275, cf. 290ff. But see O. Hofius, 'Einer is Gott—Einer is Herr,' *Eschatologie und Schöpfung*, edd. M. Evang *et al.*, Berlin 1997, 95–108, 108.

the present creation and its gifts. The 'all things' that come from the one God the Father are no different from the 'all things' that come through the one Lord Jesus Christ.

I Cor 10:1–13

I Cor 10:1–13 has a less clearly defined expository pattern than some other Pauline midrashim. But its opening summary of Exodus events (10:1–5) and its interpretive explanation of the one explicit biblical quotation (10:7) reveal its commentary form. This, its self-contained character, and its broadening of the question of food offered to idols to the more general question of idolatry lend probability to Wayne Meeks' view that the passage is 'a literary unit, very carefully composed prior to its use in its present context.'[110]

The christological question becomes explicit when the 'spiritual' following rock giving water to the Israelites in the wilderness is called Christ (10:4). By metonomy the miraculous work of God in the Old Testament can be called by the name God. But here the Rock is identified typologically[111] and surprisingly not with God but with Christ, and it is related to the typological character of other Exodus events of redemption and judgment (10:6, 11). Paul goes on to warn the Corinthians, 'Neither let us tempt Christ (Χριστόν, p^{46} D) as some of [the Israelites] tempted him' (10:9). Thus, he places Christ both at the Exodus and in the present reality at Corinth. In a change of mind[112] I now agree with Anthony Hanson that 'the real presence of the pre-existent Jesus' is Paul's meaning in I Cor 10:4.[113] If so, this preformed piece is a very early witness to the church's confession of the pre-existent Christ and, like I Cor 8:6 and Col 1:15–20, it may be related to a wisdom christology.[114]

---

[110] W. A. Meeks, '"And Rose up to Play:" Midrash and Paraenesis in I Corinthians 10:1–22,' *JSNT* 16 (1982), 65. Cf. Ellis (note 7), 79ff.; idem (note 19), 89f.

[111] Cf. L. Goppelt, 'τύπος,' *TDNT* 8 (1972), 251f. According to Goppelt 'type' is used 'technically [as an] "advanced presentation" intimating eschatological events.' See above, 115–118.

[112] Cf. Ellis, *Paul's Use* (note 2), 131.

[113] A. T. Hanson, *Jesus Christ in the Old Testament*, London 1965, 6f., 17ff., 172–178. Cf. Ellis, 'ΧΡΙΣΤΟΣ in I Cor 10:4, 9' (note 19), 89–94.

[114] Cf. Ellis (note 19), 92f.; II Cor 8:9 (γινώσκετε γὰρ ὅτι); above, note 99.

Phil 2:6-11

Phil 2:6-11 has been explained christologically in two principal ways, as a purely Adam/Christ typology like that e.g. in Rom 5:12-21 and I Cor 15:22-55,[115] and as an incarnation/exaltation christology that presupposes Christ's deity.[116] While there are some similarities to Paul's contrast between existence in Adam and in Christ, in the flesh and in the Spirit,[117] the major thrust of this hymn is quite different.

Even if J. B. Lightfoot's philosophical analogies may be questioned, his arguments and conclusion remain persuasive. The phrases, 'in the form of God' (ἐν μορφῇ θεοῦ) and 'the being equal with God' (τὸ εἶναι ἴσα θεῷ), 'must apply to the attributes of the Godhead' in the pre-incarnate Lord.[118]

The second half of the hymn (2:9-11) supports this view of the matter. It attributes to the exalted Christ 'the name that is above every name' and applies to him the obeisance due only to Yahweh (Isa 45:23) and the confession, 'Every knee shall bow . . . and every tongue confess that JESUS CHRIST IS YAHWEH to the glory of God the Father.'[119] On an Adam/Christ typology this conclusion would yield only an adoptionist christology, man becoming God. The better reading, that fits both the structure and language as well as the theology of the hymn, is an incarnation/exaltation, descent/ascent christological understanding. This understanding of Jesus as (also) a preexistent divine figure is, as Hengel has argued, the same christology that Paul had preached in Philippi c. AD 50, 'and one is tempted to say that more happened [in christology] in this

---

[115] E.g. Dunn, *Christology* (note 109), 114-121. But see C. A. Wanamaker in *NTS* 33 (1987), 179-193. R. J. Bauckham (*God Crucified*, Grand Rapids ²1999, 56-69) sees the Isaian Servant as the primary analogy or typology in Phil 2:6-11 (58-61).
[116] For the literature, interpretive options and discussion cf. P. T. O'Brien, *The Epistle to the Philippians*, Grand Rapids 1991, 186-271.
[117] E.g. Rom 8:9-17; 12:2; 13:14; Eph 4:22-24; Col 3:1ff., 9f., 12ff. Cf. E. E. Ellis, *Pauline Theology: Ministry and Society*, Lanham MD ⁴1998, 7-17.
[118] J. B. Lightfoot, *Saint Paul's Epistle to the Philippians*, Peabody MA 1993 (¹⁸1913), 127-133, 132. Similar, Strecker (note 67), 77. Cf. II Cor 8:9.
[119] Cf. Phil 2:11 with Isa 45:23; C. A. Gieschen, *Angelomorphic Christology*, Leiden 1998, 337ff., 350; D. B. Capes, *Old Testament Yahweh Texts in Paul's Christology*, Tübingen 1992, 157-160, 164f. B. F. Westcott and F. J. A. Hort, *The New Testament in the Original Greek*, Cambridge 1891, 440, and E. Nestle, *Novum Testamentum Graece*, Stuttgart ²⁴1960, placed ΚΥΡΙΟΣ ΙΗΣΟΥΣ ΧΡΙΣΤΟΣ in caps, indicating their conviction of the deity connotation of the phrase.

period of less than two decades than in the whole of the next seven centuries' (2).[120]

In I Cor 8:6 also Paul, using a preformed tradition, distinguishes, in binitarian fashion, deity from deity in terms of 'God the Father' and 'Lord.'[121] In this respect he stands in the Jewish tradition of what Aubrey Johnson called *The One and the Many in the Israelite Conception of God* (Cardiff 1961), i.e. the Old Testament teaching that God is a corporate and not a unitary being. The 'oneness' (אחד, Dt 6:4) of God was no more unitarian than the 'oneness' of Adam and Eve (Gen 2:24).[122] Probably Jewish unitarian monotheism was a development in Rabbinic Judaism, apparently in reaction to Christianity. In I Cor 8:6 and in other passages[123] the Apostle supplies us with the raw material that will later be refined and defined in the church's doctrine of the Trinity. This deity christology is not a later development of early catholicism or even of a pagan-influenced early Christianity. Nor is it limited to the Pauline mission alone. It lies at the beginnings of the church's confessions, even in the preformed traditions used by the Apostle Paul.

---

[120] M. Hengel, *The Son of God*, London 1976, 1f. = GT: 11.

[121] Elsewhere the contrast may be between God and Lord (I Cor 12:5f.; II Cor 13:14) or between God the Father and Son (I Cor 15:24–28).

[122] Cf. Ellis, 'God: Unity in Plurality' (note 9), 112–116. For current discussion on the nature of first-century Jewish monotheism cf. Bauckham (note 115); Gieschen (note 119); F. C. Holmgren, *The Old Testament and the Significance of Jesus*, Grand Rapids 1999, 139–160, and the literature cited.

[123] E.g. I Cor 12:4–6; II Cor 13:14; Eph 4:4a, 5f. Cf. Ellis (note 7), 88, 90, 106; idem (note 19), 3–94.

INDEX OF PASSAGES

I. OLD TESTAMENT

Genesis

1–7	107
1:27	108, 122, 124, 128
2:24	108, 110, 116, 122, 124, 128, 150
15:6	112
16:11	105
18:10	106, 110
21	107, 110
21:10	104, 106
21:12	106, 110

Exodus

3:6	127
3:15	127
20	116
20:10	127, 131
22:29	95
25:22	146

Leviticus

2:1ff.	126
16:2	146
18:5	108
19:18	108, 116
24:9	127

Numbers

3:11ff.	95
28:9	131

Deuteronomy

6:4	150
6:5	108
6:6f.	12
11:19f.	12
13:1ff.	129
13:1–5	129
19:15	102
24	124
24:1	109, 124
24:1–4	128
24:3	124

Judges

13:5	104
13:7	104

I Samuel

15:28	127
21:1–6	127
21:6	131

II Samuel

7	111
7:6–16	111f.
7:12–16	105, 112, 119
7:14	115

I Kings

2:27	100

II Chronicles

13:22	103
24:27	103
35:12	100

Ezra

6:13	104

Esther

—	122

Job

1:6	90
5:13	108

Psalms

2:7	115, 126
8	111, 116
8:4	116
8:4ff.	112
8:5f.	116
8:6ff.	116

32:1f.	126	52:4	32
79:6	99	52:13	33
82:6	126		
94:11	108	*Ezekiel*	
110	111	1:26ff.	116
110:1	105, 111	28:12–15	91
118:22	139	34:11	112
118:22f.	108, 130, 145		
132:11	81	*Daniel*	
147:9	126	—	229
		2:19	111
Ecclesiastes		2:24	111
—	17, 122, 138	2:34f.	108, 130, 145
12:14	123	2:44f.	108, 130, 145
		5:25f.	110
Isaiah		7:13	105, 111
—	108	7:13f.	105, 116, 127
2:2	113	7:14	105
3:25f.	32	7:27	116
4:3	105	9:2	111
5	130, 145	9:22f.	111
5:1f.	108, 130	9:27	32
5:2	108, 130	10:13	91
6:1–9:7	103, 105	10:14	113
7:13f.	105	12:2f.	113
7:14	103, 105	12:8f.	15
8:8	103	12:11	32
8:10	103		
8:14	139	*Hosea*	
9:6f.	105	6:6	131
9:11	103	11:1	112
9:14f.	110	14:1	32
11:1	104		
14:12	91	*Joel*	
28:16	139	2:28	110
29:3	32	2:32	49
45:23	149	3:5	49
49:6	54, 61, 104		
52:13	104	*Amos*	
60:21	104	9:11f.	115
62:12	105		
65:17	107	*Micah*	
66:1f.	146	4:1	113
66:22	107		
		Nahum	
Jeremiah		3:10	32
4:3	112		
6:22	55	*Zechariah*	
10:25	99	1:9f.	110
11:20	99	3:1	90
20:4f.	32		
31:31	110		

II. New Testament

Matthew

—	11f., 33, 36, 39, 41, 44, 46, 49, 101, 121, 128ff., 130f., 133f., 135–138
1:23	103
2:1–23	105, 135
2:15	112
2:23	104
3:1–17	134
3:2	113
3:3	24
3:10ff.	113
3:17	115
4:1–11	3
4:5ff.	122
4:6	101
4:14	99
5	126
5:17	40
5:17f.	122, 125
5:21	123
5:21f.	124, 135
5:27	123
5:31	123
5:31f.	124, 129, 135
5:33	123
5:38	123
5:43	123, 125
7:15	50
7:28f.	129
8:1–4	134
8:28–34	134
9:1–8	134
10:2	136
10:10	141
11:2–6	131
11:7–15	131, 134
11:15	15
12:1	131
12:1–8	130, 134
12:2	131
12:3	101
12:3f.	131
12:4f.	131
12:5	101
12:5f.	131
12:6	131
12:7	131
12:7f.	131
12:8	131
12:22–32	134
12:24	92
12:28	113
12:32	113
12:42	147
13	135
13:10–13	111
13:11	120
13:52	138
13:54	129
15:1–9	130, 134
15:4	15
15:6	125
15:18ff.	143
16:13–20	127
16:15ff.	15
16:17	120
16:17ff.	136
17:24–27	136
19:3ff.	108
19:3–9	108, 116, 124, 129, 130, 134, 135
19:4	101
19:4f.	122f.
19:4–8	128
19:5	118
19:6	108
19:7f.	109
19:8	109
21:1–16	135
21:15f.	134
21:33	108, 130
21:33–44	108, 112, 130, 134, 145
21:34–41	108, 130
21:35	108, 130
21:42	108, 130, 145
21:42ff.	108, 130
21:44	108, 130, 145
22:7	33
22:29	100, 120, 123
22:23–33	123, 134
22:33	129
22:37	11
23:34	138
24:1ff.	117
24:4–31	134
24:15	32
24:15–22	32
25:15	104
26:26ff.	118, 144

26:63f.	127	1:2	13
26:64	104	1:2f.	137
27:8	32	1:5–2:52	39
27:9	100	1:26–38	105
27:58	24	1:27	105
28:15	32	1:31	105
28:19	55	1:32	105
		1:33	105
Mark		1:35	105
—	11f., 33, 39, 41, 49, 121, 128ff., 131, 133–138	1:46–55	105
		1:68–79	105
		2:32	54
1:1	25	3:1	53
1:2	100	3:4	88
1:17	119	4:16f.	101
1:21–28	134	4:21	101
2:23–28	130	4:29	36
3:22	129	4:44	53
4:1–20	112	6:1–5	127, 130
4:10ff.	129	6:22	36
4:11	120	7:3	70
5:21–43	134	7:35	147
7:13	125	8:10	15
7:20ff.	143	9:44f.	15
8:11	129	10:7	87
8:31	104	10:9	89, 113
9:41–48	135	10:17–20	89
10:30	113	10:18	90
12:1f.	99	10:25ff.	108
12:1–12	129f.	10:25–37	108, 112, 130, 134
12:18–27	123, 129	10:27	108
12:24	122f.	10:28	108
12:26	100	10:29	108
12:28–34	129	10:29–36	108
12:35ff.	129	10:36	108
12:36	100	10:37	108
13	105	12:24	126
13:5–27	111	15–16	135
13:14	32, 136	15:3–6	112
13:14–20	32	17:26–30	117
13:26	111	18:33	104
14:22ff.	144	19:42ff.	32
14:58	116, 119, 146	20:9–19	130
14:61f.	127	20:21	88
14:62	105, 111, 116	20:27–40	123
		20:34f.	113
Luke		20:37f.	127
—	11f., 32f., 39, 40f., 46, 48f., 63, 88, 89, 92, 121, 128ff., 130f., 133–138	21:15	111
		21:20–24	32
		21:24	32
		22:19f.	144f.
1–2	137	22:20	115
1:1–4	93	22:27	85a

INDEX OF PASSAGES

22:28	145	1:1	58, 137
22:29	115	1:1–7:60	53
23:27	85a	1:8	54–58, 60f., 63, 71f., 136
23:42f.	116		
23:43	39	2:3	81
24	137	2:4	110
		2:14	70
John		2:16f.	110
—	11f., 33f., 37ff., 41, 44, 46, 49, 51, 101, 121, 128, 131, 133–138	2:17–21	61
		2:17–35	111
		2:30	139
		2:34f.	111
		3:12	70
1:14	141	3:22f.	115
1:19–34	137	3:22ff.	120
1:44	45	3:22–26	104
2:13–22	137	4:25ff.	119
2:18–22	116	4:35ff.	88
2:19	146	4:36	89
2:19ff.	119	5:3	70
2:19–22	33	6:1	76, 93
2:21f.	146	6:2	80
3:13	141	6:6	88
3:14	104	6:9	58
4:46–54	137	6:13f.	33
5:1–9	137	7	41, 146
6:1–15	137	7:47–50	33, 146
6:16–21	137	7:48	33
6:35	118	7:58	36
6:38	141	8:1	37
6:42	141	8:1–11:18	53
6:54	118	8:14	70
6:62	141	8:16	118
7:38	100	8:26	24
7:42	115	8:26–40	58
9	36f.	8:28	58
9:1–7	137	8:30	101
9:22	36	8:39	58
10:34ff.	126	9:4f.	118
10:35	122, 125	9:23	36
11:48	34	9:27	88f.
12	34	9:29	36
12:1–8	137	9:30	91, 94
12:12–19	137	9:32	70
12:32ff.	104	10:23	87
12:38–41	102	10:39	41
18–20	137	11:1	87
21:24	46, 138	11:2f.	76, 93
		11:12	87
Acts		11:19	54
—	25, 32f., 39f., 46, 49, 53, 55, 63, 67, 76, 85, 88, 89, 92	11:19–12:25	53
		11:20	58
		11:25	91
1–6	88	11:25f.	89

INDEX OF PASSAGES

11:28	33	17:5–9	92
11:29	87	17:10f.	54
11:29f.	89, 93	17:10ff.	92
11:30	70, 94	18:2	86
12:17	50, 61, 70, 87, 136	18:2f.	94
13–14	89	18:4	54
13:1	58, 89	18:7	94
13:1f.	50	18:7f.	75
13:1ff.	85, 87, 141	18:12	32
13:1–5	86	18:12–17	63
13:1–16:10	53	18:24	58, 89
13:5	85	18:24f.	88
13:7	35	18:26	93
13:16–41	111	19:1	86
13:27	126	19:1–7	88
13:33	115	19:10	54, 75
13:43	54	19:22	85a, 86
13:45	37	19:23–40	75
13:47	54, 61, 71, 136	19:26	75
13:47f.	54	19:29	94
13:50	37	19:31	35
14:1f.	54	20:4	86, 92
14:4	54, 85a, 89	20:4ff.	94
14:14	85a, 89	20:5	92
14:23	70	20:5–21:19	137
15	42	20:16	137
15:1	93	20:17	70
15:1f.	93	20:21	53f.
15:2	70, 89, 94	20:28	48, 70
15:5	93	20:31	75
15:12	89	21:16	94
15:13	70	21:17	93
15:16ff.	115	21:18	70
15:19ff.	93	21:39	91
15:22	85a, 89	22:3	36, 89, 91
15:22f.	90, 96	22:25–30	35
15:23	91	23:10	35
15:39	89	23:16	91
15:40	94	23:22–33	35
15:40f.	86	24:17	93
15:40–18:22	90	24:27	32
16:1	54	25:24–27	35
16:1ff.	86	26:27	126
16:4	13	26:30ff.	35
16:10	86, 93	26:32	61
16:10–17	137	27–28	71
16:11–19:22	53	27:1	94
16:14f.	93	27:1–28:31	53, 137
16:22	35	27:12	137
16:35–39	35	28	54, 71f.
16:35–40	63	28:15	94
16:37f.	90	28:16	35
17:1–4	54	28:24	53f.
17:5ff.	94	28:25	100

INDEX OF PASSAGES

28:30	62	10:12f.	104
28:31	58	10:13	49
		10:18–21	102
Romans		11:2	100, 145
		11:9f.	119
—	18, 23, 39, 43, 49f.,	11:26	101
	54, 69, 78, 85f., 133f.,	11:33–36	147
	139f., 143f.	11:36	147
1:1	85a	12:2	149
1:11f.	50	12:4f.	145
1:16	53	12:6ff.	94
1:17–4:25	107	12:8	70
1:29ff.	141	12:20	147
2:24	117	13:1	91
3:10–18	102, 126	13:8ff.	77, 116
3:19	126	13:14	120, 149
3:21	126	14	94
3:30	147	14:17	113
4:1–25	117, 140, 143	15:8	85a
4:7	126	15:9–12	102
5	115	15:24	59, 63, 71, 136
5:3	141	15:25ff.	93
5:3ff.	140	15:28	59, 63, 136
5:12–21	140, 149	16:1	85a, 88, 93
5:14	115	16:3	86, 93
6:3	118	16:3ff.	85b, 94
6:6	81	16:3–15	50
6:17	13, 94	16:5	75
6:23	85a	16:6	85b, 93
7:12	116	16:7	85a, 85b, 91f.
8:9–17	149	16:9	85b–86
8:17	141	16:10f.	75
8:29	81	16:11	92
9–11	54, 102, 109	16:12	85a, 85b, 93
9:6f.	106	16:13	93
9:6–29	106, 109	16:14f.	75
9:7	147	16:15	93
9:7ff.	110	16:15f.	93
9:9	106	16:17	94
9:10–28	106	16:21	26, 85b–86, 92
9:12	106, 124	16:22	14, 47, 79, 96
9:13	106	16:23	75, 85b–86
9:15	106	16:25f.	111, 120
9:17	106		
9:24ff.	106	*I Corinthians*	
9:25–28	106		
9:27	106	—	18, 40, 43, 49f., 66,
9:29	106		78, 85f., 133f., 139,
9:30–10:21	139		140, 143f.
9:32f.	145	1:1	85a, 87, 142
9:33	101, 139	1:11	75
10:4	77, 115	1:12	42
10:9	49	1:13	118
10:11	104	1:18–31	107, 111

1:18–3:20	9, 107	10:13	81
1:18–31	107, 111	10:16f.	144
1:23f.	53	11:2	13, 94
2:1–5	107	11:3–16	47, 140
2:6–16	47, 107, 111, 120, 139, 142, 143	11:16	50
		11:20ff.	145
2:8	91	11:23	13
2:9	104	11:23–26	144
2:14f.	24	11:25	115
3:1	85a	11:26	144
3:1–17	108	11:27	145
3:5	85a, 87f., 90	11:27–34	145
3:8	86	12:1	78
3:9	85b–87	12:4ff.	150
3:16	33, 119, 145	12:8	143
3:18ff.	108	12:4–11	47, 141, 146
3:22f.	24	12:5f.	150
3:22–4:1	88	12:27	118, 145
4:1	24, 111	12:28	70, 94
4:3	24	13	139
4:9	85a, 88f.	14:21	126
4:17	26, 73, 90, 95	14:29	24, 78
5:1	145	14:33	50
5:9f.	69	14:34f.	47f., 79, 81, 139, 140
6:4	24		
6:5	24	14:36f.	28
6:9f.	81, 141	14:37	90
6:15	145	14:37f.	24, 78
6:15f.	145	15:1ff.	13, 50
7:1	78	15:3–7	141, 146
7:22	85a	15:5–8	88
7:25	78	15:6	88
8:1	78	15:8	91
8:6	140f., 146ff., 150	15:10	85b
9:1	88	15:12	76
9:1ff.	24	15:22	118, 120
9:3	78	15:22–55	149
9:5f.	85a, 89	15:24–28	150
9:6	89	15:27	111f., 116
9:7	85b	15:45	116, 120
9:9–14	141	16:1	78
9:14	87	16:3	93
10:1–4	117	16:3f.	94
10:1–5	148	16:10	26, 85b
10:1–13	140, 143, 146, 148	16:12	50, 78, 85a, 86
		16:15f.	75, 95
10:2	118, 120	16:15ff.	85a, 85b
10:4	148	16:16	87
10:6	115, 148	16:18	87
10:6–10	117	16:19	75, 94
10:7	148	16:19f.	25, 87
10:9	148	16:21–24	79
10:11	115, 148	16:22	14
10:11f.	117	16:23f.	25

INDEX OF PASSAGES

II Corinthians

—	18, 40, 43, 49f., 85, 133f., 139f., 143f.
1:1	25f., 69, 85a, 87
1:5ff.	85b
1:7	139, 141
1:19	26
2:13	26, 85a, 87
2:15ff.	28
3:2	90
3:6	85a, 88
3:7f.	116
3:9	117
3:12–18	15
3:14	115
3:14ff.	120
5:1	118, 145f.
5:17	118
5:18f.	95
6:1	87
6:2	119
6:4	85a, 87f.
6:14–7:1	47, 139, 142
6:16	33
6:16ff.	102, 104, 119
6:18	111, 115, 119
7:6	73
7:8	69
7:12f.	73
8–9	93
8:9	148
8:16	95
8:16ff.	85a
8:16–24	91
8:18	87
8:19	94
8:22f.	87
8:23	26, 85b–86, 89, 91, 95
10–13	144
10:17	111
11:3–6	144
11:4	90
11:5	90
11:12–15	144
11:13	24, 50, 90, 144
11:13ff.	90
11:14f.	91
11:15	88, 90
11:22	93, 144
11:23	88
11:24	53
11:25	36
12:1	144
12:11f.	24, 144
12:17f.	26
12:18	86, 95
13:11	25
13:14	25, 150

Galatians

—	18, 20, 40, 43, 49f., 85, 87, 133f., 139f., 143f.
1:1	24
1:1f.	87, 142
1:2	69
1:6	90
1:12	24
1:17	24
1:18	50, 70
1:21	91
2	42, 136
2:1	26, 85, 89, 94
2:4	70
2:4f.	93
2:7ff.	50
2:8f.	24
2:9	70, 89
2:9f.	93
2:10	93
2:12ff.	93
2:13	85, 89
2:17	85a
3:6–14	117, 143
3:12	147
3:16	147
3:24f.	77
3:27	120
4	107
4:9	76
4:9f.	76
4:21f.	107
4:21–5:1	107, 140, 143
4:22	107
4:22ff.	110
4:23	107
4:23–29	107
4:25	107
4:25f.	117
4:26	107
4:27	107
4:28	107
4:30	100, 104, 107
4:30ff.	107

4:31	107	*Philippians*	
5:2ff.	77		
5:13–21	76	—	18, 39, 42, 49f., 85, 133f., 139f., 143f.
5:14	116		
5:17	24	1:1	39, 42, 48, 70, 85a, 87f., 95, 142
5:19–23	141		
5:25–6:10	140	1:14	87
6:6	70, 88, 94f., 141	1:22	24
		2:6–11	47, 49, 141f., 146, 148
6:11	14, 47	2:7	85a
6:11–18	79	2:9ff.	149
6:15	94	2:11	149
6:18	25	2:19	86
		2:25	73, 85a–86, 92
		3:20f.	141
Ephesians		4:2	95
—	14, 19, 21, 25, 39, 41f., 49f., 78, 85, 86, 133f., 139f., 143f.	4:2f.	85b, 93
		4:21f.	87
		4:22	75
1:1	25	*Colossians*	
1:3–14	141		
1:20	111	—	14, 19, 39, 42, 49f., 85, 86, 96, 133f., 139, 140, 143f.
1:21	113		
1:22	111f.		
1:22f.	145	1:1	85a, 87, 96, 142
2:20	33	1:2	87, 96
3:1	26	1:7	85a, 88
3:3f.	26	1:7f.	95
3:3ff.	111, 120	1:12–20	47
3:5	88	1:13	113
3:7	88	1:15–20	146ff.
3:7f.	88	1:16	147
4:4	141, 150	1:23	88, 90
4:4ff.	147	1:24	118
4:5f.	141, 147, 150	1:25	28
		2:1	95
4:7–16	145	2:6ff.	13
4:11	94	2:8	94
4:12	145	2:17	76
4:16	145	2:18	76
4:22ff.	120, 149	2:23	76
4:25	26	3:1ff.	149
4:25–5:14	140	3:5–15	141
5:5	81, 139	3:9f.	149
5:22–6:9	140	3:12ff.	149
5:29–32	145	3:15	145
5:29ff.	118	3:16	95
5:31f.	110	3:18–4:1	140
6:5–9	75	4:7	85b–86
6:6	85a	4:7f.	73, 86
6:20	26	4:7ff.	95
6:21	85a, 86	4:9	85a
6:21f.	26, 73, 95	4:10	85a, 86, 89f.
6:23f.	25, 87		

INDEX OF PASSAGES

4:10f.	85b, 94	1:3–20	82
4:11	85b	1:7	77
4:12	85a, 95	1:9f.	27, 80f., 139, 141
4:14	53, 75, 85b–86, 93	1:15	80f., 83, 101
4:15	87, 93	1:17	80, 82
4:15f.	87	1:18	26
4:16	69, 78, 95, 96, 139	1:19f.	72
4:17	85a	2:1f.	73
4:18	79	2:5f.	80, 82f., 141
		2:7	90

I Thessalonians

		2:9–12	140
—	14, 18, 40, 49f., 85, 96, 133f., 139f., 143f.	2:9–3:1	47, 80ff., 101f.
		2:11–15	48
1:1	86f., 90, 142	3:1	50
1:4f.	81	3:1–13	47, 80, 82
2:4	99	3:2	48, 69
2:6	90	3:8	88
2:7	85a	3:14	26, 47, 73, 82
2:12ff.	42	3:15	75
2:13	28, 78	3:16	47, 79, 80, 82, 141, 146
2:14	36		
3:2	85a, 86, 95	4:1	70, 79f., 90, 101
3:6	95	4:1f.	27, 72
4:5	99	4:1ff.	77
5:12f.	70, 87, 95	4:1–5	47, 80
5:20f.	140	4:1–10	82
5:27	78	4:3	76
		4:6	47, 82, 88, 101
		4:9	101

II Thessalonians

		4:9f.	81
		4:11	82
—	40f., 49f., 65, 85, 96, 133f., 139f., 143f.	4:13	26, 73
		5:3–25	82
1:1	90, 142	5:5f.	82
2:1f.	96	5:9	41
2:2	24	5:9f.	82
2:2f.	25	5:13	75
2:3f.	117	5:14	26
2:13	95	5:17	69, 87
2:15	28, 69, 78, 94	5:17f.	80, 141
3:1–15	96	5:17–20	82
3:6	94	5:18	87
3:6–11	95	6:1f.	75, 82
3:10	87	6:3–10	82
3:17	14, 24, 47, 79	6:7f.	82
		6:10	82

I Timothy

		6:11f.	80
—	14, 19–22, 25f., 39, 40ff., 48ff., 51, 65–73, 75–79, 81f., 85, 96, 101, 133f., 139f., 143f.	6:11–16	82
		6:13	83
		6:13f.	26
		6:14	83
		6:15f.	80
1:3	73, 95	6:17f.	75
1:3ff.	77	6:20	72, 77, 144
1:3–7	72	6:20f.	79

INDEX OF PASSAGES

II Timothy

—	19–22, 25f., 40f., 42, 48–51, 65–71, 74–79, 81f., 85, 96, 101, 133f., 139f., 143f.
1:2	86
1:6	27
1:7	82
1:8	27, 73
1:9f.	80, 82f.
1:11f.	27
1:13	27
1:15f.	77
1:15ff.	27
1:15–18	72f.
1:16	75
2:3	73, 85b
2:6	85b, 87
2:8	83
2:11f.	83
2:11ff.	80f.
2:14	81f.
2:14–4:5	82
2:16f.	72
2:18	76
2:19ff.	80
2:24	85a
3:1–5	81
3:6f.	76
3:6–9	72
3:11	27
3:15	80
4	27
4:3f.	72
4:6	27
4:6f.	74
4:8	83
4:9ff.	27
4:10	72f., 86, 95
4:10f.	86
4:10ff.	86
4:11	53, 79, 85a, 86, 92
4:12	86, 95
4:13	69, 73
4:16f.	73
4:18	83
4:19	73, 75
4:19f.	86
4:19–22	25, 79
4:20	72ff., 86

Titus

—	14, 19–22, 25, 39, 41f., 48ff., 51, 65–73, 75–79, 81f., 85, 96, 101, 133f., 139f., 143f.
1:4	86
1:5	69, 72f., 86
1:5–9	82
1:7	48, 69
1:7ff.	82
1:9	81, 102
1:10	76f., 93
1:10f.	72, 77
1:10–16	72
1:10–2:1	82
1:12	80, 99
1:14	102
1:15	76
1:11	75
2:2–14	82 *bis*
2:11–14	80, 82
2:13	x, 83
2:15	82
3:1	73
3:1–8	82
3:3–7	80
3:3–8	81, 102
3:9ff.	72, 82
3:10	39
3:12	72f., 86, 95
3:13	86, 89
3:15	79

Philemon

—	18, 47, 49f., 65, 78, 85, 86, 133f., 139, 140, 143f.
1	85a, 85b, 142
1f.	93
2	75, 85a, 85b, 94
7	85a
17	85b
19	14, 47
19–25	79
23	85b
24	53, 85b–86, 90, 92

Hebrews

—	17ff., 33, 39, 116, 133f., 139f., 143f.
1	102
1:5	111, 115, 119

INDEX OF PASSAGES

2:6–9	111	3:1–6	81
2:8f.	112	3:1–7	140
2:10	147	3:3–6	47, 140
2:11f.	85a	3:13	35
3:1	85a	3:18	141
4:11	117	3:22	141
6:10	85a	4:3f.	141
7:9f.	118	4:13	141
8:4	33	5:1	27
8:13	33	5:1ff.	70
9:6f.	33	5:2	141
9:11	118	5:12	47, 50, 90
9:26	113	5:12f.	27
10:1	115	5:13	55, 90
10:1–4	33		
10:9f.	115	*II Peter*	
11:28f.	117	—	18ff., 22f., 25, 29, 33, 39, 41f., 44, 51, 133f., 139f., 143f.
13:7	28		
		1:1	39
James		1:16ff.	27
—	18ff., 32, 39, 42, 44, 50, 133f., 136, 139f., 143f.	1:20	139
		1:20–2:1	28
		1:20–2:22	140, 143
1:1	25	2:1	70
1:3	139	2:1ff.	143
1:3f.	140	2:3	28
2:20–26	47, 143	2:5f.	117
3:13–18	139, 141	2:21	13
5:14	39, 70	2:22	143
5:16	39	3:1f.	28
		3:2	28
I Peter		3:3	139
—	18f., 21, 23, 25, 29, 39, 41f., 44, 48, 133f., 139f., 143f.	3:3f.	107, 143
		3:3–13	47, 107, 140, 143
		3:5	107
1:1	27	3:5f.	107
1:2	70	3:6	107
1:6f.	140f.	3:7	107
1:11f.	111	3:7–12	107
1:18	139	3:8	107
1:23ff.	28	3:9	107
2:1	27	3:10	107
2:4–8	139, 145	3:12	107
2:5	119, 146	3:13	107, 143
2:6ff.	139	3:15	28
2:6–9	102	3:15f.	28, 50, 120
2:9f.	119		
2:11f.	27	*I John*	
2:13–17	35		
2:18f.	140	—	18f., 39, 51, 133f., 139f., 143
2:18–3:7	140		
2:21–25	140	3:2	141

INDEX OF PASSAGES

4:1	50, 140
4:2f.	141

II John

—	18f., 39, 51, 133f., 139f., 143

III John

—	18f., 39, 51, 133f., 139f., 143

Jude

—	18f., 32f., 39, 41, 51, 133f., 139f., 144
1	25
3	13
5	139
5–19	143
7	117
8f.	90
17	28
17f.	38

Revelation

—	33, 35, 38f., 43, 104, 140, 143
1:1	25
1:4	25
1:9	25
1:17f.	141
2:2	50
2:6	50
2:14	50
2:20ff.	50
4–22	40
4:8	141
5:9	141
9:20	141
11:2	32
11:8	117
13:1–10	117
17:5–10	55
21:2	25, 117
21:8	141
22:6	81
22:8	25
22:15	141

III. APOCRYPHA AND PSEUDEPIGRAPHA

APOCRYPHA

Wisdom of Solomon

—	17, 138
9:1f.	147

Ben Sira = Sirach = Ecclesiasticus

46:15	81
48:22	81
51:23	103

PSEUDEPIGRAPHA

Ascension of Isaiah

4:2ff.	74

I Enoch

—	21f.
6	90

IV Ezra

—	21f.

Jubilees

—	107

Psalms of Solomon

8:15	55

Testaments of the Twelve Patriarchs

Levi

13, 2	12
18	116

IV. Dead Sea Scrolls

1Q27 (Book of Mysteries)

1:3–8	113
1:8	81

1QGenApoc (Genesis Apocryphon)

—	107

1QH (Hymns of Thanksgiving)

12:11ff.	111

1QM (War of the Sons of Light with the Sons of Darkness)

—	113
1:1	91

1QpHabakkuk

—	110
2:3–7	110
2:10–6:12	55
3:1ff.	109
7:1–8	111
7:2	110

1QS (Manual of Discipline)

—	78
4:22f.	116
5:15	100

6:14	70
6:20	70
6:25	36
7:1f.	36
8:14	100
10:21–26	143

4QFlorilegium

—	110
1:2f.	110

4QMidrEschat[a, b]

—	113

4QTestimonia

—	102

11QTemple

—	28
54:8–18	129

CD (Covenant of Damascus)

4:14	110
10:16	109
12:2f.	91, 129

CD-A

13:7–13	70

V. Early Jewish Writings

Josephus

—	14

Against Apion

1, 38–42	17, 122
1, 67	60
2, 204	12

Antiquities

4, 211	12
18, 252	63
20, 200f.	32

Jewish War

2, 183	63
3, 53–58	53
6, 354–364	33

Philo

de cherubim

99	56
127	147

de confusione linguarum

24	143

de legatione ad Gaium = Embassy to Gaius

115	12
210	12
371	89

de migratione Abrahami

118	100
181	56

de sacrificiis Abelis

8	147
22	143
27	143
76–86	106

de somniis

1, 134	56

de vita Mosis

1, 2	59

in Flaccum

53	89

quod deterius potiori insidiari soleat

54	147

quod deus sit immutabilis

79	59

VI. Ancient Christian Writings

Acts of Paul

—	23, 62
9f.	74
9ff.	71
11	74

Acts of Peter (Vercelli)

—	67
1ff.	62, 71f., 136
40	71, 136

Aphraates

—	143

Apocalypse of Moses

17:1	90

Apocalypse of Peter

—	23

Augustine

Letters

# 71	51
# 75	51

Epistle of Barnabas

6:13	118
16:1–5	33
16:3f.	143

Clement of Alexandria

Stromata = Miscellanies

1, 1, 11	135
2, 11, end	66
2, 20	89

Clement of Rome

—	66

I Clement

—	143
1:1	59, 74
5	67, 71, 74
5:1–7:1	34f.
5:6f.	59, 72
5:7	60ff., 136
6:1	75
42:1	28
60:4	35
61:1f.	35

III Corinthians

—	23

Correspondence of Paul and Seneca

—	23

Didaché

—	143

INDEX OF PASSAGES

Epiphanius

Panarion

26, 6, 5	136
29, 7, 8	32
29, 9, 2	37
51, 12, 2	35, 136
51, 33, 7ff.	136
51, 33, 9	35

Weights and Measures

15, 2–5	32

Epistle of the Apostles

—	23

Epistle to the Laodiceans

—	23

Eusebius

Ecclesiastical History (HE)

1, 12, 1	89
2, 1, 4	89
2, 15, 1	136
2, 22, 1–8	72
2, 22, 2	72
2, 25, 3ff.	34
2, 25, 5–8	74
2, 25, 8	74
3, 1, 3	72
3, 5, 2f.	32
3, 18, 1f.	35
3, 25, 4–7	23
4, 26, 9	35
4, 26, 13f.	122
5, 8, 4	136
6, 12, 3	23, 65
6, 14, 5ff.	136

vita Constantini

1, 8, 3f.	59

Gospel of Peter

—	23

Hippolytus

Refutations

6, 20	136

Ignatius

—	66, 143

ad Ephesios

14:1	65

ad Magnesios

8–11	77

ad Romanos

4:3	28

ad Trallianos

9	77

Irenaeus

Against Heresies (AH)

1, 16, 3	65
2, 14, 7	65
3, 1, 1	136
3, 3, 3	72
3, 14, 1	65
5, 30, 3, end	35

Jerome

—	51

adversus Jovinianum

1, 26	35

Commentary on Isaiah

5:18	37
49:7	37
52:4	37

Commentary on Titus

preface	66

Letters

120, 11	41

Lives of Illustrious Men = de viris illustribus

1	74
5	74
9	35
12	74

prologus in liber Salomonis
120, 11   29

Justin Martyr

Dialogue with Trypho
16:4   37
40   33
69   129
137:2   37

Muratorian Canon
—   23, 62, 67, 71, 136
9–16   46
39–68   35

Origen
—   93

Commentary in Matthew
Matt 23:37ff.   29

Papias
—   66

Polycarp
—   66, 143

ad Philippenses
4:1   65, 81

Preaching of Peter
—   23

Epistula
2:4   25

Contestatio
5:2   25

Pseudo-Hippolytus

On the Seventy Apostles
24   89
50   89

Sulpicius Severus

Chronicle II, 29   34

Tertullian

adversus Marcionem = Against Marcion
4, 5   25
5, 21   66

Apology
5   34f.

On Baptism
17   23

To the Pagans
1, 7   34

Theophilus of Antioch

ad Autolycum
3:14   65

Victorinus

On the Apocalypse
10:11   35, 38

VII. Mishnah, Tosefta, and Babylonian Talmud

Mishnah

Aboth
3:7   100

Baba Bathra
3:2   63

Berakoth
4:3   36

Makshirim
6:3   63

Sanhedrin
10:1   123

INDEX OF PASSAGES

Shabbath

22:2   63

Tosefta

Sanhedrin

7:11   126

Babylonian Talmud

Berakoth

28b   36

Megillah

7a   122
17b   36
32a   78

Rosh Hashanah

17a   123

Sanhedrin

11a   17
43a   129
100a   122

VIII. Other Jewish Writings

Aboth de Rabbi Nathan

37, 10   126

Midrashim

Genesis Rabbah

20:4   37

Sifra Leviticus

2:1ff.   126

Targums

Job   28

Jonathan

—   28

Onkelos

—   28

Twelfth Benediction = Shemoneh Esreh = Birkath ha-Minim

—   35f.

IX. Greco-Roman Writings

Aeschylus

Prometheus Bound

665   56

Marcus Aurelius

Meditations

4, 23   147

Chrysippos

—   see Stobaeus

Cicero

—   14

epistulae ad Atticum

13, 25, 3   47

Letters to Friends

2, 4   78
7, 25, 1   69
16, 18, end   69

Dio Cassius

Roman History

67:14   35

Diodorus Siculus

History

25, 10, 1   57

INDEX OF PASSAGES

Galen

On His Own Books

—   17

Herodotus

History

3, 25   56

Livy

History

21, 43, 13   60
23, 5, 11   60

Pausanius

Description of Greece

4, 26, 5   57
4, 29, 13   57
6, 18, 4f.   17

Philostratus

vita Apolloni

4, 47   60
5, 4   60
6, 1, 1   56

Pliny the Elder

Natural History

3, 1, 3–7   60

Pliny the Younger

Letters

10, 96   34
10, 96, 9f.   75

Procopius

History of the Wars

2, 3, 52   56
2, 22, 7   56
6, 30, 9   56

Quintilian

institutio oratoria

10, 3, 19   142
10, 3, 31   79

Stobaeus

Eklogai

1, 1, 26   147

Strabo

Geography

1, 1, 5   57
1, 1, 6   56f.
1, 1, 8   57
1, 2, 24   57
1, 2, 31   56ff., 60
1, 4, 6   57, 60
2, 1, 1   60
2, 3, 5   56
2, 4, 2   56
2, 4, 3   60
2, 4, 4   60
2, 5, 14   57
3, 1, 2   60
3, 1, 4   57
3, 1, 8   57
3, 2, 1   63
3, 4, 3   63
3, 5, 3   62
3, 5, 5   60

Suetonius

Lives of the Caesars

Nero

16   34

Tacitus

Annals

15, 44   34, 75

Histories

4, 3, middle   60

INDEX OF MODERN AUTHORS[1]

Aalders, G. C. **6**
Aichele, G. **3**
Aland, K. **20**, **21**, **69**, **139**
Albertini, E. **63**
Albright, W. F. **6**, **34**
Alexander, J. A. **54**
Alexander, P. S. **78**
Allison, D. C., Jr. **108**, **134**
Applebaum, S. **63**
Ashcraft, M. **ix**
Audet, J. P. **25**
Aune, D. E. **80**, **137**

Bacher, W. **37**
Baird, W. **2**
Baltensweiler, H **49**
Balz, H. R. **21**, 24
Barclay, J. **130**
Barnard, L. W. **59**
Barnikol, E. **20**
Barrett, C. K. **125**, **138**
Barth, K. **8**
Bauckham, R. J. **19**, **149**, 150
Bauer, B. 18
Baur, F. C. **6**, **7**, 8, 13, **18**, 19, **20**, 21, 26, 29, **41**, **42**, 43, 48, **66**, 67ff., **140**
Beard, C. A. **5**
Beare, F. W. **21**
Beasley-Murray, G. **138**
Becker, C. L. **5**
Beckwith, R. T. **108**
Behm, J. **19**
Bellinger, W. H. **108**
Betz, O. **10**, **44**, **62**, **71**, **104**, **129**
Bihel, P. S. 61
Billerbeck, P. **36**, **123**, 125, 129
Black, D. A. **19**
Black, M. **113**
Blaiklock, E. M. 61
Blass, F. 61
Bloch, R. **100**, 103
Bock, D. L. **146**
Bockmuehl, M. **130**

Bornkamm, G. **7**
Borgen, P. **106**, **138**
Bousset, W. **43**, 44
Bowker, J. W. **130**, **133**
Bowman, J. W. **7**
Braude, W. G. **130**, **142**
Braun, H. **28**
Brown, R. E. **3**, **19**, **36**
Brownlee, W. H. **34**, **78**, **136**
Brox, N. **17**, 21f.
Bruce, F. F. **24**, **54f.**, **92**, 113
Büchsel, F. **24**
Bultmann, R. 4, **9**, 10, 44, **48**, **118**, **128**, **146**
Burney, C. F. **136**
Bussmann, C. **x**
Butler, J. T. **1**, 14
Byrskog, S. **96**, **142**

Calloud, J. **3**
Calvin, J. 16, **29**, **39**, 41
Campenhausen, H. v. **48**
Candlish, J. S. **17**, 22
Carmignac, J. 3
Capes, D. B. **49**, **149**
Carson, D. A. **125**
Cary, M. **55**
Cassuto, U. **6**
Catchpole, D. **146**
Charles, R. H. **17**
Charlesworth, J. H. **34**, **136**
Charlesworth, M. P. **63**
Childs, B. S. **6**
Churchill, W. 11
Cludius, H. H. **41**
Commager, H. S. **4**
Conzelmann, H. **48**, **53**, **54**, **68**, **96**
Crim, K. **21**
Crossan, J. D. **6f.**
Cullmann, O. **4**, **13**, **46**, 50, **114**, 117, 119
Culpepper, R. A. **50**

Dahl, N. 133
Dalman, G. **45**

---

[1] **Bold text** refers to first citation of work.

INDEX OF MODERN AUTHORS

Daube, D. **101**, **124**, 125, 129
Davies, W. D. **34**, **36**, **108**, **125**, **134**, 136
Davis, J. **5**
Deissmann, A. **62**, 92
Delitzsch, F. **54**
Denniston, J. D. **17**
Derenbourg, J. **37**
Dibelius, M. **68**, 76, **128**, 139, **141**
Didier, M. **99**
Deissmann, G. A. **77**
Dockery, D. S. **19**
Dodd, C. H. **32**, **34**, **102**, 105, 111, **136**, **137**, **139**, **140**
Doeve, J. W. **101**, 111, **128**, 129, **135**
Donelson, L. R. **26**, **68**
Doyle, A. C. 33
Dulles, A. **9**
Droysen, G. 4
Dugmore, C. W. **36**
Duhm, B. **54**
Dunn, J. D. G. **19**, 21, **22**, **48**, **92**, **147**, 149

Easton, B. S. **22**
Edersheim, A. **146**
Edmundson, G. **34f.**, **59**, 61, **67**, 71, 74
Eichhorn, J. G. **1**, 2, **41**
Eissfeldt, O. **6**
Eldredge, L. **1**, 2
Ellis, E. E. **ix**, **x**, **3**, 7, **8**, **10**, 12, **13**, 14ff., **18**, 20, **22**, 23, **24**, **28f.**, **32f.**, 35., 38, 42, **43**, 44ff., **46**, 47, **49**, 50f., **53**, 59, **61**, 62, 63, **65**, **66f.**, 69, **70**, 71f., 74f., 76ff., 79, 80, **81**, 82f., **85**, **86**, 87f., **88f.**, 89f., 92f., **94**, 95, 96f., **99**, 100, **100f.**, 102, 103, 104, **105**, 106ff., 109f., 111f., **113**, 116, 118, 120, **121**, **122**, **126**, **128**, **129**, **130**, **131**, **133f.**, **135f.**, **137**, 138–148, **149**, 150
Eltester, W. **33**
Ernesti, J. A. 2
Evang, M. 147
Evans, E. F. **23**
Evanson, E. **18**, **39**, 39ff., 43

Falconer, T. **40**
Fanning, B. M. **146**
Farkasfalvy, D. **3**
Farmer, W. R. **x**
Fee, G. D. **74**, **144**, 145f.

Feine, P. **19**
Filson, F. V. 61
Finegan, J. **12**, 61
Fiorenza, E. S. **93**
Fischer, B. **29**
Fischer, D. H. **5**
Fitzer, J. **42**
Fitzmyer, J. A. **45**, **50**, **141**
Foakes Jackson, F. J. **55**
France, R. T. **4**, **100**, 105
Frend, W. H. C. **34**, 35
Fritz, K. v. **17**, **138**
Furnish, V. P. **86**

Gabler, J. P. **1**, 2, 8f.
Gardner-Smith, P. **138**
Geiger, W. **20**
Georgi, D. **88**
Gerberding, K. A. **93**
Gerhardsson, B. **13**, **134**, **135**
Gieschen, C. A. **149**, 150
Ginsberg, L. **143**
Godet, F. **92**
Gooch, G. P. **4**
Goodenough, E. R. **45**, 61
Gooding, D. W. **103**
Goodspeed, E. J. **19**
Goppelt, L. **21**, **27**, **47**, **117**, 118, **148**
Goulder, M. D. **8**, **19**, **48**
Graves, R. **28**
Gray, G. B. **56**
Green, W. S. **100**
Greenwood, D. S. **3**
Grotius, H. **39**
Guelich, R. **25**, **124**
Guthrie, D. **16**, 67, **68**
Güttgemanns, E. **135**

Haenchen, E. **53**, 55, **138**
Hammond, N. G. L. **17**, 28
Hanson, A. T. **148**
Hare, D. R. A. **37**
Harnack, A. **20**, **23**, **59**, **61**, 62, **68**, 69, 71, 74, 82, **86**, 87
Harrington, D. J. **85**
Harris, H. **8**, **18**, 20, **42**, 43
Harrison, E. F. 61
Harrison, P. N. **27**, **68**
Hartlich, C. **9**
Hartman, L. **99**, **105**
Hawthorne, G. F. **10**, **44**, **62**, **71**
Hays, J. H. **121**
Hays, R. B. **99**

Hegel, G. W. F. 5, 42, 48
Hemer, C. J. **50**, **53**, 61f., **75**, **92**, **137**
Hengel, M. **10**, **21**, **25**, **44**, **49**, **50**, **53**, **123**, **136f.**, **138**, **150**
Herbert, E. (Lord Cherbury) 2
Herder, J. G. 12
Herford, R. T. **37**
Heyne, C. G. 2
Hilgenfeld, A. **18**, 19, **140**
Hillard, T. W. **32**
Hodgson, P. C. **42**
Hoehner, H. W. 146
Hofius, O. **141**, **147**
Holmgren, F. C. **150**
Holtzmann, H. J. **55**, **66**, 67f.
Horrell, D. **x**
Horst, P. v. d. **44**, 45
Hort, F. J. A. 19, **35**, **149**
Hübner, H. **99**
Hughes, P. E. **45**
Hume, D. **9**
Hurst, L. D. **125**
Hyatt, J. P. **9**

James, M. R. **55**
Jastrow, M. **104**
Jeremias, J. **34**, **70**, **135**, **144**
Jervell, J. **49**, **54**
Johnson, A. R. **119**, **150**
Johnson, F. **99**, 102
Juel, D. **105**
Jülicher, A. **19**, 21

Kahle, P. **36**
Kaiser, O. **6**
Kaminsky, J. S. **118f.**, **145**
Kasher, A. **89**
Keck, L. E. **48**
Kee, H. C. **45**
Kelber, W. H. **13**
Kelly, J. N. D. **27**, **70**, 72, 76, 82
Kenyon, J. **4**
Kern, F. H. **20**
Kikawada, I. M. **6**
Kim, S. **127**, **147**
Kimball, C. A. **108**, **130**
Knight, G. W., III **69**, **79**, **83**
Knowling, R. G. **55**
Knox, J. **19**
Koch, D. A. **109**
Koch, K. 40, **21**
Kraus, H. J. **6**
Krentz, E. **3**

Kümmel, W. G. **2**, **12**, **18f.**, 27, **39**, 40, **41**, 42f.
Kuhn, K. G. **123**

Lake, K. **55**
Lane, W. L. **129**
Lategan, B. C. **3**
Laurentin, R. 19
Lea, T. D. **19**
Leiman, S. Z. **121**, 122
Lewis, D. **19**
Lewis, J. P. **121**
Lietzmann, H. **136**
Lightfoot, J. B. **8**, **11**, 19, **20**, **23**, **32**, **35**, **59**, 60, 62, **66**, 68, 69, 77, **136**, **149**
Lincoln, A. T. **21**
Lindars, B. **138**
Locke, J. 2
Lohmeyer, E. **139**, 141
Loman, A. D. 18
Lona, H. E. **59**
Lonergan, B. **7**
Longenecker, R. N. **45**, 61, **87**, 88, 94, **99**
Lüdemann, G. **8**, **19**, **48**
Luther, M. 16, **38**

Maier, G. **3**
Malherbe, A. J. **78**
Manson, T. W. **136**
Marshall, I. H. **19**, **68**, 69
Martin, R. P. **19**, **26**, **141**
Martyn, J. L. **19**, **36**
Matill, A. J. 61
Maybaum, S. **130**
Mays, J. L. **26**
McKim, D. K. **8**
McRay, J. **34**
Meade, D. G. **17**, 19, 21
Meeks, W. A. **129**, **133**, **148**
Mentz, A. **47**
Metzger, B. M. **17**, **19**, **22**, **23**, **29**, **79**
Meyer, A. **21**
Meyer, H. A. W. **55**
Meyer, R. **45**
Michaelis, J. D. **40**
Mielziner, M. **126**
Miller, J. D. **27**, **68**
Mitton, C. L. **21**
Moffatt, J. **19**, 21
Möhler, J. A. **42**
Mommsen, T. **63f.**

Moo, D. **91, 108**
Morgan, R. **1**
Morris, L. **138**
Motyer, A. **54**
Moule, C. F. D. **49, 79**
Mueller-Vollmer, K. **4**
Mulder, M. J. **78, 121**
Munck, J. **43**, 61
Murphy, R. E. **14**
Murphy-O'Conner, J. **14, 63**

Neander, A. **8, 20**
Neill, S. **8**
Neirynck, F. **138**
Nestle, E. **149**
Neusner, J. **123, 126, 143**
Newman, R. C. **122**
Nicoll, W. R. **17, 55**
Nöldeke, T. **122**
Norden, E. **147**

O'Brien, P. T. **149**
Oertel, F. **62**
Ollenburger, B. **1**
Ollrog, W. H. **96**
O'Neill, J. C. **139**
Ormond, H. A. **55**
Oswalt, J. **54**

Packer, J. I. **28**
Paige, T. **x**
Parker, P. 61
Parsons, W. **51**
Patte, D. **3**
Paulus, H. E. G. **9**
Perriman, A. C. **119**
Plessner, M. **143**
Polzin, R. M. **3**
Pölzl, F. X. **85**
Potterie, I. d. l. **3**, 15
Poythress, V. S. **3**
Priestley, J. **40**
Prior, M. **67**

Quinn, A. **6**
Quinn, J. D. **68**

Rackham, R. B. 61
Radl, W. **x**
Raleigh, W. 4
Ranke, L. v. **4**
Redlich, E. B. **85**
Reicke, B. **12, 32, 53, 55**, 61, **71, 137f.**

Reimarus, H. S. 6
Rengstorf, K. H. **33**
Resch, A. **56**
Reventlow, H. G. **2**, 8
Richards, E. R. **14, 46, 69**, 70, 73, 79, **96, 142**
Richardson, A. **2**, 9
Riesenfeld, H. **13**
Riesner, R. **12**, 13, **32, 135**
Robertson, A. T. **24**, 61
Robinson, J. A. T. **29, 31, 33**, 34f., 37, **49**, 51, **59**, 61, **67**, 71
Robinson, H. W. **119**
Rogers, J. B. **8**
Rogerson, J. W. **6, 119**
Roller, O. **14, 46, 70**, 79, **142**
Rordorf, W. **4, 62, 71**, 74
Ryle, H. E. **55, 121**

Sachs, W. **9**
Sandys-Wunsch, J. **1**, 2
Schaff, P. **143**
Schlatter, A. **11, 62**
Schleiermacher, F. D. E. **39**, 41f.
Schmid, J. **19**
Schmidt, J. E. C. **39, 41**
Schmidt, P. L. **78**
Schmithals, W. **92**
Schmitz, L. **60**
Schneck, R. **108**
Schneemelcher, W. **23**
Schneider, G. **53**, 58
Scholder, K. **41**
Schrage, W. **144**, 145, 146
Schürer, E. **32, 45, 70, 123**, 126
Schweitzer, A. **6**, 7, 9, **18**
Scott, E. F. **21**
Selwyn, E. G. **90**, 96
Sevenster, J. N. **45**
Sherwin-White, A. N. **14, 62**
Sigal, P. **130**
Silva, M. **141**
Simcox, W. H. **21**
Simpson, D. **40**
Sint, J. A. **17**
Smalley, S. S. **49, 138**
Smend, R., Jr. **6**
Smith, D. M. **138**
Smith, M. **17, 138**
Snyder, P. L. **5**
Son, S. W. A. **118, 145**
Speyer, W. **18**, 22, 28
Spicq, C. **62, 74**, 79
Stanley, C. D. **102**

Steinmann, A. E. **22**
Stemberger, G. **126**
Stendahl, K. **9**, **46**, 50, **102**, 110
Stenning, J. F. **104**
Steudel, A. **113**
Stibbs, A. M. **145**
Strachotta, F. **39**
Strack, H. L. **36**, **37**, **123**, **126**
Strauss, D. F. **9**
Strecker, G. **133**, 134, **141**, 149
Strobel, A. **79**, **129**
Strout, R. F. **138**
Stuckenbruck, L. T. **9**
Stuhlmacher, P. **10**, **16**, **133**, **146**
Sukenik, E. L. **45**
Swete, H. B. **35**

Tajra, H. W. **62**
Thackeray, H. St. J. **14**
Theron, D. **23**
Thielicke, H. **8**
Thiering, B. E. **70**
Thiselton, A. C. **3**
Thornton, T. C. G. **58**
Tindal, M. 2
Tittmann, C. C. **42**
Torm, F. **22**
Torrance, T. F. **9**
Torrey, C. C. 61, **136**
Trebilco, P. **93**
Treitschke, H. v. 4
Trestemont, C. 3
Trevor-Roper, G. R. 4
Trobisch, D. **65**
Trummer, P. **21**, 26
Tuckett, C. x
Turpie, D. M. **99**

Unnik, W. C. v. **55**, 56

Van Manen, W. C. **18**, **39**
Van Segbroeck, F. **46**
Van Seters, J. **6**
Vatke, W. 6
Vine, V. E. 61
Vorster, W. S. **3**

Wacker, W. C. **68**
Wagner, G. **44**
Walker, W. O., Jr. **139**
Wansbrough, H. **12**, **46**, **134**
Warfield, B. B. **101**
Weil, G. **143**
Weinfeld, M. **70**
Weiss, B. **19**
Weiss, J. **19**, **62**
Welborn, L. L. **59**
Wellhausen, J. **6**, 7
Wenham, D. **4**
Wenham, G. J. **6**
Westcott, B. F. **19**, **23**, **29**, **149**
Westermann, C. **54**
Wette, W. M. L. d. 41
Wikenhauser, A. **19**
Wilkins, M. J. x
Williams, F. **37**
Wink, W. **3**
Witherington, B. **75**, **137**
Wolter, M. **26**, **68**
Workman, H. D. **34**
Wrede, W. 6
Wright, R. B. **56**
Wright, T. **8**

Zachariae, G. T. 2
Zahn, T. **8**, **11**, **20**, 29, **32**, **51**, **62**, **67**, 68, 71, 72f., 74, **90**
Zeller, E. **42**
Zerwick, M. **24**
Ziegler, K. **78**

ADDITIONS TO THE INDEX OF MODERN AUTHORS

Morgan, T. D. 42
Semler, J. S. 42

INDEX OF SUBJECTS

Apostles of Jesus Christ
  status in the early church 22ff., 88
  include Apollos, Barnabas and Silas
    88ff.
Apostles of the Churches 91
Authorship
  Gospels 138
  New Testament letters 13f., 142.

Baur, F. C.
  school of 7f., 18, 41ff., 66
  tradition of 18-22
Biblical Authority 100-102, 122-126
Biblical Criticism
  contemporary (twentieth century)
    44-49
  history of 1-16, 38-44
Biblical Expositions—see Midrash
Biblical Interpretation
  historical-literary method 1-16
  presuppositions 112-120
  principles 126-128
  of Jesus—see Jesus
Biblical Quotations
  forms and techniques 102-103
  introductory formulas 100-102
  testimonia 111-112
Birkath ha-Minim—see Jewish Prayer
  against Heretics

Canonical Status
  Old Testament 121f.
  Paul's letters 78
Charismatic Exegesis 110f., 120
Christology of Paul 144-150
Corporate Personality 118ff.
Coworkers of Paul
  activities of 94-97
  Apostles 88-90
  general 85-97
  kinsmen 91-93
  women 93
Critical Method—see Historical-
  Literary Criticism
Critical Orthodoxy
  axioms of 38
  critique of 2-10, 44-51

Dating the New Testament
  Acts 33, 35, 60-63
  general 31-51, 142-144
  Gospels 32-34
  historical evidence for 32-37
  letters 33, 35
  I Peter 35
  Pastoral Epistles 71-74
  Revelation 35
Domitian, Emperor
  persecution of Christians 35

Eighteen Benedictions—see Jewish
  Prayer against Heretics
Expositions—see Midrashim

False Teachers 76f., 90f., 93f., 143f.
Forgery—see Pseudepigrapha
Form Criticism, Gospels 12-13, 128f.

Gospels
  biblical expositions in 108f., 130f.,
    134f.
  dates of 32-34
  formation of 134-138

Hegelian Philosophy
  influence of 6-8, 47-49
Hillel's Rules—see Biblical
  Interpretation, principles
Historical Knowledge
  subjectivity of 4-5
Historical-Literary Criticism
  contemporary 10-22, 49-51
  early literary criticism 1-3, 5-10,
    38-44
  history of 1-16
History of Religions School 43f.

Jerusalem
  fall of 32-44
Jesus
  attitude toward his Bible 122-126
  Bible received by 121f.
  expositions of Scripture 130f., 134f.
  his interpretation of his Bible
    121-132

principles of biblical interpretation 126–128
Jewish Prayer against Heretics 35–37

Method
  importance of 10–14
  limitations of 14–16
Midrashim 103–112, 128–131, 130f., 134–135, 140, 148f.

Nero, Emperor
  persecution of Christians 34f.
New Testament letters
  authorship of 13f., 142
  biblical expositions in 106–108, 140f.
  preformed traditions in 140f., 144–150

Old Testament Quotations—see Biblical Quotations
Old Testament Exposition—see Midrash
Old Testament Testimonies—see Biblical Quotations
Opponents—see False Teachers

Pastoral Epistles
  authorship 65–71
  composition 77–79
  historical setting 75f.
  occasion and date 71–74
  preformed traditions in 77–82
  situation in Paul's ministry 72ff.
  themes 82f.
Paul
  authorship of the Pastoral Epistles 65–71
  co-workers 76, 85–97
  letters, canonicity of 78
  mission to Spain 53–63
  opponents of 76f., 90f., 93f., 143f.
  origins of his christology 144–150
  release from First Roman Imprisonment 62
  use of preformed traditions 138–141, 144–150

Persecution of Christians
  Domitian 35
  Nero 34f.
Preformed traditions—see Traditions
Pseudepigrapha
  apostolic, deceptive character of 24–29
  attitude toward, in antiquity 22ff., 65f.
  pseudonymity and canonicity 17–29

Qumran 109ff., 120
Quotations—see Biblical Quotations

Rabbinic Exegesis 106–109
Rationalism 8–10
Revelation 14ff.

Salvation History 113ff.
Secretaries 13f., 67, 70, 79, 96
Shemoneh Esreh—see Jewish Prayer against Heretics
Spain
  as the 'end of the earth' 58ff.
  Gades 57f., 60, 62f.
  Paul's Mission to 53–63, 71f.

Testimonia 111f.
Traditions
  biblical expositions (midrashim) 80, 103–112, 130f., 148
  christological 80, 82, 133–150
  church order 80, 82f.
  confessions 80
  hymns 80, 141, 149f.
  implications for authorship and dating of documents 142–144
  implications for origins of Paul's christology 144–150
  in Gospels 130f., 134–138
  in letters 14, 67, 70, 79–82, 138–141
  soteriological 81
  vice and virtue lists 141, 143
Typology 115–118

www.ingramcontent.com/pod-product-compliance
Lightning Source LLC
Chambersburg PA
CBHW031313150426
43191CB00005B/212